THE OTTOMAN EMPIRE AND SAFAVID IRAN,
1639–1682

The Royal Asiatic Society was founded in 1823 'for the investigation of subjects connected with, and for the encouragement of science, literature and the arts in relation to Asia'. Informed by these goals, the policy of the Society's Editorial Board is to make available in appropriate formats the results of original research in the humanities and social sciences having to do with Asia, defined in the broadest geographical and cultural sense and up to the present day.

The Monograph Board

Professor Francis Robinson, CBE, DL, Royal Holloway, University of London (Chair)
Professor Tim Barrett, SOAS, University of London
Dr Barbara Brend, Royal Asiatic Society
Dr Evrim Binbas, Institute of Oriental and Asian Studies, University of Bonn
Professor Anna Contadini, SOAS, University of London
Professor Michael Feener, National University of Kyoto
Dr Gordon Johnson, University of Cambridge
Dr Firuza Melville, University of Cambridge
Dr Taylor Sherman, London School of Economics
Dr Alison Ohta, Director, Royal Asiatic Society

For a full list of publications by the Royal Asiatic Society see www.royalasiaticsociety.org

THE OTTOMAN EMPIRE AND SAFAVID IRAN, 1639–1682

DIPLOMACY AND BORDERLANDS IN THE EARLY MODERN MIDDLE EAST

Selim Güngörürler

EDINBURGH
University Press

To Lokum

Edinburgh University Press is one of the leading university presses in the UK. We publish academic books and journals in our selected subject areas across the humanities and social sciences, combining cutting-edge scholarship with high editorial and production values to produce academic works of lasting importance. For more information visit our website: edinburghuniversitypress.com

© Selim Güngörürler, 2024, 2025

Edinburgh University Press Ltd
13 Infirmary Street
Edinburgh EH1 1LT

First published in hardback by Edinburgh University Press 2024

Typeset in 11/13pt JaghbUni Regular by
Cheshire Typesetting Ltd, Cuddington, Cheshire

A CIP record for this book is available from the British Library

ISBN 978 1 3995 1010 3 (hardback)
ISBN 978 1 3995 1011 0 (paperback)
ISBN 978 1 3995 1013 4 (webready PDF)
ISBN 978 1 3995 1012 7 (epub)

The right of Selim Güngörürler to be identified as author of this work has been asserted in accordance with the Copyright, Designs and Patents Act 1988 and the Copyright and Related Rights Regulations 2003 (SI No. 2498).

Contents

Acknowledgements		vi
	Background and Outline	1
1	Settings and Trends of the Ottoman–Safavid Detente	15
2	1639–1643: Baghdad	36
3	1644–1660: Armenia and Azerbaijan	90
4	1660–1682: The Persian Gulf	141
	Afterword	176
Bibliography		179
Index		190

Acknowledgements

The seeds of this book were first sown as I was preparing to embark on a doctoral disseration about Habsburg–Ottoman relations in the early eighteenth century. Amidst a discussion of our syllabus, my doctoral advisor and mentor, Gábor Ágoston, wondered if I could academically use my knowledge of Persian, which I had hitherto studied purely for literary enjoyment, and it was this suggestion that triggered the quest leading up to my changing tracks towards research on a different geography and time. It was Prof. Ágoston also who, by heartening me to delve into the scholarship on Ottoman–Safavid relations, motivated me to formulate the research questions that yielded first the dissertation and now the present book. Since 2011, he has taught and guided me more than a doctoral student could expect from an advisor. I have benefitted much from his combination of constructive support and encouragement to stand on my own two feet. The privilege of having been his student I will always carry as a mark of pride.

Giorgio Rota, first as my dissertation committee member and more recently as my project director, has an equally principal share in the fruition of the almost ten-year work behind this book. He wholeheartedly mentored me by introducing sources, commenting on publications, pointing out potential gaps, and reading my drafts, no less painstakingly than I myself did, to save me from the pitfalls of a young academic's over-enthusiasm. It is thus a source of particular pleasure that in 2020 I began working beside him, which has thus enabled me to continue benefitting from his generous expertise, to which this book is immensely indebted. I cannot thank him enough for the advice and wisdom he has shared with me. His dear fellowship continues to be a reason for me to stay in academia.

From my former supervisor and director, Derin Terzioğlu, I have learned a lot. I should particularly note here how she has trained me to contextualise my findings and tighten my arguments. It was she and Selçuk Akşin Somel who suggested early on that I might have the skills needed to

Acknowledgements

pursue a career in academia. I am grateful for their support. I am indebted to Judith Tucker for the time she spent on reading and commenting on my dissertation draft. From Paolo Sartori, who was the first to motivate me to shape what later became my ongoing project, I have benefitted beyond what I could imagine when we had first met. Although we did not have a formal advisor–advisee relationship, his friendly mentorship has contributed so much to my scholarship that it deserves to be mentioned alongside that of my supervisors. It is thanks to his intellectual and editorial advice that I could work further on my teaching, writing and argumentation. He is also the originator of the idea to prepare this book's first proposal and submit it to the EUP through the Royal Asiatic Society. Velizar Sadovski readily shared his scholarly wisdom throughout the conception, late-stage research, and writing of this book.

Florian Schwarz, as director of the Institute of Iranian Studies at the Austrian Academy of Sciences, has provided me with a comfortable and productive research environment. I thank him for facilitating my work since I joined the Institute. I am likewise grateful for the similar support I received from Chris Roosevelt during my fellowship at Koç University's Research Center for Anatolian Civilizations. I had the privilege of consulting and receiving valuable advice on many occasions from Claudia Römer, and from the late Bert Fragner while he was in active retirement. Evrim Binbaş did not spare his help in steering my book proposal through the Royal Asiatic Society towards the EUP. I have benefitted greatly from the collegial inspiration and friendship of Ulfatbek Abdurasulov, Viola Allegranzi, Arturo Annucci, Elçin Arabacı, Jo Ann Hoeppner Moran Cruz, Laura Goffman, Faisal Husain, Andrzej S. Kaminski, Bruno De Nicola, Yiğit Alp Özalkuş, Michael Polczynski, Lukáš Rybár, M. Habib Saçmalı, James Shedel, Ceren Temizyürek, Fuat Cem Topcu, Davide Trentacoste, Leili (Afsane) Vatani, Elizabeth Williams and Guglielmo Zucconi.

This research was funded in part by the Austrian Science Fund (FWF) [P 32696-G]. Earlier research that afforded a groundwork for this book had been facilitated by financial support from Georgetown University, Austria's Agency for Education and Internationalisation, German Academic Exchange Service, and Koç University – RCAC, in chronological order. Primary source research was conducted at the Ottoman Archives (Istanbul), Süleymaniye Manuscript Library (Istanbul), Austrian National Library – Manuscript Collection (Vienna), and Berlin State Library – Oriental Section. I am grateful to the friendly staff of all four institutions for making sure that requests were processed as smoothly as possible.

During my doctoral study abroad, my mother Tijen devoted herself to picking up my never-ending book orders from within Turkey, and never failed me whenever I needed her to make scans and forward them to me. My sister Eda not only helped my mother in performing these tasks but also printed out large amounts of necessary material and brought it to me during my time in Istanbul; in thus saving me time she generously sacrificed her own, which was no less valuable given her commitments. My father Ibrahim played his part in Izmir by obtaining publications. Our beloved dog Lokum gave me soul-cherishing and unconditional love. The years I spent away from her vicinity hurt the most, as I could explain the reason of my absence to everyone but her.

My work on this book since 2018 has been stamped above all by my better half, Setare, for whose companionship I cannot be grateful enough. Since the day we met, her existence has inspired me to discover and foster new sides of myself that I had thitherto not been acquainted with. I can only consider myself lucky that she and I have crossed paths in the journey of life.

Background and Outline

Premodern polities dominating Greater Iran and the eastern Mediterranean lands clashed with one another for millennia: Medes vs Lydians, Achaemenids vs Greeks, Parthians vs Romans, Sassanids vs Romans, Sassanids vs Arabs, Arabs vs Romans/Byzantines, Seljuks vs Byzantines, Mongols vs Seljuks, Timurids vs Ottomans, Akkoyunlus vs Ottomans, and so on. Rulers rose and fell, wars were fought, countries changed hands, and treaties were made, but structural basics such as geographical conditionality (though not determinism) swaying power relations abided. The so-called Persian–Roman, or to be more precise, Iranian–Levantine contrast remained an invisible but constant factor in power relations between polities controlling these lands. This contrast did not determine the balance of power by itself, but was so weighty that it has to be calculated in and used as a scale in understanding what a given status quo in power relations indeed meant.

These structural continuities are worth bearing in mind as we consider the history of Ottoman–Safavid relations. The Ottoman–Safavid match-up introduced new factors to the picture. In many ways, such as the two sides' shared cultural, demographical and political worlds, this match was profoundly unlike anything that had taken place before. But again, in many other respects, such as military strategies and land disputes, these two monarchies simply picked up from where their forerunners in western Iran and Anatolia left off. From a macro-historical perspective, therefore, the Ottoman–Safavid confrontation can be seen as a chapter within the larger narrative of relations between Anatolian and Iranian polities, as well as an episode from the phenomenon of the polities conquered, established, ruled and sustained by Turkish dynasties and militaries across the Middle East of the second millenium CE.

The present book explores Ottoman–Safavid diplomacy and political relations from 1639 to 1682, to the exclusion of trade,[1] which is a mostly standalone subject not only thematically but also in terms of actors and sources involved,[2] and to the exlusion of religious affairs, which I handle elsewhere.[3] Of course, readers will be aware that relations between these two parties go back almost two centuries prior to this period. But 1639 is a significant date, for it constitutes the beginning of a sustained timespan of unbroken peace, distinguishing it from what had come before; both the earliest phase of relations (before 1501) in which the Safavids were not yet a monarchy, and from the second phase (1501–1639), which was marked by recurring struggles, wars and truces. The period 1639–82 is furthermore notable, as we shall see, for constituting a historiographical lacuna, which the present book seeks to redress. This is again in contrast with the aforementioned earlier two phases, both of which have been the subject of considerable research, and are thus largely familiar to readers.

The historiography handles the first two periods up to 1639 fairly well, though it lacks some crucial levels of analysis, especially in diplomacy and diplomatics. In offering by way of background a brief historical overview of Ottoman–Safavid relations, I confine myself to a short chronology of political relations that led to war, change of territory, and peace, so as to lay out the factual groundwork of the topic at hand.

The Ottoman monarchy's dealings with the House of Safi began when the latter, under its chieftain Junayd (r. 1447–60), converted itself from the Sufi order it had been into a religious-military entity with claims to territorial sovereignty and political power. The movement recruited its overwhelmingly Turkish warriors and believers in Anatolia, Azerbaijan and northern Syria. Ottoman and Akkoyunlu lands thus became both a source and a target for the House of Safi. Junayd was eventually driven out from the order's headquarters, Ardabil, after which he migrated westwards into Anatolia, showed up in Iconium (Konya), capital of the central-Anatolian principality of the Karamanids, and set up indirect contact with the Ottoman monarch Murad II. However, neither the Karamanids nor the Ottomans gave him shelter. Reaching a capacity to raid into the post-Byzantine rump 'Empire' of Trebizond, Junayd increased the political clout of his House by marrying into the Akkoyunlu dynasty ruling central and western Iran, and his movement grew militarily so much that he could campaign against the Shirvanshahs. Under his son Haydar's chieftainship (1460–88), the House of Safi's Kızılbaş religious teaching was coupled with its followers' ideological rejection of Ottoman subjecthood, while the order's militarisation peaked as it put together an army of warrior-believers with an operational capacity in Azerbaijan, southern Caucasus, and to the east of Anatolia. Under Haydar's underage successor and son Ismail, the order gathered its warriors in 1500 to Erzincan and launched their leader's 'emergence' to become a sovereign. In 1501, the shaykh became shah and by 1510, the whole of Greater Iran came under Safavid sway. The Kızılbaş's becoming the ruling class and military nobility in Safavid Iran had profound consequences on relations with the Ottomans. Because many of the Kızılbaş were from Anatolia, and thus regarded this region as their homeland, it became a site of Ottoman–Safavid competition over sovereignty, territory, subjecthood and ideology.[4]

Once the Safavids set up a kingdom over a territory more or less overlapping greater Iran, the Ottoman monarch Bayazid II (r. 1481–1512), to cut off the Safavids' ties from Anatolia, resettled, cordoned off and mobilised against Safavid-follower subjects of the Ottoman state. These earliest Ottoman measures yielded results, though in conventional terms. But the Safavids employed a wide repertoire of asymmetric tactics, such as breaching the borders, harbouring runaway Ottoman princes and, most notably, stirring up uprisings among Kızılbaş loyalists in Ottoman territory, who laid waste to Anatolia, slaughtered dwellers, defeated the Ottoman army and killed the grand vizier. It was only a matter of time, therefore, before the actual state of affairs would be openly acknowledged as war and and the ongoing proxy struggle would give way to direct conflict. And unmediated war did break out. Selim I (r. 1512–20), wresting the Ottoman throne from his father for this sake, first struck back against the Anatolian Safavid-followers and then trampled Shah Ismail's army (r. 1501–24) in 1514 at the Battle of Chaldiran, eastwards from Van at western Azerbaijan, whereafter he entered the Safavid capital Tabriz and held court there. Northern Kurdistan and western Armenia thus became part of the Empire in this first wave of Ottoman expansion against the Safavids. Selim I then put a ban on the movement of goods and persons from Safavid Iran, keeping up the state of war. Shah Ismail's last years and the first decade of the reign of his son and successor Tahmasp (r. 1524–76), roughly coinciding with the first decade also of the Ottoman emperor Sulayman I (r. 1522–66), witnessed backroom dialogue through agents and underhand support of each other's unruly frontier strongmen in Azerbaijan and Iraq on one side, and Kurdistan and Anatolia on the other.[5]

Fierce war restarted in 1533. Unlike Selim, who had thrust straight on for a head-to-head confrontation and knockdown, Sulayman first contained and then pushed the Safavids further east. And in 1534, once again, the Ottoman troops entered Tabriz and the Ottoman monarch held court at the Safavid capital. Tahmasp withdrew before the Ottoman advance, shunning engagement and instead resorting to scorched-earth tactics to tire out the invaders. By 1535, the Ottomans called off the occupation of Azerbaijan, but the second wave of Ottoman conquests materialised and would be lasting: new gains in western Armenia, southern Kurdistan and middle Iraq became organised as the Ottoman provinces of Erzurum and Baghdad. War reawakened in 1548–9 as Tahmasp's brother Alqas took shelter at the Ottoman court (1547) and campaigned alongside Sulayman, whose goal was to install the Safavid prince as an Ottoman-friendly shah and to wrest some further territory for the Empire from Iran. Once again, Tahmasp, instead of giving battle, laid waste to eastern Armenia and Azerbaijan in line with his scorched-earth policy. Though Sulayman again had to pull out from Azerbaijan after holding court yet another time at the Safavid capital Tabriz, the Empire captured and was able to keep for good the fortress city of Van and its hinterland at the intersection of Armenia, Azerbaijan and Kurdistan. The two-year war also saw Ottoman campaigns in Georgia (where permanent conquests were also made), Shirvan and Kurdistan. When a last campaign to Nakhchivan in 1553–4 did not bear any outcome other than the by now habitual cycle of the shah's devastating his own lands and the padishah's occupation followed by evacuation, the Peace of Amasya in 1555 confirmed the Ottoman's conquests since 1533. The border between the Empire and Iran, as set by this writ, would hold good for centuries notwithstanding brief handovers of territory in later wars and treaties. The 1555 Peace of Amasya was notable also as the first document to lay the groundwork for neighbourly, if not friendly, relations between the Ottomans and the Safavids.[6]

Sulayman I's son Bayazid took shelter at Shah Tahmasp's court in 1559 after losing the struggle against his brother Selim to become their father's heir-apparent. Intensive correspondence, diplomacy and bargaining between the two sides ended up in the shah's handover of Bayazid to an Ottoman delegation in 1562 in return for a handsome payment in gold and the heir-apparent Selim's issuing a prospective writ of peace for the shah. During the time of peace after 1555, Safavid agents continued to gather donations and build up allegiance networks in Ottoman Anatolia in the name of the Safavid shah. This in turn kept up the drain of finance and manpower from the Empire to Iran. The clash of dynastic claims to legitimacy thus went on even in the absence of military conflict.[7] Indeed, it is perhaps not too fanciful to speak of these decades as a sort of early modern Middle Eastern cold war.

After Ismail II (r. 1576–7) succeeded Tahmasp and an Imposter Shah Ismail arose in Anatolia (1577), war broke out in 1578, and went on for the next twelve years. By the end of the first campaign in 1579, Ottoman armies had overcome the Safavids, taken Kars, and occupied most of Shirvan along with middle and eastern Georgia. In 1583, after winning the Battle of Torches, the Ottomans captured the province of Çukursaᵓd with its metropolis Erivan, and Baku. By 1585, the Ottomans had fully conquered Azerbaijan including Tabriz, former capital of the Safavid kingdom. Karabakh also fell to the Empire with its metropolis Ganja in 1588. After the new shah Abbas I (r. 1588–1629) pleaded for peace by sending his nephew, Haydar Mirza son of Hamza Mirza, as diplomatic hostage to the imperial court, Murad III (r. 1574–95) issued a writ of peace[8] in 1590 confirming all Ottoman conquests, after which the new border was demarcated on the spot by joint committees. In 1603, from a position of strength at home and relative advantage abroad, Abbas I broke the peace, whose conditions were in open belittlement of the Safavids, and, by 1604, he had taken back Tabriz, Nakhchivan and Erivan. Next, beating a disorderly Ottoman army at the Battle of Sufiyan in 1605, Abbas's troops drove out the Ottomans from Azerbaijan, Shirvan, Karabakh and eastern Georgia. Shunning a battle with Ottomans throughout following campaigns, the shah could hold on to Safavid recoveries and have the 1555 borders acknowledged with the Ottoman writ of peace of Nasuhpasha in 1612, but at the cost of accepting to pay a yearly tribute to the padishah.[9]

War broke out once again in 1615, this time sparked by border disagreements in the Caucasus. Over the course of the ensuing conflict, the Ottomans fruitlessly beleaguered Erivan, a Crimean raid laid waste to northwestern Iran, Abbas I resorted to scorched-earch tactics and burned down much of Azerbaijan, and the Ottomans, thrusting into this ravaged land, entered the Safavids' now-former capital Tabriz for yet another time, while the Safavids beat an Ottoman contingent. Nevertheless, even as the fighting continued, the two sides bargained on for peace. The Serav writ of pledge[10] issued in 1618 near Ardabil restored the terms of the 1612 Peace of Nasuhpasha, though with less tribute to be presented to the Ottoman monarch. Over the next few years, the two sides exchanged missions, abided by the terms of peace and upheld an outward friendship.

However, truce was undone in 1623 as the Safavids ended up taking possession of Baghdad via rebel usurpers from the Ottomans' Local Military Corps who had wrested the control of the city and hence the province in disobedience of imperial orders. Abbas I claimed to not have broken the peace for he had taken Baghdad from a rebel ringleader rather than the padishah, and therefore he asked the padishah to name his son the Safavid prince as governor of Baghdad. Nevertheless, this far-fetched justification could not forestall the war. The long-drawn-out Ottoman siege of Baghdad in 1625–6 and the subsequent clash of the two sides' armies proved inconclusive. In the meantime, the rebel pasha of Erzurum, Abaza Mehmed, defected to Iran, undermining the Ottoman war effort. Notwithstanding such disruption, the Ottomans invaded Ardalan (easternmost Kurdistan) and raided Hamadan as a counterstrike. Despite gaining the upper hand with their follow-up victory at the Battle of Erivan, the Ottomans were again unable to prevail in their second siege of Baghdad (1630). The Safavids' siege of Van (1633) proved even less effective. Almost each campaign in this fifteen-year war was preceded and followed by diplomatic contacts between the parties. Breaking the deadlock, the Ottoman army led by Murad IV (r. 1623–40) himself captured Erivan in 1635. Marching southwards, the padishah also entered Tabriz, but eventually withdrew from the wrecked Azerbaijan. In 1636, Shah Safi (r. 1629–42) recaptured Erivan after a winter siege. The definitive campaign to end the war victoriously for the Ottoman side materialised in 1638: after a heavy beleaguerment, Murad IV reconquered Baghdad, and hence Iraq. Under the immediate threat of further Ottoman advance into Iran, Shah Safi appealed for peace. The Peace of Zuhab (a.k.a. Qasr-i Shirin) signed in 1639 re-established the pre-1623 borders, which were indeed those established by the 1555 Peace of Amasya, with certain modifications in favour of the Empire.[11]

The Peace of Zuhab, which ended the last war between the Ottoman Empire and Safavid Iran (1623–39), marks, after Selim I's Iranian, Syrian and Egyptian conquests (1514–17), the second watershed that shaped the balance of power in the early modern Middle East. It proved to be the only peace document of the age that would not become overridden by a resumption of the feud it had ended. It held good as long as both signatories remained in existence, namely throughout the eighty-four years until the overthrow of the Safavid kingdom in 1722. Thanks to the regime begotten by the Peace of Zuhab, the principle of territoriality took on its full form in the Middle East because, with the resultant interstate stability, the Ottoman monarchy formally acknowledged the Safavid Iranian polity's existence as legitimate and unbounded by time.

Thus arose in Islamdom a new order whereby neighbouring, sovereign, independent states could co-exist with the legal fiction that they would live on forever. And even after the Treaty of Zuhab's natural invalidation by the downfall of one of the two signatories, it remained in indirect force. For the surviving signatory (the Ottoman Empire) and the defunct signatory (the Safavid State)'s successors (the Afşarid and later the Kajarid kingdoms of Iran) grounded their later treaties (of Kerden in 1746 and of Erzurum in 1823 as well as 1847) on the terms of Zuhab. It continued to serve as the point of reference drawing the border and conceiving sovereign statehood, in word as well as in deed. It built an international peace of unmatched resilience in the Middle East, going far beyond its original purpose of setting up a truce and settling the border.

Background and Outline

We have long assumed, implicitly, that the Ottomans and the Safavids scarcely dealt with each other after 1639. Our received knowledge holds that once the on and off fighting of almost one and a half centuries (1501–1638) ended with the Ottomans' taking back Baghdad (1638), neither side wished to become entangled with the other, that they were content with upholding the peace resting only upon a truce and a sketchy border. But this is not in fact the case. While it is true that for the years after 1639 we find nothing like the density of war-referenced military, diplomatic, financial and literary records as that pertaining to Ottoman–Safavid relations in the period prior to this date, closer investigation yields a host of lesser-known sources that attest to how this relationship lived on and required constant upkeep on both sides. Peace, after all, demands investment: it needs information and communication, in the absence of which it is liable to break down.

We perhaps best get a sense of how the maintenance of peace was itself an active process by thinking in terms of detente, that is the principle of diplomatic engagement and accommodation that underlay first the European interpower relations in the run-up to World War One and then, more famously, East–West relations in the latter decades of the Cold War. Of course, we should be aware of the limitations of this analogy. There was no Nixon figure in the mid-seventeenth-century Ottoman Empire, nor a Safavid Willy Brandt. But thinking in terms of detente does usefully draw our attention to the fact that peace between the Ottoman and Safavid states was not simply an absence of war: it was a delicate state of affairs that called for active management.

The present study reconstructs the history of Ottoman–Safavid diplomacy, political dealings and borderland contacts in the forty-four years after the Peace of Zuhab. It establishes the narrative on this uncharted field almost from scratch, with documents that were not necessarily drawn up to shed light on this subject. It demonstrates that, far from being static, as is often assumed, Ottoman–Safavid relations during the period in question were eventful and dynamic. In particular, over the chapters that follow I attempt to reconstruct how ambassadors, envoys and diplomatic heralds bearing messages and letters shuttled between monarchs, heads of government, border governors and military commanders.

The agenda of this busy diplomacy involved negotiations between host statesmen and incoming missions, talks between one of the parties and the other side's adversaries, embittering demands, declarations of goodwill and thankfulness, mistaken mobilisations, provocations, empty threats, shows of might, initiations of state of war with fielded armies, and reassurances in the face of potential tensions. It was also asymmetric. In its long-term state policy, the Ottoman Empire deemed its relations with Safavid Iran to be of purely secondary importance, and sought simply to maintain the peace at as cheap a price as possible. The Safavids, by contrast, regarded that their relations with the Ottoman Empire were vital for their well-being. Therefore, they readily made concessions to uphold the peace and build a working relationship with their western neighbour. Having internalised the conclusions drawn from their earlier fights with the Empire, they were furthermore aware of what was at stake here, and what they stood to lose if hostilities were to flare up once again.

Marginal elements still breached the borders, frontier entities occasionally raided into the other side, not only state troops but also vassals and even tributaries took military actions, central courts as well as their border governors and commanders disputed the territory, demarcation and fortified positions. Yet, the aftermaths of all these strifes bear witness to a simple reality: central courts could set the course of relations without necessarily giving in to the fait accomplis of frontier elements. The borderland brought forth content for the states to deal with, but at the end of the day, central courts could steer relations towards their direction of choice. This is why great upheavals by the borders could end up fostering a cooperative friendship between the two sides, and why lesser breaches could bring them to the brink of war. Besides, border contacts also show that diplomatic business by frontier governors (though not that by vassals or tributaries) was coordinated with, not alternative to, state centres.

My exploration of Ottoman–Safavid diplomacy and political relations in this period is divided into four chapters. In lieu of an introduction and conclusion, Chapter 1 plunges straight into the action and offers a broad overview with thematised inferences based on the findings put together in the rest of the book, handling the period as a whole. Focusing not on individual events but on structural dynamics and the logic of practice, it outlines the hierarchical foundation of relations marked by a principle of seniority–juniority on every platform, highlights the key concepts of legal personhood, representation and delegation that underlay diplomatic missions, and delineates the different categories of missions that were exchanged. It proceeds then to explore the use of language in official communications. Next it thematises foreign policy, status quos, the borderland, balance of power, harmony and strife. In doing so it depicts how busily Constantinople and Isfahan (then the capital of Safavid Iran) dealt with each other after the definitive peace. Proceeding with a degree of abstraction, Chapter 1 thus familiarises the reader with the post-1639 peacetime interactions between the Ottoman and the Safavid states.

Background and Outline

Chapter 2 moves into a granular approach and delves into the events of 1639–43, beginning with the immediate setting that came into being after the truce. Both sides prioritised a military withdrawal with minimal entanglement, and therefore pushed to upgrade their bare border protocol to a treaty with almost no change throughout its enactment. But the signing in 1639 of the border protocol of Zuhab did not, in fact, translate into an immediate end to the state of war. It took serious time and challenge for the text to be ratified and promulgated as a formal peace treaty. This episode, among others, also reflected the disparity of interest between the two parties. The defeated Safavids and the victorious Ottomans both wanted to end the war, but whereas the hard-pressed Safavids needed the peace and readily made concessions for its sake, the Ottomans, in their position of strength, deemed the peace a desideratum only on their own chosen terms. Not because of these conflicting priorities though, an unforeseen halt interrupted the ratification steps. A diplomatic 'interregnum' struck just as the prisoners of war were being exchanged, after the last ratification was sent out and before it reached its destination. Therefore, the formal state of war dragged on for a few more years after the fighting had stopped. The Ottomans swiftly built up the fortress of Baghdad, and manned it with troops as strong as the army of a lesser kingdom. Top dignitaries likewise kept their wartime titles of command. Besides the two envoys, commissioners, the ratificatory writ of pledge, a peace letter, and a few other diplomatic letters exchanged after the signing of the protocol, it took the sides two further ambassadors and two more envoys as well as at least twelve further diplomatic letters, a few espionage undertakings, backstage deals, and political executions of high-ranking personages to work out the finalisation of the peace, whose fulfilment had meanwhile become even more tangled owing to a demarcation strife and a border breach. Also thereby, the Ottomans in polite but steely fashion made clear to the Safavids, buoyed by the news of Murad IV's unexpected death in February 1640, that the Empire retained the upper hand. As the confident grand vizier Avlonyalı Kemankeş Kara Mustafa Pasha tried to reassure his restless new monarch Ibrahim (r. 1640–8) of the Empire's steady position of strength, the Ottomans set about cleansing middle Iraq of the traces of the bygone Safavid occupation (1623–38) and stamping it anew with marks of their own lordship.

Chapter 3 explores the seventeen years (1644–60) that followed the Treaty of Zuhab's coming into full effect. After the Cretan War broke out in 1645, the Republic of Venice sent emissaries to talk the Safavids into joining the anti-Ottoman alliance, all of which the Shahdom sent back empty-handed. After 1640, each time the Ottomans' European foes called on Iran to wage war against the Empire, the Safavids would decline, owing to their conviction that the Empire was essentially stronger than Iran, that gains at its expense could not be lasting, and that upholding the peace was in Iran's best interests under any circumstances. Yet, other developments too helped the Safavids make up their mind as such. For instance, the Ottomans created a military command of the Iranian front at Erzurum in 1646 and fielded an army by the border at Armenia, at the same time as fighting another war across the Mediterranean. Nevertheless, in the next few years the two sides teamed up to advance their common interests over Mughal India and the Bukharan Uzbek Khanate. One borderland that remained a persistent source of tension was the Persian Gulf hinterland, where both sides of the border were then a hotbed of local factions, which frequently played the two monarchies off against each other. Safavid plans in 1651 for a campaign against Ottoman-tributary Basra could likely have sparked a direct confrontation between the two states. But it was instead the Basran principality's infighting that shook the two states' sprouting neighbourship, as it triggered an Ottoman intervention from Baghdad, which the anti-Ottoman faction in Basra confronted with warriors recruited from Iran. Yet, after setbacks, the Ottomans could turn the tide: the Sublime Porte did away with the Basran principality's tributary status and converted it into a hereditary fiefdom within the Empire. In 1656, the Ottomans, against indirect Iranian hostility from the early 1650s, set up another military command of the Iranian front, this time at Van, and fielded an imperial army near the border at Azerbaijan. As before, the Safavids gave up their claims once this military command sent emissaries across the border to Iranian governors and to the shah himself. Assured that the Safavids posed no threat, in 1656 the Sublime Porte rejected overtures from the Mughals to invade and split Iran. For the Ottomans, their line of demarcation with Safavid Iran was worth preserving.

Chapter 4 deals with the last twenty-three years spanned by this book (1660–82), when the nexus of entanglements shifted altogether from the north and the middle to the southern flank of the border. Once again, Basra was a particular upsetter of rest. Against the Ottomans' regime makeover in the principality of Basra, three uprisings broke out in the 1660s, once again backed up with troops recruited from Iran. The Ottomans had to undertake three imperial campaigns to crush the Basran establishment's insubordination for good: in the end Basra became fully annexed as a province. In 1666, the Ottoman and the Safavid grand viziers exchanged letters to underscore the two states' neighbourship tested by the ongoing clashes in southern Iraq. By fielding secondary imperial armies near the Persian Gulf while fighting full-fledged wars in Europe and the Mediterranean, the Ottomans effectively browbeat the Safavids. Even after the Basran upheaval was settled, the Sublime Porte asserted itself with the Shahdom in 1669 through a letter of victory recording the fulfilled conquest of Crete from Venice.

Perhaps somewhat cowed by such assertions of Ottoman mastery, the Safavids made a point of denying asylum to the defeated Basran leaders. While it remained mutually accepted practice for both parties to offer refuge to individual defectors, to receive mass defections from across the border was much likelier to stir up a war, particularly when, as in the Basran instance, the defectors proposed also to transfer territory and revenue from one state to the other. Even when presented with the lucrative prospect of acquiring Basra, the Safavids were reluctant to risk a clash with their Ottoman neighbours, choosing instead to prioritise stability over the riskier possibility of marginal gain. As the Cretan War was going on in the 1660s, Iran rejected another round of Venetian offers to fight against the Empire, and turned down a further call, this time from Poland and Russia, in the 1670s. This latter decade was in fact not entirely peaceful, and on several occasions both the Ottomans and the Safavids mobilised against each other when borderland hearsay triggered false alarms and led to states of emergency. The greatest threat to diplomatic stability was often inadvertent human error. By the early 1680s, peace was restored, both along the frontier and in communications between the courts of the two states. But this was only the calm before the storm, for a revolution in Middle Eastern diplomacy was about to break out without the slightest foretoken.

As for our current knowledge on post-1639 Ottoman–Safavid relations, the present book engages with existing scholarship extensively. This it does, however, not by discussing the literature in the body text, but by using and, when need be, quietly setting aright these works in the chapter endnotes, for the sake of keeping the book's flow as free as possible from historiographical debates and as refined as possible in establishing hitherto-unknown facts upon the new information unearthed during research. The same goes for primary sources, which I draw on heavily and, whenever necessary, correct quietly in the endnotes, instead of diverging the flow to discuss a particular source. These choices are made in line with the intended function of the work: most of the facts found in the body text, no matter how 'factual' they may seem at first glance, are new discoveries, and whereas I thematise and contextualise them, the originality of the knowledge they reveal is a main strength of the book that will presumably have a longer lifespan than the historiographical debates that come along. The visibility of primary sources and secondary literature are therefore confined to endnotes, and engagement with them to references.[12]

Notes

1. For an introduction to Ottoman–Safavid trade in the handled period, see Suraiya Faroqhi, 'Trade between the Ottomans and Safavids: The Acem Tüccarı and Others', in *Iran and the World in the Safavid Age*, ed. Willem Floor and Edmund Herzig (London: I. B. Tauris, 2012), 237–52.
2. For instance, again from the post-1639 decades, I have a pile of likewise new, unexploited archival records sitting on my shelf, with which a separate monograph on Ottoman–Safavid trade might be written.
3. For an overview of the religious dimension of Ottoman–Safavid relations after 1639, see Selim Güngörürler, 'The Qizilbash in Anatolia after 1630: Sidelined and Estranged', in *Iranian/Persianate Subalterns in the Safavid Period: Their Role and Depiction: Recovering 'Lost Voices'*, ed. Andrew J. Newman (Berlin: Gerlach Press, 2022), 83–98; Güngörürler, 'Islamic Discourse in Ottoman–Safavid Peacetime Diplomacy after 1049/1639', in *Historicizing Sunni Islam in the Ottoman Empire*, eds Tijana Krstic and Derin Terzioğlu (Leiden: Brill, 2020), 470–500.
4. Hanna Sohrweide, 'Der Sieg der Safawiden in Persien und seine Rückwirkungen auf die Schiiten Anatoliens im 16. Jahrhundert', *Der Islam* 41 (1965): 95–223; Adel Allouche, *The Origins and Development of the Ottoman–Safavid Conflict 906–962/1500–1555* (Berlin: Schwarz, 1983); Faruk Sümer, *Safevi Devletinin Kuruluşu ve Gelişmesinde Anadolu Türklerinin Rolü* (Ankara: Güven Matbaası, 1976); Michel M. Mazzaoui, *The Origins of the Safavids: Şhiism, Sufism, and the Ghulat* (Wiesbaden: Franz Steiner Verlag, 1972); Rustam Shukurov, 'The Campaign of Shaykh Djunayd Safawî against Trebizond (1456 AD/860 H)', *Byzantine and Modern Greek Studies* 17, no. 1 (1993): 127–40; Ayfer Karakaya-Stump, *The Kizilbash/Alevis in Ottoman Anatolia: Sufism, Politics and Community* (Edinburgh: Edinburgh University Press, 2020); Ayşe Baltacıoğlu-Brammer, 'The Formation of Kızılbaş Communities in Anatolia and Ottoman Responses, 1450s–1630s', *International Journal of Turkish Studies* 20 (2014): 21–48; Baltacıoğlu-Brammer, *Politics of Sectarianism in the Middle East: Ottoman Sunnism, Safavid Shiism, and the Kızılbaş* (forthcoming).
5. Feridun Emecen, *Zamanın İskenderi, Şarkın Fatihi. Yavuz Sultan Selim* (Istanbul: Yitik Hazine Yayınları, 2010); Şahabettin Tekindağ, 'Yeni Kaynak ve Vesikaların Işığı Altında Yavuz Sultan Selim'in İran Seferi', *İstanbul Üniversitesi Edebiyat Fakültesi Tarih Dergisi* 17, no. 22 (1968); Jean-Louis Bacque-Grammont, 'The Eastern Policy of Süleyman the Magnificent', in *Süleyman the Second and His Time*, eds Halil İnalcık and Cemal Kafadar (Istanbul: The Isis Press, 1993); Reha Bilge, *1514 Yavuz Selim ve Şah Ismail: Türkler, Türkmenler ve Farslar* (Istanbul: Giza Yayınları, 2010); Roger M. Savory, 'Tajlu Khanum: Was She Captured by the Ottomans at the Battle of Chaldiran, or not?' in *Irano-Turcic Cultural Contacts in the 11th–17th Centuries*, ed. E. M. Jeremias (Piliscsaba: The Avicenna Institute

of Middle Eastern Studies, 2003); Refet Yinanç, *Dulkadir Beyliği* (Ankara: Türk Tarih Kurumu, 1989); Benjamin Weineck, *Zwischen Verfolgung und Eingliederung: Kızılbaş-Aleviten im osmanischen Staat (16.–18. Jahrhundert)* (Ergon Verlag: Baden-Baden, 2020).

6. M. Tayyib Gökbilgin, 'Arz ve Raporlarına Göre İbrâhim Paşa'nın Irakeyn Seferi'nde İlk Tedbirleri ve Fütuhatı', *Belleten* 21, no. 83 (1957): 449–82; İsmet Parmaksızoğlu, 'Kuzey Irak'ta Osmanlı Hakimiyetinin Kuruluşu ve Memun Bey'in Hatıraları', *Belleten* 37, no. 146 (1973): 191–230; Rhoads Murphey, 'Süleyman's Eastern Policy', in *Süleyman the Second and His Time*, eds Halil İnalcık and Cemal Kafadar (Istanbul: The Isis Press, 1993); Walter Posch, *Osmanisch-safavidische Beziehungen (1545–1550): Der Fall Alkas Mirza*, vol. 1–2 (Wien: Verlag der Österreichischen Akademie der Wissenschaften, 2013); A. Ekber Diyanet, *İlk Osmanlı-İran Anlaşması (1555 Amasya Musâlahası)* (Istanbul: İstanbul Üniversitesi Edebiyat Fakültesi, 1971); Remzi Kılıç, *Kanuni Devri Osmanlı-İran Münasebetleri 1520–1566* (Istanbul: IQ Kültür ve Sanat Yayıncılık, 2006); Dündar Aydın, *Erzurum Beylerbeyiliği ve Teşkilatı: Kuruluş ve Genişleme Devri, 1535–1566* (Ankara: Türk Tarih Kurumu, 1998); Menuchihr Parsadust, *Shah Tahmasb-i Avval* (Tehran: Shirkat-i Sahami-yi Intishar, HS 1381).

7. Şerafettin Turan, *Kanuni'nin Oğlu Şehzade Bayezid Vak'ası* (Ankara: Türk Tarih Kurumu, 1961); Josef Matuz, 'Vom Übertritt osmanischer Soldaten zu den Safawiden', in *Die islamische Welt zwischen Mittelalter und Neuzeit: Festschrift für Hans Robert Roemer zum 65. Geburtstag*, ed. Ulrich Haarmann (Beirut: Orient-Institut der Deutschen Morgenländischen Gesellschaft, 1979), 402–15; Elke Eberhard, *Osmanische Polemik gegen die Safawiden im 16. Jahrhundert nach arabischen Handschriften* (Freiburg im Breisgau: Klaus Schwarz Verlag, 1970); Istvan Nyitrai, 'The Third Period of the Ottoman–Safavid Conflict: Struggle of Political Ideologies (1555–1578)', in *Irano-Turcic Cultural Contacts in the 11th–17th Centuries*, ed. E. M. Jeremias (Piliscsaba: The Avicenna Institute of Middle Eastern Studies, 2003); Colin Imber, 'The Persecution of the Ottoman Shiites According to the Mühimme Defterleri 1565–1585', *Der Islam* 56 (1979): 245–73; Erhan Afyoncu (ed.), *Venedikli Elçilerin Raporlarına Göre Kanuni ve Şehzade Mustafa* (Istanbul: Yeditepe Yayınevi, 2015); Rudi Matthee, 'The Ottoman–Safavid War of 986–998/1578–90: Motives and Causes', *International Journal of Turkish Studies* 20, no. 1–2 (2014): 1–20.

8. *sulhnâme-i humâyun*.

9. Bekir Kütükoğlu, *Osmanlı-İran Siyasi Münasebetleri (1578–1612)* (Istanbul: Fetih Cemiyeti Yayınları, 1993); Faruk Söylemez, 'Anadolu'da Sahte Şah Ismail İsyanı', *Erciyes Üniversitesi Sosyal Bilimler Enstitüsü Dergisi*, no. 17 (2004): 71–90; Abdullah Gündoğdu, 'Türkistan'da Osmanlı İran Rekabeti (1583–1598)', in *Uluslararası Osmanlı Târihi Sempozyumu (8–10 Nisan 1999) Bildirileri*, ed. Gökçe Turan (İzmir: Türk Ocakları İzmir Şubesi, 2000), 141–52.

10. ᶜahdnâme.
11. Özer Küpeli, *Osmanlı-Safevi Münasebetleri (1612–1639)* (Istanbul: Yeditepe Yayınları, 2014); Claudia Römer, 'Die osmanische Belagerung Bagdads 1034–35/1624–25. Ein Augenzeugenbericht', *Der Islam* 66 (1989): 119–36; Elke Niewöhner Eberhard, 'Machtpolitische Aspekte des osmanisch-safawidischen Kampfes um Bagdad im 16./17. Jahrhundert', *Turcica* 6 (1975): 103–27; Rhoads Murphey, 'The Functioning of the Ottoman Army under Murad IV (1623–1639/1032–1049): Key to the Understanding of the Relationship between Center and Periphery in Seventeenth-Century Turkey' (PhD diss., University of Chicago, 1979).
12. For an evaluation of the bulk of the sources and scholarly works I reference in the book, see the 'Introduction' to Selim Güngörürler, 'Diplomacy and Political Relations between the Ottoman Empire and Safavid Iran, 1639–1722' (PhD diss., Georgetown University, 2016).

1

Settings and Trends of the Ottoman–Safavid Detente

Beyond all that befell the Ottomans and the Safavids after the Peace of Zuhab, a set of overarching fundamentals governed how the two sides dealt with each other. The foremost one of these mutually acknowledged fundamentals was that it was not egalitarianism but Ottoman primacy that framed the relations. This unequal relationship stamped every platform on which the two sides interacted. It was clearly manifest, for example, in the status of the two states' diplomatic missions. Ottoman and Safavid ambassadors, envoys and heralds were one another's mutual counterparts, but they were not peers. Ottoman dignitaries were hierarchically superior to their Safavid counterparts, as a token of the Ottoman monarchy's supreme imperial[1] dignity against the kingly[2] or lesser imperial rank[3] of the Safavids. This disparity branded each step of diplomatic conduct, such as right of correspondence, titulature, order of precedence and applicable class of protocol. A mark of real power relations in diplomatic hierarchy, Ottoman primacy was by no means an obsolete artefact of olden days, or a one-sided claim targeting a domestic audience without currency at interstate level. The correlation between diplomatic titulature and order of precedence reflected the power relations and the status quo.

The highest and most binding form of Ottoman–Safavid diplomacy was correspondence between two sovereigns. One should not attribute the highest level of diplomatic representation to the monarchs though, for they were the heads of not only their states but also of the dynasties which themselves were *the* states.[4] Therefore they did not represent their respective states; their selves were rather the embodiments of their respective states, which were principal parties to diplomacy.[5] The sovereigns hence stood above the highest level of diplomatic representation. When wording the parties to relations, diplomatic writs identified the dynastic establishments specifically for this reason.[6] This finds its best utterance within official correspondence in the names of the polities in question vis-à-vis the names of the respective realms over which they held sway: Ottoman State[7] and Safavid State. In contrast, the (Ottomans') Empire was called

Rûm, namely the (former eastern) *Roman* (Empire), hence *Byzantium*.[8] The then-standard use of Rûm, as had been the case for centuries by the later Safavid period, denoted the territory of the empire that controlled first and foremost Anatolia, and whenever applicable, also its neighbouring lands. Especially in the Persian of the day, but also in Turkish as well, Rûm identified, politically, geographically and in terms of subjects, the Ottomans' realms, namely the Empire.[9] Equating Rûm with Ottoman subjects and the Empire was standard not only in unofficial prose and poetry but also in official diplomatic writings. In other words, Rûm was the sole name by which the Empire as a whole was called, both officially and unofficially.[10] In turn, both sides called the kingdom of the Safavids *Iran* and *Ajam* interchangeably.[11]

Alongside these territorial identifications, there are of course also the ethnicised names *Persia* and *Turkey*, customarily used in European languages to denote (Safavid) Iran and the Ottoman Empire. Europeans called the Ottoman realms as a whole the *Turkish Empire* and the Ottoman monarch the *Turkish emperor* in diplomacy and in scholarship, besides the Ottomans' own terminology, while they referred to the Safavids' kingdom as *Persia*. On the face of it, the use of these terms is perfectly understandable. The Turkness of the Ottoman dynasty and the primacy of Turkishness in the workings of the Ottoman establishment was beyond dispute. The same goes for the centrality of all things Persian in Safavid Iran. The use of *Persia* and *Turkey* for (Safavid) Iran and the (Ottoman) Empire, however, were not only nonexistent in Persian- and Turkish-language primary sources, but are also misleading when used to this end today. In fact, reference to 'Turkey' and 'Persia' in our context obscures more than it reveals. These dynasties reigned over lands that were too manifold to be named after an ethnicity: politically, early modern Ottomans did not call themselves Turks nor their empire Turkey, except when sometimes quoting from the speech of Europeans. Likewise, the Safavids did not call themselves Persians or their kingdom Persia, which comes only on top of the fact that the Safavids were a Turkish/Turkified dynasty and had made their overwhelmingly Turkish military the ruling class of Iran. In both territories, people used the identifications Persian and Turk to name ethnic, cultural, demographic, historical and political phenomena, but not to name their realm or state.

In Ottoman–Safavid dealings, there was no state of Iran nor an Empire existing autonomously from the dynasties that reigned over them. Parties to diplomacy were thus institutionalised dynasties, not the realms that they ruled. An ambassador sent from Isfahan, for example, embodied not Iran but the Safavid shahdom, just as an envoy sent from Constantinople embodied not Rûm the Empire but the Ottoman emperor.[12] This was because the two dynasties did not occupy the thrones of pre-existing sovereignties; they ruled new states of their own making. It is true that the territorial outline of the Ottoman Empire resembled that of the Eastern Roman Empire and Safavid Iran that of greater Persia. But this was a matter of geography, not of statehood. The realm had a continuity transcending the state in the spheres of geography, territory, borders, subjecthood of dwellers and even monarchy (throne and crown). Nevertheless, relations, diplomacy, treaties and deals took place between the dynastic Ottoman and Safavid institutions, not between the realms of Iran and Rûm. Pacts were made between the monarchs themselves, and if these contracts were to remain in force for perpetuity, they bound the future successors of the institutionalised embodiments of the two dynasties, namely the states. What we are dealing with here is then interstate diplomacy between institutionalised dynastic establishments, not between countries, nations or realms.

At many levels of analysis, equating the dynasty with the state would be somewhat anachronistic, too literal an observance of an old concept that gainsaid many of the realities of the later seventeenth and the early eighteenth centuries. In Ottoman–Safavid diplomacy, however, this equation continued to hold true, and rested upon reality rather than an artificial thought. Even though the state had by then become a mostly standalone institution in Europe and the Middle East, in Ottoman–Safavid dealings the dynasties still constituted the reason of state, whereby states were corporate embodiments of these ruling houses. Ottoman–Safavid diplomacy, while taking place during early modernity, still clung on to the earlier setting in which state was the institutionalised household of the dynasty. Were the ruling house to cease to exist, the state would thus cease to exist also: the end of a dynasty thus would entail the invalidation of the treaties to which said dynasty was party. The ruling house was not a constituent of the crown within a state establishment; the wider network of the dynasty was itself the state.

This construct, which in many ways had become outdated by the mid-seventeenth century, was by no means obsolete in Ottoman–Safavid dealings. It almost single-handedly defined the state, which was party to diplomatic dealings, and by extension delimited the realm, whose continuity in other respects was acknowledged without attributing it legal personhood. Therefore, the role of a monarch when conducting diplomacy was not to represent the state or to act on its behalf. Rather, it was in the monarch's capacity as head of the dynasty to embody the state in diplomatic interactions. And while individual monarchs differed in the extent to which they personally participated in the policy-making, they uniformly conferred authority on policy by the mere dint of articulating it in word, be it spoken or written.

It was furthermore in these communications that Ottoman hierarchical primacy likewise manifested itself. This hierarchical relationship was clear from the earliest diplomatic communication to ratify the protocol of 1639 into a peace treaty. In composing the shah's writ of pledge, the Safavid chancellery stuck to a deferential style, while the Ottoman chancellery chose a rather haughty wording for the padishah's peace writ in answer. The inequality of this relationship was not acquired but inbuilt from the outset. Although in the Peace of Zuhab the Sublime Porte remarked the Safavids' lordship over Iran, thus acknowledging them as the rightful sovereigns of a neighbouring, standalone territory, it did not bestow on them any title that could hint that there were two equal sides corresponding with each other: the padishah's titles were supreme imperial and those of the shah were kingly. Nor, furthermore, were these expressions of hierarchical inequality simply a reflection of the fact that the Ottomans had won and the Safavids had lost the war of 1623–39. Shifting nuances aside, such expressions of Ottoman superiority had broadly been a constant in Iranian–Ottoman dealings ever since the 1510s and would continue even after the fall of the Safavids. Every letter that the two sides sent to each other after 1639 likewise shows the unequal positions of the Ottoman 'shah-of-shahs' and the Safavid 'shah'. Both sides had internalised the principle that in their relations with one another they stood unequally.

In a setting where the heads of states were formally themselves the states rather than its representatives, the highest degree of diplomatic representation lay with the heads of government. In their capacity as premiers, and absolute deputies of their monarchs, Ottoman grand viziers and Safavid chief viziers conducted top level, official and binding diplomacy without needing credentials to bestow plenipotentiary powers upon them. Separate diplomatic deeds of a monarch and his premier of course expressed a single political will. But communications between premiers struck a different tone from those between monarchs. Whereas exchanges between sovereigns tended to be highly abstract, focusing on underlying and overarching fundamentals of relations, communications between premiers were often more granular in detail, discussing specific novelties, challenges or adventitous occurences.

As a continued reflection of Ottoman primacy vis-à-vis the Safavids, Ottoman grand viziers, who ranked at a more-or-less kingly level, stood above Safavid chief viziers, who mostly ranked at a level comparable to

European grand dukes.[13] This is shown not only by diplomatic letters but also by the template *inscriptio* that Ottoman correspondence compilations set down for use when addressing Iran's premier.[14] Safavid chief viziers were not entitled to write to the Ottoman monarch, let alone receive letters from him, whereas Ottoman grand viziers both wrote to and received letters from the Safavid shah, and this correspondence was by no means just ceremonial. The padishah's absolute deputy held direct political talks with the shah, and was empowered to go so far as to warn the shah against taking a specific step, and threaten him, albeit with due courteousness, with retaliation.[15]

Precedence and hierarchy aside, correspondence from premiers had a specific function in diplomatic communications. Both monarchs and premiers could send letters at the same time, offering complementary elements of a single message. Their letters generally covered much the same ground, each confirming and emphasising the upshot of the other. On occasion, however, the two letters might underscore different aspects of the question at hand, thereby demonstrating the complexity of the issue. And sometimes the two writs might even contradict one another outwardly, promises of amity sitting alongside threats of reprisal in a sort of good cop/bad cop set-up, simultaneously assuring the addressee of what they might hope and warning them of what they should fear.

Below the premier was a range of dignitaries and diplomats who might engage in diplomatic activities such as communicating messages and entering into pledges. Unlike premiers, these functionaries required credentials in order to act. One notable class of credentialed dignitaries were the governors-general at the borderland. In their capacity as regional 'deputy of the monarchy', the Ottoman governors-general of Baghdad and Erzurum and the Safavid governors-general of Çukursaʾd (Erivan) and Azerbaijan (Tabriz) were empowered to play a leading role in borderland diplomacy. They introduced themselves to their opposite number with letters of friendship that initiated their credentials to interact on behalf of the monarchy with the neighbouring state. Borderland governors-general also exhanged letters to resolve local cases of strife, regulate cross-border faring of convoys, warn of potential dangers and coordinate joint operations.[16] This cross-border interaction between frontier governors constituted an essential line of Ottoman–Safavid diplomacy. It ensured that transfrontier communications continued even at times when no active contact was present between monarchs and premiers, and that borderland diplomacy continued with an almost constant exchange of correspondence and missions,[17] even though next to nothing of this documentation has come down to us today.

The letters of friendship that Ottoman frontier governors sent across the border upon taking up office too show how matching Ottoman and Safavid posts were counterparts but not peers. Letter templates that were logged in correspondence compilations hint at how established it was for Ottoman border governors-general to correspond with the shah,[18] and likewise did Safavid shahs and chief viziers exchange missions with Ottoman governors,[19] while it was out of the question for a Safavid governor to correspond with the Ottoman padishah, or even the grand vizier. Exhibiting the same hierarchical disparity in Ottoman–Safavid diplomacy, an Ottoman governor ranked as prince.[20] If created marshal, then he enjoyed high princely,[21] and sometimes a kind of sovereignly dignity. On the other hand, a plain governor of the Safavids ranked as a kind of lesser margrave as seen in the below-princely *inscriptio* chosen when an Ottoman governor wrote to him.[22]

The next category of functionaries who ran the diplomatic business between the Ottoman and the Safavid states after the Peace of Zuhab were ad hoc diplomats. Ranking highest within this group, ambassadors[23] were authorised to fully represent the monarch and the state. Aside from conveying correspondence, they could wield their plenipotentiary powers to stop wars, bargain for new deals, amend the status quo and promulgate ratified peace treaties. At the end of the credentials section of the diplomatic letters entrusted to them, it was further noted that ambassadors-extraordinary were commissioned to raise in spoken discussion topics not mentioned in the written text itself.[24] Among diplomats, only the ambassador-extraordinary had the capacity to negotiate and strike a deal, or make a binding pledge. At such talks, the ambassador was authorised to go beyond the broadly worded content of the letter that he had brought with him. There was a culture of secrecy within both the Ottoman and Safavid diplomatic practices, with ambassadors empowered to negotiate certain matters that were never set down in writing. While chronicles and mission reports notarised the formalities, ceremonies and non-political gatherings in detail, negotiations were not written down.

In contrast to ambassador, an envoy,[25] while officially representing the state, was only authorised to reconfirm the status quo by handing in a letter or to forward a message letting the other side know of a new happening. Typical tasks that could be commissioned to an envoy were forwarding ratifications, announcing peace (re-)confirmations, bearing letters tackling disputes, ceremonially symbolising new deals or reconciliations, and wishing well on accessions.[26] An envoy was not empowered to raise any matters not itemised in the missives entrusted to him; nor could he bargain for and strike deals, or make binding pledges beyond the authorisation defined for him in the accompanying correspondence. If an envoy was dispatched to let the other party know of a new development, an amendment, or a protest, this was written in full within the accompanying document(s) as a mark of the envoy's non-authorisation to negotiate changes to the status quo or to go beyond reconfirming it.[27]

As the lowest-ranking of mission leaders, diplomatic heralds[28] carried messages, first confirmations of protocols, premiers' letters unaccompanied by a letter from the monarch, or unofficial procurement orders. They were not given audiences with monarchs. Instead, premiers received them with a ceremonial gathering. Diplomatic heralds thus dealt with the host premier and other relevant dignitaries, without engaging the sovereign.[29] One function performed by diplomatic heralds was to inform the other state of an instance of regnal succession following the dethronement of the former monarch. In instances of succession resulting from natural death, by contrast, no such diplomatic mission was undertaken, and the new monarch simply awaited congratulations from his counterpart.[30]

The question of who congratulated whose enthronement in which way was another instance of the hierarchy operating between the two states. After 1639, the shahs sent ambassadors to congratulate the newly enthroned padishahs.[31] In contrast, the padishahs did not even send envoys, let alone ambassadors, to the newly enthroned shahs. Rather, the Ottomans waited until the next incoming Safavid embassy, and once it was returning to Iran, they sent along a legation of congratulations.[32] Thus the Ottoman court asserted its own superiority on these occasions too. This practice rested on that convention of Eastern diplomacy that primacy was shown off by receiving, not sending, the higher-ranking mission.

A further consequence of this hierarchy was that Safavid accessions did not trigger a reconfirmation or renegotiation of the peace, whereas Ottoman accessions did. As only ambassadors could negotiate amendments and strike new deals, any reconfirmation of the status quo and changes to it would be shaped and enacted at the padishah's court – not at the shah's. In addition, the shah also sent non-congratulatory embassies on great occasions.[33] This too upheld the unspoken principle that no deal would be finalised at the Safavid court. Negotiations could be held either at the frontier or the imperial court, but the imperial court retained a prerogative to put agreements into force.

As a rule, Ottoman envoys were picked from among elder Outer Court *agha*s – such as a master-gatekeeper[34] or a patrician[35] of the imperial court. Safavid ambassadors were mostly *xan*s,[36] namely governors matching non-vizier Ottoman pashas of two standards,[37] and exceptionally a highly prestigious *soltan*, such as the deputy-master of the Kızılbaş-Safavid order, corresponding to an Ottoman *bey* at the level of provincial sub-governor. A Safavid envoy would normally be a Royal Court *beyg*, in turn on a par with an Ottoman Court *agha*. Diplomatic heralds handled official business between premiers and private correspondence between monarchs. Ottoman heralds ranked below an Outer Court *agha*, and would therefore hold the rank of *çavuş* – an Imperial Council sergeant,[38] or lower – such as a palace-guard.[39]

All Safavid ambassadors, envoys and establishable heralds sent to the Sublime Porte from 1639 to 1682 were from the Turkish clans of the Kızılbaş military-political nobility. The same was probably true for the staffers of these missions. Although there is no official record to indicate that Kızılbaş lineage was a formal criterion in being chosen for diplomatic missions, it is such a constant feature that it is unlikely to have been a coincidence. The Ottomans, while sometimes remarking the Kızılbaş-ness of an incoming Safavid diplomat, seem not to have been particularly attentive to what Kızılbaş clan the diplomat or his staffers hailed from, so, when mentioning them other than in official letters of answer, they generally skipped clan surnames.

In any instance of diplomatic interchange, communications between guest missions and host statesmen required mastery of Persian and Turkish in conversational and literary registers. Ottoman diplomats who visited Safavid Iran, plus many of the Ottoman officials tasked with hosting Safavid missions, had studied Persian as graduates of the Inner Imperial Court; they could not only speak but also read, and if particularly gifted, compose literature in Persian, besides a self-explanatory mastery of Turkish.[40] Second to Turkish, Persian was maybe the most prestigious language in the Ottoman Empire, such that it, together with Arabic, was regarded as an integral part of an educated person's cultural repertoire. It was thus not deemed foreign despite being non-native. Persian literature in prose and poetry was the model for those composing in the *divan* jargon of Turkish. Persian chancellery and literary sayings were not only borrowed straightforwardly into Turkish *divan* terminology but also innovated within Turkish itself by Persophone Turks/Ottomans. Persian was widely taught and, in the field of poetry, it thrived in the Empire both within Turkish and through compositions in Persian. In diplomacy, Persian was a lingua franca for many Eastern courts.[41] In the Turko-Persian world stretching from Hungary to east-central Asia, Persian enjoyed a similar, if not identical, prestige and function as Latin did in Europe. This cultural, linguistic and artistic integratedness in courtly life and diplomacy also had parallels in the waning but still ongoing scholarly exchange between Greater Iran and Rûm.[42]

The linguistic situation on the other side of the frontier was somewhat different. Unlike the case with Persian in the Ottoman Empire, Turkish had been implanted long ago in Iran as a widespread native tongue, thanks to the presence of a politically and militarily dominant minority of Turks. Turkish was the language of not only the Kızılbaş nobility but also the Safavid dynasty and the extended royal household itself. Turkish thus remained the working tongue of speech at the shahly court, in the military and, throughout not only the first century but the whole Safavid period, among the ruling elite, even including those who were not ethnic Turks, and at provincial courts.[43] While Persian was the preferred language for chancellery composition and learned production in Safavid Iran, knowledge of the spoken lingua franca of the ruling class, namely Turkish, was essential for officials to be able to function at the shah's court, in provincial administration and in the military. This did not mean, furthermore, that Turkish was a purely instrumental language; indeed, there remained in Safavid Iran a tradition of composing and enjoying literature in Turkish.

Therefore, the Ottoman Empire and Safavid Iran were culturally intertwined to the utmost, thanks to the outstanding positions that both sides' official and native tongues enjoyed in each other's realms. This intertwinement was so broad and rooted that it left bold marks on diplomacy.

In official correspondence, the Ottomans wrote to the Safavids in Turkish, and the Safavids wrote to the Ottomans in Persian. It is noteworthy that throughout the timespan under study, the Safavid chancellery seemingly did not draw up any letter to the Sublime Porte in Turkish, even though it occasionally issued Turkish official documents to its own functionaries and diplomatic letters to foreign states. The Sublime Porte too, although still drawing up documents in Persian in other spheres, likewise never wrote to the Safavids in Persian. Yet, in letters addressed to Iranians, the Ottoman chancellery chose a much more florid, poetical style and a remarkably more Persianate Turkish than was already the case in genres employing the *divan* jargon.[44] In diplomatic correspondence between the Ottomans and the Safavids, a more-or-less standardised Arabo-Persian vocabulary was used particularly for certain formal components such as *inscriptio*, *intitulatio*, final *salutatio*, and the terminology identifying the status quo; as a consequence, some fixed elements of these diplomatic writs in Persian and in Turkish were almost identical in wording. This Persianising tendency in communications with the Safavids seems to have been a deliberate policy. In letters addressed to European courts over the same timespan, the Ottomans used by contrast a more Turkish terminology, a vocabulary which did not make its way into the jargon that the Ottomans employed when writing to the Safavids.[45]

As noted above, an instance of Ottoman dynastic succession required the Safavids to send an embassy and a royal letter. Such ceremonial contacts may on the face of it seem like a pure formality, but in fact they were freighted with significance, as to be inferred from the accompanying correspondence, negotiations, and the outcomes thereof.[46] Although much of the content of this congratulatory diplomacy was conventional, laden as it was with stock phrases expressing mutual regard, these communications also conveyed a more substantive message, serving to reconfirm or modify existing contractual undertakings. The accompanying letters exchanged between the Ottoman and the Safavids monarchs and premiers did not however itemise every single peace condition and treaty clause then in force, unlike in the Ottomans' dealings with European states. Rather, in their correspondence the Ottomans and the Safavids simply acknowledged, through keyword mentions, the validity of the Peace of Zuhab, and remarked, in the most ornamental wording possible, any modification to the treaty. Other than when ratifying a treaty, reconfirmations between the Ottomans and the Safavids did not include full texts of treaties and amendment clauses. While in the Ottomans' relations with Poland or the Habsburgs not only the resultant pact but also later reconfirmations were mostly writs of pledge bargained by the two sides but issued by one side, and sometimes also ratified by the receiver, in relations with the Safavids after 1639, later reconfirmations of ratified deals were promulgated by monarchical letters, which explains the shorter texts.

After the hostilities ended in 1639, the two parties did not simply stop dealing with one another. Thereafter too did monarchs, premiers, marshals and governors-general send each other missions of all scopes, headed by ambassadors, envoys, heralds and emissaries. And through these missions, these statesmen swapped with their addressees a range of diplomatic missives, such as protocols, ratifications and letters. The extent of this interaction is difficult to quantify, because it is clear that the vast majority of communications between the two sides were never set down in writing, or, when they were, have since been lost; the extant documents that I have been able to identify in this book are a small amount of what was a greater corpus. Therefore, judging the frequency of the diplomatic activity by counting the documents identified in this book will underrepresent the full breadth, because, for example, most instances of the seemingly continuous border diplomacy were never logged into registers or chronicles. Moreover, even the extant sources that document Ottoman–Safavid dealings after 1639 are much richer than the quantifiable pieces of official correspondence.

This was a multi-focal diplomatic environment. The most obvious hubs of diplomatic activity were the two metropoles and they could determine the course of relations as long as they chose to. A fait accompli staged by borderland actors and then dropped in the state's lap could not upset Ottoman–Safavid neighbourship politically, unless statesmen were involved in plotting it. The frontier could furnish the state centres with capital stock to bargain on, but even the most peace-threatening and treaty-breaching events from the borderland could not harm relations between the two states so long as the centres did not let this happen.

Away from the capital, meanwhile, governorates were key agents in implementing the central court's will in the frontier. On the western side of the border, the governorates of Baghdad in the south and Erzurum in the north stood out as military bulwarks and embodiments of state authority. On the eastern side of the border, the province of Çukursaʾd (with its metropolis Erivan) was effectively a counterpart in Armenia to Erzurum, just as the Tabriz-centred province of Azerbaijan offset Ottoman Van. Southwards, across Iraq, although the Safavids lacked in the border province of Kirmanshah a bulwark to counter Baghdad, this gap was easily filled by the nearby Isfahan, the heartland of Safavid Iran where the kingdom's strength and resources were concentrated. As a difference between the two sides of the border, in the south the Safavids had more vassal principalities than regular provinces, and were thus hampered by not having a single governorate-general capable of harnessing the rest of the frontier to implement the centre's will. The northernmost flank of the Ottoman–Safavid frontier was in Georgia, with vassal petty kingdoms and principalities (all fractions of the medieval kingdom of Georgia) on each side of the border. These realms were somewhat unbiddable, and there were frequent cases of upheavals, encroachments and coups on both sides. However, such instances of local disorder rarely became a subject in Ottoman–Safavid diplomacy, with neither metropole seemingly wanting to get entangled in contention over the rather unforeseeable actions of Georgian dynasts.

Though peace reigned with Iran, the Empire held the Iranian frontier in an undeclared state of war by fielding an imperial army[47] under the command of a specially appointed marshal and by deploying extraordinary Sublime Court contingents[48] during a total of eight years out of forty-three.[49] Notwithstanding these deployments, however, as the states never wished for war, even the tensest situations did not escalate into an armed conflict between the two states. Both sides were determined to uphold their peaceful neighbourship.

Given that the Shahdom and the Sublime Porte were capable of setting the direction of relations despite the regional and local power holders at their respective borderlands, not the content but the course of Ottoman–Safavid diplomacy was determined more by long-term metropolitan strategy than by the actions of the man on the ground. As noted above, each state abided by a distinct and coherent policy. On the one hand, the Safavids were committed to upholding the peace with the Ottomans at almost whatever cost and furthering the relations even when this cost their own side more sacrifices and concessions than it did the Ottomans. The Shahdom accepted its juniority in this relationship, and sought to maximise its interests within the established unequal order. The Sublime Porte, by contrast, had a different priority. The Ottomans were keen to maintain the peace, though in light of their other interests elsewhere, relations with the Safavids were not of the utmost importance, and their commitment to upholding peaceful relations was limited. While peace was desirable, it was certainly not worth undermining the principle of Ottoman superiority. In pursuing relations, the Sublime Porte was less ready to make sacrifices than the Shahdom was; and there were even instances when some Ottoman dignitaries, out of self-interest, plotted faits accomplis to start a war with the Safavids,[50] seemingly on the calculation that even in the worst-case scenario Iran would undergo significantly greater losses than the Empire would. In contrast, the Safavids' state policy was so entrenched that even factions against the Ottomans did not venture a move that could lead to a head-on confrontation with the Empire.

Because the Sublime Porte did not prioritise relations with the Shahdom, factionalism stemming from differing policies towards Iran did not have a tangible presence at the imperial court. We also get a sense of Iran's marginality for the Ottoman State in Ottoman chronicles, where interactions with the Safavids seldom feature in the main annalistic narrative, and are rather noted in passing only as marginal addenda in the format 'this year, so and so also happened'. Unlike when recounting dealings with the Habsburgs, Poland, or Venice, Ottoman chroniclers did not bother explaining the political background to developments regarding the Iranian borderland.

The role of third parties was also a factor to be reckoned with in bilateral relations. Throughout the Safavid rule, European foes of the Ottomans in a given war – such as Germany,[51] Poland, Russia or Venice – kept on calling Iran into an alliance against the Turks. In one or two instances, the Safavids might in fact have accepted such proposals, lending their weight to a larger anti-Ottoman coalition and increasing the likelihood of scoring gains at the Empire's expense. However, after 1639, the Shahdom rejected all such offers, even when the Empire's armies were tied up on faraway European fronts and the prospect of a swift Ottoman retaliation was thus unlikely. The internalisation in Iran of the Empire's superiority in strength had Iranian dignitaries decline any proposal that would lead to war. Wariness and contentment with the established order defined the Safavids' Ottoman policy. Even the prospect of immediate gains at the Empire's expense was insufficient to merit drawing the Ottomans' wrath, for sooner or later the Ottomans would overcome. Thus, the Shahdom, considering that it had more to lose from a war with the Empire than it had to win, did not embark on such a risky venture.

Espionage was an inbuilt part of peacetime dealings. Although there were no centrally run spy networks, states commissioned single tasks to borderland governors, who in turn sent their own agents to gather news in disguise to targeted spots across the border, such as the other side's capital, residence of the court, army encampment, province or frontier, either on his own or attached to a diplomatic mission. Aside from such tasks, Ottoman frontier governors forwarded to the grand vizierate relevant news from Iran and their own observations from across the border.[52] For the individuals involved, espionage was a dangerous business, and spies if captured were liable to be put to death. But revealed cases of espionage and executions of the individuals in question did little to impede the two sides' political friendship.

Generally speaking, both polities sought to maintain control over their borderlands by using inducements and rewards to foster the loyalty of their respective vassals or using the nearby instruments of state authority as checks. Sometimes, persons of weight defected to the other side, but even when their new lords gave them office, these acts alone did not lead to a showdown between the two states. Such defections happened even at the level of governor, but as long as the episode could be regarded as a 'personal' matter stemming from an individual dignitary's political estrangement or fear of punishment, defection from the original lord and admission by the new lord did not trigger a feud between the monarchies.[53]

Similarly, instances where vassals on one or the other side breached the borders or defied treaty terms, which happened regularly, did not break the peace between the Ottoman and the Safavid states. When vassals such as princes, viceroys or tribes committed a breach, the states were held liable but not responsible. The punishment of wrongdoers and recompense for the injured were deemed enough to fulfil the obligations born out of this liability. For a breach to be regarded as a violation on the part of the state, which happened only rarely, certain conditions had to be met: it had to be initiated by a governor and to involve central state troops, fielded artillery and a playing military band.[54] In cases of such exceptional breaches, there was furthermore a protocol for de-escalation: the state in question was held politically responsible, and the injured party raised accusation demanding compensation.

The hierarchical relationship, as embodied in the two parties' uneven concessions and commitments, was also reflected in their attempts to seize opportunities at the expense of the other and the other side's retaliation thereto. There was a sharp contrast, for instance, in how the two states responded to large-scale, mass defections. The Ottoman punitive action that followed up sooner or later would not only crush the movement and thereby hinder a loss of territory but also swallow the thitherto self-governing unit into the centrally governed provincial system by undoing its tributary or autonomous status. Thus, whereas cases of unrest were handled with the general policy of spending the minimum possible effort for tributaries and vassals, those who set about defecting from Ottoman to Safavid overlordship found themselves sooner or later part of a regular imperial province.[55] After the annexation, any Safavid attempt at building up influence at the borderland in question would be deemed an intervention into the padishah's realm, and therefore, it could even justify a declaration of war. The Safavids, on the other hand, were simply not strong enough to undo and centralise a self-governing frontier province if it rose up to cast off Isfahan's overlordship. This not only put them at a disadvantage against the Ottomans along the border but also would prove deadly in the events leading up to their downfall later on.

Thus, so as not to draw more Ottoman deployment to the frontier, the Shahdom kept aloof from backing up anti-Ottoman dynamics across the border once the autonomy of the concerned region became undone. The Ottomans' ability to respond also forestalled later Safavid ventures in still autonomous tracts of the borderland, as the Safavids found out that sooner or later, their attempts to build up influence across the border at the expense of the Ottomans would only lead to the growth of imperial sway there, even when the Empire had to shoulder the financial burden of annexing and handling the tribal countryside. Thus, Safavid attempts at cross-border interventions only pushed forward the gradual elimination of potential Iranian fifth columns at the Empire's eastern edge, as the Safavids did not have the fieldable strength to follow up on their opening bid. In their own share of tributary governments, the Safavids could not step in with enough forces to upset the status quo in the Shahdom's favour and at the expense of local dynasties along Iran's western edge.

When the Safavids went beyond helping or sheltering Ottoman rebels and gathered troops for one reason or another near the border, and likewise when the Ottomans got false intelligence of Safavid military movement at the frontier,[56] the Sublime Porte responded by putting together a secondary imperial army, creating a marshal, and fielding further Household companies, artillery and ammunition. These imperial armies, though engaging the rebels, did not set on the Safavids. They, however, staged shows of might by holding military parades at spots chosen for the Iranians to behold. These show-offs daunted the Safavids, who did not reciprocate but cowered whenever faced therewith. Normal peacetime figures of the Household, Local, provincial and governor's troops kept in the borderland were high enough on their own to hold the Safavids in check and undertake punitive expeditions if need be.

Nor was it only along the frontier that the Ottomans set forth to the Safavids their military superiority: news of Ottoman victories from faraway fronts communicated a similar point. When the Sublime Porte triumphed against foes in Europe, it sent letters of conquest to the Shahdom.[57] These letters, which recounted the Empire's successful operations, sieges, battles, troops and resources, repeated in writing the same message hinted at in the shows of strength by armies fielded near the Iranian border. Although these letters of conquest formally announced to the friendly Safavids the glad news of victories won elsewhere, they also reminded the Shahdom of what it would have to cope with if it were to take on the Empire. Festivities held at borderland metropolises on the occasions of such victories, as well as on the occasions of imperial accessions and births, offered a more scenic version of the same message.[58]

Notes

1. Denoted by the titles *shahenshâh, saltanatu'l-uzmâ, sultânu's-salâtîn, khaqanu'l-khawâqin, pâdishâh-i rûy-i zamîn, pâdishâh-i Islam, sâhib-qirân, khilâfatu'l-kubrâ, zillullah, farmân-farmâ-yi zâmin, tâj-bakhsh-i khusravân* and *Iskandar-i thânî*, among others.
2. Denoted by the titles *ᶜâlî-hadrat, shah, khan* and *melik*, among others.
3. Denoted by the titles *aᵓlâ-hadrat, jihân-bân, jihân-dâr, jihân/ᵓâlam-panâh, sultân, pâdishâh, khaqan, qaan, caesar, humâyûn* and *khilâfat*, among others.
4. *Dawlat*.
5. Even in contemporary Western concepts of state, according to which monarchy was one of the pillars of state rather than the state itself, the monarch still embodied the state in the ceremonial sense. William Roosen, 'Early Modern Diplomatic Ceremonial: a Systems Approach', *The Journal of Modern History* 52, no. 3 (1980): 455.
6. Thus, although the Safavids revived the pre-Islamic monarchy of Iran in terms of territory and the concept of kingship, they did not set up or reign

The Ottoman Empire and Safavid Iran

over a Persian state. Savory claims that the polity of the Safavids was a Persian state: see Roger M. Savory, 'The Emergence of the Modern Persian State under the Safavids', reproduced in his *Studies on the History of Safavid Iran* (London: Variorum Reprints, 1987), chapter VII. However, his use of *Persian* rather stands for *Iranian*. Aside from whether and in what ways *Persia* and *Iran* can still be used in each other's stead, the distinction between them is too clear to overlook in a conceptual argumentation. The Safavids did revive the old Persian kingship and did reign over a kingdom of Iran, which might be called *an* Iranian state, but not a Persian state, for reasons that even Savory himself lays out in the rest of his article.

7. See Abulqasim Haydar Beyg Evoğlu, *Majmaᶜuᵓl-Inshâ*, from British Library Ms. Add. 7668, ff. 277b–278a; ff. 283a–283b.
8. Nevertheless, in cultural and geographical references, Rûm denoted a narrower territory, namely Anatolia and the Balkans, excluding the Empire's Hungarian, Crimean-Ukrainian, Caucasian, Kurdistani and Arab lands.
9. If used in a more restricted, cultural meaning, it then referred to the non-Arab Ottomans of Anatolia and the Balkans.
10. *Rûm* continued to also carry its earlier medieval meaning of 'Roman/Byzantine' and the much-less used leftover thereof, meaning 'Greek Orthodox', but only when the context explicitly made room for this reading. Particularly in Turkish, its use as a noun or adjective, along with the suffixes it did or did not have, would determine which of these alternative meanings it conveyed. Rûm as a noun meant the (Eastern) Roman/Ottoman Empire in general. When used as a noun but in a possessive construction with *ayâlat* of *beylerbeyi*[*lik*], it then meant the Ottoman province in mid-northern Anatolia covering Sivas, Amasya, Canik, Divriği, Arabgir, Çorum and Bozok. *Rûm* as adjective stood for Greek/Byzantine/Orthodox-Christian – however the context must explicitly specify this usage. The Rumlu were a Turkish clan that had migrated from Anatolia to Safavid Iran. *Rûmî* referred to someone who is from or who lives in the Ottoman/Byzantine realm in general, or Anatolia in particular. When presented in contrast to Arab, it referred to non-Arab Ottomans from Anatolia and the Balkans. See also Cemal Kafadar, 'A Rome of one's own: reflections on cultural geography and identity in the Lands of Rum', *Muqarnas* 24, [History and Ideology: Architectural Heritage of the 'Lands of Rum'] (2007): 7–25 for an overview of the evolution of the terms *Rûm* and *Rûmî* after the coming of the Turks to Anatolia. Kafadar's argument, that in the official language *Rûm* did not denote the Ottoman lands (see ibid., 12), holds true for internally issued documents, but not for the official language used in diplomatic writings, especially in diplomacy with Iran.
11. See Sarı Abdullah Efendi and İbrahim Çelebi Cevri, *Dastûruᵓl-Inshâ*, from Süleymaniye Kütüphanesi, *Nur-ı Osmaniye*, no. 4304, the untitled entry following the entry titled 'bu canipten Şah Abbas-ı Sani tarafına gönderilmek için sabıkan reisülküttap olan Abdullah Efendi müsvedde ettiği namedir,

lakin bu mektup gönderilmeyip badehu yazılan gönderilmiştir'; *Asnâd u Mukâtabât-i Siyâsî-yi Îrân az Sâl-i 1038 ta 1105*, ed. AbdulHusein Navâî (Tehran: Bunyâd-i Farhang-i Îrân, HS 1360), 203–8, 250–7; *Majmûʿa-i Makâtib*, from Staatsbibliothek zu Berlin, *Orientabteilung*, Ms. or. quart. 1577, ff. 68b–70a.

12. In seventeenth-century Europe too, where the crown institution was by law not the state itself but one of the pillars thereof, ambassadors and envoys formally represented their monarchs, not the state or realm of which the monarchy in question was a constituent. See William James Roosen, *The Age of Louis XIV: the Rise of Modern Diplomacy* (London: Routledge, 1976), 5, 51–3.
13. Denoted by the titles *âlî-janâb*, *dawlat*, *farmân-rân*, *farmân-ravâ*, *farmân-farmâ* and *shahryâr*, among others.
14. *Majmûʿa -i Mukâtabat*, from Österreichische Nationalbibliothek, *Orientalische Handschriften*, Cod.Mixt. 371, ff. 31b–32a.
15. Evoğlu, *Majmaʿuʾl-Inshâ*, ff. 276b–277b.
16. See, for instance, BOA, *Sadaret Mektubi Kalemi Belgeleri*, 1/56; Evliya Çelebi b. Derviş Mehemmed Zılli, *Evliyâ Çelebi Seyahatnamesi* (Istanbul: Yapı Kredi Yayınları, 2011), 2/115, 4/176–7, 4–201.
17. For some cases, see Evliya Çelebi, *Seyahatname*, 2/111, 115, 4/177–9, 186–92, 201–10.
18. See *Majmûʿa -i Mukâtabat*, ff. 20b–21a.
19. Evliya Çelebi, *Seyahatname*, 4/177–9, 190–2; Silahdar Fındıklılı Mehmed Ağa [Fındıklılı Mehmed], *Zeyl-i Fezleke*, published in Nazire Karaçay Türkal, 'Silahdar Fındıklılı Mehmed Ağa. Zeyl-i Fezleke (1065–22. ca. 1106/1654–7 Şubat 1695)' (PhD diss., Marmara Üniversitesi, 2012), 499–501; Mühürdar Hasan Ağa, *Cevahirüʾt-Tevarih*, published in Ebubekir Sıddık Yücel, 'Mühürdar Hasan Ağaʾnın Cevâhirüʾt-Tevârihi' (PhD diss., Erciyes University, 1996), 396; Jean Chardin, *Chardin Seyahatnâmesi: İstanbul, Osmanlı Toprakları, Gürcistan, Ermenistan, İran 1671–1673*, trans. Ayşe Meral, ed. Stefanos Yerasimos (Istanbul: Kitap Yayınevi, 2013), 413.
20. Denoted by the titles *janâb*, *amârat* and *beğ*, among others.
21. Denoted by the additional title *iyâlat*.
22. *Majmûʿa -i Mukâtabat*, f. 32a.
23. [*büyük*]*elçi/safîr*[-*i kabîr*].
24. Evoğlu, *Majmaʿuʾl-Inshâ*, ff. 277b–278a; Sarı Abdullah (and Cevri), *Dastûruʾl-Inshâ*, entry title: 'Şehinşah ... Sultan İbrahim ... taraf[ına] ... Şah Abbas-ı Sani canibinden gelen namedir'.
25. [*orta*]*elçi/rasûl*.
26. Muhammad Masûm b. Khâjagî-Isfahânî, *Khulâsatuʾs-Siyar*, ed. Iraj Afshar (Tehran: Intishârât-ı ʿIlmî, 1358), 294; Iskandar Beyg Türkman Munshî, *Zayl-i Târîkh-i ʿÂlam-ârâ-yi ʿAbbâsî* (quoting from Muhammad Yusuf Walih Kazvini-Isfahani's *Khuld-i Barîn*), ed. Ahmed Suhayli Khvânsârî

(Tehran: Châpkhâna-i Islâmiya, 1317), 250–1; Evoğlu, *Majmaʿuʾl-Inshâ*, ff. 283b–284a; Abdülkâdir Efendi [Kadri Efendi], *Topçular Katibi Abdülkâdir (Kadrî) Efendi Târihi*, vol. II, ed. Ziya Yılmazer (Ankara: Türk Tarih Kurumu, 2003), 1169; Mustafa Naima Efendi, *Târih-i Naʾîmâ*, ed. Mehmet İpşirli (Ankara: Türk Tarih Kurumu, 2007), 961; Muhammad Tahir Wahid Kazvini, *ʿAbbâsnâma, yâ Sharh-i Zindagânî-yi 22-Sâla-i Shâh ʿAbbâs-i Sânî (1052–1073)*, ed. Ibrahim Dihgân (Erâk: Kitâb-furûshi-yi Dâvûdî-yi Erâk, 1329), 45; Sarı Abdullah (and Cevri), *Dastûruʾl-Inshâ*, the untitled entry following the entry titled 'bu canipten Şah Abbas-ı Sani tarafına gönderilmek için sabıkan reisülküttap olan Abdullah Efendi müsvedde ettiği namedir, lakin bu mektup gönderilmeyip badehu yazılan gönderilmiştir'; *Dastûruʾl-Inshâ*, letter title: 'balada mestur olan mufassal olmakla gönderilmeyip tekrar muma-ileye Abdullah Efendi müsveddesiyle ber-vech-i ihtisar bu name tahrir olunup Sadrazamʾdan Şah-ı Acemʾe gönderilmiştir'; [Şair] Abdurrahman Abdi Paşa, *Vekâyi-nâme*, ed. Fahri Ç. Derin (Istanbul: Çamlıca, 2008), 20; Karaçelebi-zade Abdülaziz Efendi, *Ravzatüʾl-Ebrar Zeyli*, ed. Nevzat Kaya (Ankara: Türk Tarih Kurumu, 2003), 26; Vecihi Hasan Efendi, *Tarih-i Vecihi*, f. 44a in Buğra Atsız, *Das Osmanische Reich um die Mitte des 17. Jahrhunderts. Nach den Chroniken des Vecihi (1637–1660) und des Mehmed Halifa (1633–1660)* (Munich: Dr. Dr. Rudolf Trofenik, 1977); Nazmizade Murteza, *Gülşen-i Hulefâ: Bağdat Tarihi 762–1717*, ed. Mehmet Karataş (Ankara: Türk Tarih Kurumu, 2014), 262; Müneccimbaşı Derviş Ahmed Dede Efendi, *Sahâifuʾl-Akhbâr*, ed. Ahmed Nedim, vol. III (Istanbul: [Matbaa-i Amire], 1285), 713; Kazvini, *ʿAbbâsnâma*, 222–3; Muhammad Yusuf Walih Kazvini-Isfahani, *Khuld-i Barîn [Îrân dar Zamân-i Shâh Safi vu Shâh ʿAbbâs-i Duvvum]*, ed. Muhammad Rizâ Nasiri (Tehran: Anjuman-i Âsâr u Mafâkhir-i Farhangî, 2003), 587.

27. This capacity of envoyship, and the lexical equivalence of *risâlat* with *envoyship* also show themselves in the use of *rasûl* and *risâlat* as legal concepts in the Ottoman Empire. They meant that the person in question was only to convey the entrusted message as it was, without having the authorisation to add, take out, or change anything. See the entries 'resul' and 'risâlet' in *Kubbealtı Lügatı*, ed. İlhan Ayverdi (Istanbul: Kubbealtı Neşriyatı, 2011).
28. küçükelçi/nâma-bar/nâma-rasân.
29. Kazvini-Isfahani, *Khuld-i Barîn*, 454; Walî-kulu b. Davud-kulu Shamlu, *Qisasuʾl-Khâqânî*, ed. Sayyid Hasan Sâdât Nâsiri (Tehran: Sâzmân-i Châp u Intishârât-i Vazârat-i Farhang u Irshâd-i Islâmî, 1371), 313; *Asnâd u Mukâtabât 1038–1105*, 209–11; Fındıklılı Mehmed, *Zeyl-i Fezleke*, 423–4; Mühürdar Hasan Ağa, *Cevahirüʾt-Tevarih*, 294–5; Müneccimbaşı, *Sahâifuʾl-Akhbâr*, 743; Abdi Paşa, *Vekâyi-nâme*, 227; *Asnâd u Mukâtabât 1038–1105*, 250–64.
30. *Majmûʿa-i Makâtib*, ff. 68b–70a; *Asnâd u Mukâtabât 1038–1105*, 203–5.
31. Kazvini-Isfahani, *Khuld-i Barîn*, 301, 585; Bîzhan [*Sahîfa-i Girâmî*], pub-

lished in Giorgio Rota, *La vita e i tempi di Rostam Khan (Edizione e Traduzione Italiana del Ms. British Library Add 7,655)* (Vienna: Verlag der Österreichische Akademie der Wissenschaften, 2009), 417; *Asnâd u Mukâtabât 1038–1105*, 206–8; Kazvini, ʿ*Abbâsnâma*, 222.

32. Sarı Abdullah (and Cevri), *Dastûruʾl-Inshâ*, entry title: 'balada mestur olan mufassal olmakla gönderilmeyip tekrar muma-ileyhe Abdullah Efendi müsveddesiyle ber-vech-i ihtisar bu nâme tahrir olunup Sadrazamʾdan Şah-ı Acemʾe gönderilmiştir'; Kadri Efendi, *Tarih*, II, 1158.
33. Kazvini, ʿ*Abbâsnâma*, 222; Kazvini-Isfahani, *Khuld-i Barîn*, 585; *Asnâd u Mukâtabât 1038–1105*, 206–8.
34. *Dargâh-i ʿÂlî kapıcıbaşısı*.
35. *mutafarriqa-i Dargâh-i ʿÂlî*.
36. To differentiate between the Safavids' devalued use of this title from its original, sovereign meaning, I transcribe the Safavid-devalued term as *xan*, whereas I spell the historical and contemporary use for sovereign rulership as the more customary *khan*.
37. *tuğ*.
38. *Dîvân-ı Humâyûn çavuşu*.
39. *bostâncı*.
40. Ülker Akkutay, *Enderun Mektebi* (Ankara: Gazi Üniversitesi Basın-Yayın Yüksekokulu Basımevi, 1984), 63–5, 124–51.
41. See Bert G. Fragner, *Die 'Persophonie': Regionalität, Identität und Sprachkontakt in der Geschichte Asiens* (Berlin: Das Arabische Buch, 1999) for an analysis of Persian's position in Islamdom. See Muhammad Amîn Riyâhî, *Zabân u Adab-i Fârsî dar Qalam-rav-i Osmânî* (Tehran: Intishârât-i Pâzhang, 1369) and Sara Nur Yıldız, 'Ottoman Historical Writing in Persian, 1400–1600', in *A History of Persian Literature*, vol. X, ed. Charles Melville (London: I. B. Tauris, 2012), 436–502 for an evaluation of Persian's influence on Turkish and its position in the Ottoman Empire.
42. See Florian Schwarz, 'Writing in the Margins of Empires – the Huseinabadi Family of Scholiasts in the Ottoman–Safawid Borderlands', in *Buchkultur im Nahen Osten des 17. und 18. Jahrhunderts*, eds Tobias Heinzelmann and Henning Sievert (Bern: Peter Lang, 2010), 151–98.
43. See Tourkhan Gandjei, 'Turkish in the Safavid court of Isfahan', *Turcica* 21–3 (1991): 311–15, 317–18; John Perry, 'The historical role of Turkish in relation to Persian of Iran', in *Iran and the Caucasus V. Research Papers from the Caucasian Centre for Iranian Studies, Yerivan*, ed. Garnik Asatrian (Tehran: International Publications of Iranian Studies, 2001), 193–4, 198; Perry, 'Cultural currents in the Turco-Persian world of Safavid and post-Safavid times', in *New Perspectives on Safavid Iran*, ed. Colin P. Mitchell (London: Routledge, 2011), 87.
44. The chancellery Turkish used in the Sublime Porte's compositions addressed to the Safavids could be so Persianate that in many long sentences, if the one-word Turkish verb was to be replaced with its Persian counterpart, the

whole composition itself could be deemed Persian. Ironically, the Persian within the Ottomans' technically Turkish diplomatic letters written to Iranian addresses was in many cases more flowing and sophisticated and less artificial than the Persian in Safavid-composed letters.
45. The rank-denoting Turkish vocabulary for diplomats – *büyükelçi*, *ortaelçi* and *küçükelçi* – which the Ottomans employed in their contemporary diplomacy with European states, do not come up in their diplomacy with the Safavids, and were instead replaced by the Arabic/Persian counterparts *safârat*, *risâlat* and *nâma-barl-rasân*.
46. As to be seen in Johann Rudolf Schmid, *Finalrelation 1–4 vom 12. November 1643*, published in Peter Meienberger, *Johann Rudolf Schmid zum Schwarzenhorn als kaiserlicher Resident in Konstantinopel in den Jahren 1629–1643* (Bern: H. Lang: 1973), 259.
47. *Ordu-yi Humâyûn*.
48. Hacı Halife Mustafa Katib Çelebi, *Fezleke*, published in Zeynep Aycibin, 'Kâtib Çelebi. Fezleke. Tahlil ve Metin. I-II-III' (PhD diss., Mimar Sinan University of Fine Arts, 2007), 897, 901; Naima, *Tarih-i Naima*, 894; Karaçelebizade Abdülaziz Efendi, *Ravzatüʾl-Ebrar*, published in İbrahim Özgül, 'Ravzatüʾl-Ebrâr [Kara Çelebi-Zade Abdülaziz Efendiʾnin Ravzaüʾl-Ebrâr Adlı Eseri (1299–1648) Tahlil ve Metin]' (PhD diss., Atatürk University, 2010), 338; Kadri Efendi, *Tarih*, II, 1112, 1140.
49. Evoğlu, *Majmaʿuʾl-Inshâ*, ff. 276b–286a; Evliya Çelebi, *Seyahatname*, 1/133–4, 2/87–115, 4/109–210; Abdi Paşa, *Vekâyi-nâme*, 236, 257, 328; Nazmizade, *Gülşen-i Hulefâ*, 277–80, 283–4, 288–90; Fındıklılı Mehmed, *Zeyl-i Fezleke*, 456, 495–6, 499–501, 574; BOA, *Sadaret Mektubi Kalemi b.*, 1/61; Mühürdar Hasan Ağa, *Cevahirüʾt-Tevarih*, 396.
50. See Evliya Çelebi, *Seyahatname*, 1/133–4, 4/176, 188.
51. Using *Germany* for the Habsburg monarchy is anachronic in many instances. Besides, there were Hungarian, Czech, Serbian, Croation, Italian, and so on, elements in the Holy Roman Emperor's forces. Therefore, whenever the referent is the monarchic state made up of the Habsburg crowns held in personal union, the name *Habsburgs* is used. However, this naming sometimes falls short of describing the referent. As a rule, the Holy Roman Empire of the German Nation was not a state but a system in which sovereign states of various hierarchical positions operated in the early modern age. A few of the Ottoman wars, owing to the targeted lands, triggered that single clause of the German 'constitution' that could still bring about a relatively concerted action by most of these otherwise separate German states: 'defense of the realm'. This was the case in the Great Turkish War, in which not only the realms of the Habsburgs' composite monarchy (which included Germany's Austria and Bohemia) but also the sovereign principalities of Bavaria, Saxony, Brandenburg, Baden, Hanover, and so on, sent commanders and sizable troops to the German imperial armies. The use of Germany in this book is for the sake of exactness whenever needed by the occasion.

The Ottoman–Safavid Detente

The Hungarian element does not necessarily undermine this usage either, as Hungary, though not in equal shares, was present on both sides of the warring parties with its territory, inner politics and manpower.

52. Topkapı Sarayı Müzesi Arşivi, *Evrak*, zarf 3420 evrak 1 [dosya 640 gömlek 5]; Topkapı, *Evrak*, z.7022 e.249 [d.796 g.32]; Topkapı, *Evrak*, z.7022 e.193 [d.795 g.82]; Topkapı, *Evrak*, z.4590 e.1 [d.698 g.8]; Evliya Çelebi, *Seyahatname*, 4/207–10.
53. Kazvini, ʿ*Abbâsnâma*, 227; Kazvini-Isfahani, *Khuld-i Barîn*, 593; Karaçelebi-zade, *Ravzatüʾl-Ebrar Zeyli*, 325–7.
54. Evliya Çelebi, *Seyahatname*, 4/188–9.
55. Nazmizade, *Gülşen-i Hulefâ*, 234, 288–9; *Tarih-i Naima*, 955; Mühürdar Hasan Ağa, *Cevahirüʾt-Tevarih*, 294; Evliya Çelebi, *Seyahatname*, 1/85, 4/302–5; BOA, *Sadaret Mektubi Kalemi b.* 1/61, 2/13; Abdi Paşa, *Vekâyinâme*, 328; Raşid Mehmed Efendi and Çelebizade İsmail Asım Efendi, *Tarih-i Raşid ve Zeyli*, eds Abdülkadir Özcan, Yunus Uğur, Baki Çakır and Ahmet Zeki İzgöer (Istanbul: Klasik, 2013), 102; BOA, *İbnülemin – Şükrü-Şikayet*, 47; BOA, *Divan Beylikçi Kalemi Belgeleri*, 53/3, 53/21, 53/24, 57/16.
56. *The Journal of Zakʾaria of Agulis*, ed. and trans. George A. Bournoutian (Costa Mesa, CA: Mazda Publishers, 2003), 117–18; Abdi Paşa, *Vekâyinâme*, 426–7; *Tarih-i Raşid*, 181; Topkapı, *Evrak*, 243; BOA, *Divan Beylikçi Kalemi b.* 72/98 (H 1085); *Majmûʿa-i Mukâtabat*, 21b–22a; Sarı Mehmed Paşa, *Zübde-i Vekâiyât: Tahlil ve Metin (1066–1116/1656–1704)*, ed. Abdülkadir Özcan (Ankara: Türk Târih Kurumu, 1995), 48; Fındıklılı Mehmed, *Zeyl-i Fezleke*, 659; BOA, *Cevdet – Askeriye*, 43935.
57. *Asnâd u Mukâtabât, 1038–1105*, 250–64; Rami Mehmed, *Munshaʾât*, from Österreichische Nationalbibliothek, HO 179, ff. 19a–21a.
58. Topkapı, *Evrak*, z.7022 e.110 [d.794 g.105]; Nazmizade, *Gülşen-i Hulefâ*, 235, 239, 241–2, 270, 273, 291, 295.

2
1639–1643: Baghdad

25 December 1638. The Ottomans wrest Baghdad from the Safavids at the end of a deadly struggle. Throughout the forty-day siege, overseen by the padishah himself, the Ottomans have lost not only thousands of soldiers and officers but also Grand Vizier Tayyar Mehmed Pasha himself, shot dead by Safavid defenders two days ago while leading a forlorn hope[1] of Janissaries in a near-suicide mission against the fortifications in the kill zone. Kemankeş Kara Mustafa Pasha becomes the new grand vizier, assuming duty literally where his forerunner fell, to drive home the thrust.[2]

Bektaş Xan Mirimanidze, Safavid governor of Baghdad, steps out of the fortress, and proceeds through the regiments of Ottoman soldiers and ranks of court officers ceremoniously lined up all the way from the gates of Baghdad to Murad IV's war council in the Imperial Marquee. After Bektaş kisses the ground before the throne, Murad rhetorically asks: 'who are you, why did you come, what is your name?'[3] The fallen commander answers: 'Long live my monarch! I am Your servant Bektaş Xan, who is the commander of Baghdad. I came to give my monarch Baghdad and the fortress of Baghdad.'[4] Thereupon Murad says: 'I did not come here to slay the Kızılbaş. This fortress of Baghdad is Our patrimony, I came therefor. I wish you had served [Us] from the outset and not confronted Us so long. I hereby give quarter to you and your troops. And, you did the utmost service to your lord [the shah].'[5] Bektaş Mirimanidze not only yields himself and his fortress but also seeks admission into Ottoman service. Murad IV accepts Bektaş's troth, promises him viziership, and, as a token thereof, puts a jewelled aigrette on him, clothes him with sable fur, and girds him with a jewelled dagger.[6] By 26 December 1638, Baghdad is back in Ottoman hands. The Ottoman Empire thus regains Iraq from Safavid Iran, as the final battle in the war of 1623–39 comes to an end.

1639–1643: Baghdad

From War to Truce

As soon as taking hold of Baghdad and before anything else, Murad IV ordered the war-torn bulwarks to be built up, at the same time as he commanded his troops to march onwards into Iran. Two days after the conquest, as governor of Baghdad he installed Küçük Hasan Agha commander of the Janissary Corps,[7] who in the siege had fought in the grand vizier's column deployed against the White Gate to the east of the fortress.[8] The Janissary chief-of-staff[9] Arnavut Bektaş Agha, who as second general[10] of the Corps had commanded a division of 6- or 7,000 against Iran at the siege of Erivan back in 1635,[11] was to man the fortress of Baghdad at the head of 8,000 Janissaries as a wartime measure.[12]

In early January 1639 Bektaş Xan Mirimanidze, the surrendered Safavid governor of Baghdad, having pledged himself to Ottoman service and awaiting to leave Baghdad as Ottoman vizier beside Murad IV, suddenly died. Why and how he lost his life never came to light, though the word of mouth narrowed down the unknown to a few probabilities: one was that he died naturally, according to some because of pleurisy and according to others owing to a brain stroke triggered by depression. The other rumour was that he died of poisoning, either through suicide out of shame or at the hands of his wife, Lur Husein Xan's daughter, who, being a hard-line Shiite, did not accept her husband's defection.[13] Murad IV set out from Baghdad on 17 January 1639, leaving his grand vizier both as commander-in-chief[14] for the war and as plenipotentiary[15] for the upcoming peace talks.[16]

Kemankeş Kara Mustafa of Avlonya was an outstanding soldier who had shone out in the last Iranian war. At the siege of Erivan back in 1635, he had fought as commander of the Janissary Corps, and the artillery in his column had wrecked almost one-fourth of the fortress. In the 1638 campaign too, in which he had partaken as grand admiral, he had stood out: arguing that the region's river regime was unforeseeable, he had insisted that not all but only some of the artillery be shipped from Mosul towards Baghdad by river and that some go over land with the army. Murad IV's acting on this plan had proved critical in retaking Baghdad, because, later, the shipped artillery could not make it to the siege on time. During the siege itself, he had commanded a column set against the fortress's bulwark and distinguished himself in the trench operations that followed.[17] He would go on to become a well-respected statesman not only for the Ottomans but also in the eyes of the Iranians.

Back in 1637, amidst the war, Shah Safi had sent Maqsud Soltan Karadağlu, his deputy-chieftain[18] of the Kızılbaş order,[19] as ambassador extraordinary to the imperial court. Murad IV had withheld the ambassador in Constantinople, taken him along on the Baghdad campaign in 1638, left him in Mardin on the eve of the siege, and had him brought to Mosul after the conquest.[20] When Murad stopped by Mosul on his way back from Baghdad to Constantinople on 27 January 1639, he received Maqsud Karadağlu in audience, entrusted him with two letters to the shah, and sent him to the commander-in-chief to be forwarded to the Safavid court together with Ottoman envoy Hamzapaşaoğlu Mehmed Agha (a patrician of the imperial court).[21] The embassy's fifty-men staff and baggage were likewise shipped from Mardin to Baghdad on 3 February. Karadağlu reached Baghdad on 5 February, and on the 8th Kara Mustafa sent him, alongside Hamzapaşaoğlu, off to Iran.[22]

Safi had been waiting for this mission since it had first been announced: Rustam Xan Saakadze, the field-marshal[23] of Iran, who had been watching the Ottomans' movements closely, had given the shah the news of the upcoming emissaries the very next day after they had been ordered to get ready. At the head of a large detachment, Begdilli Karakhan Beyg Shamlu (brother of Janibek Xan Shamlu, the head of the royal guard)[24] and Taqi Beyg Ustajlu (the shah's chief military aide-de-camp)[25]) welcomed the joint mission halfway and guided the two emissaries to the royal court. When Murad IV's envoy arrived on 11 February 1639, Shah Safi greeted him with a feast, where Hamzapaşaoğlu Mehmed Agha handed over the padishah's and grand vizier's letters to the shah.[26] Murad wrote:

> Prince Safi ... the ruler of the Iranians ... When my decree ... arrives, it shall be known so: ... affairs arising from your side stirred Our imperial zeal ... and ... We augustly campaigned towards Baghdad ... When I came with my victorious troops, ... there was no sign of you or your vanquished legion, you hid behind towering mountains ... The conquest of the fortress of Baghdad was fulfilled in little time, ... grand vizier Mustafa Pasha ... along with the triumphant troops ... are assigned for its keeping, and ... [I] have headed out towards Diyarbekr ... Our august mind has augustly decided that Erivan, Nakhchivan, and Azerbaijan shall soon become an encampment for the tents of my triumphant warriors and trampled by ... the flood of horses of my victorious soldiers ... If [you wish to] spend an effort to ... make up for what happened and seek to appease Our august heart, ... Our august consent permits that the borders in [the treaty from] the time of ... Sultan Suleiman Khan ... be taken as the principle of reconciliation. Otherwise, be ready for the rendezvous. Whatever is hidden behind the veil of destiny ... will materialize ... In the letter brought by Maqsud Soltan who had been sent as ambassador, there was no word of Yours upon which good interactions could be built ... Now, whatever your answer is, communicate it to my Imperial Court.

1639–1643: Baghdad

... When the august epistle of required-conformance arrives, it shall be known so: you had formerly sent your man Maqsud the deputy-grandmaster and wished for peace. The reason that We put off your emissary for some time was that We were a bit preoccupied. We have now dealt with that business of Ours. Hence, if you wish for peace, ... you shall hand back to our governors-general the lands that were under our blissful rule in the time of our great forefathers, ... and my victorious legions shall go ahead to take possession of them ... If not, it is determined that I winter at this frontier and come upon your country and lands ... in the springtime with sea-like legions. If you are a man, show up. Sitting behind curtains is unfitting for those who allege leadership. And for those who fear [battle], it is a mistake to mount a horse and gird on a sword. Whatever is destined from pre-eternity will happen. Grieve not, come forth.[27]

The grand vizier's letter to the shah backed up Murad IV's message, blaming the Safavids for the deaths in Azerbaijan and Baghdad caused by war and threatening them with heavier blows if they did not settle for the pre-war borders.[28]

This, then, was the Ottomans' first peace proposal, offering realistic conditions but including an open threat and a belittling challenge. Murad IV's message to Safi thus shows what the Sublime Porte's Iranian policy looked like in early 1639. Now that the Ottomans had taken back the territory which had been the centrepiece of the war, they were willing to make peace if the Safavids gave up all claims from the last fifteen years. Victorious but tired of campaigning on a front so far away from the Empire's heartland and against an enemy whose geopolitical strength, unlike their own, lay near the front, the Ottomans chose to dictate the terms based on the new status quo, and not to demand things yet outside their reach. But if the Safavids would not settle for this offer, by accepting which they would acknowledge defeat and Ottoman superiority but keep their kingdom intact, the Ottomans seemed ready to take the war into Iran itself.

Notwithstanding whether there would be peace or war, building up the fortress of Baghdad was the Empire's foremost business of the day. And it began forthwith, drawing on the Imperial Army's manpower and the expertise of its technical staff.[29] The work on the bulwarks was completed on 18 February 1639. To commemorate his triumph over Iran, Murad IV had poems dating and celebrating his conquest of Baghdad engraved on the arches above the fortress gates and newly raised buildings. Again, to betoken the reinstated Ottoman sway, a full-fledged military band was set up at Baghdad, which was said to be the best of its kind in all Ottoman frontier provinces (including the famous one at Cairo), playing twice daily.³⁰ Future enthronements, births of imperial princes, and victories at faraway frontiers would be celebrated in Baghdad with well-wrought festivities.³¹ The care taken in Baghdad went beyond merely stamping provincial centres with marks of Ottoman lordship. Rather, it served to present this metropolis to neighbouring Iran as a beacon of Ottoman might.

Kemankeş Kara Mustafa Pasha himself oversaw the works before starting the onward march into Iran. Abundant supplies, ammunition and money were also stockpiled³² for times of need. The fortifications were thus improved beyond what had been there before 1638. On the day of the Imperial Army's departure, 12,000 new soldiers were enlisted for the Local Service,³³ besides the 8,000-strong Janissary force headed by Chief-of-staff Arnavut Bektaş Agha and the 1,000-strong Court Cavalry³⁴ contingent appointed to stand watch at this borderland stronghold.³⁵ The Imperial Army aside, the Baghdad garrison itself had become a force almost equal to a lesser kingdom's military.

The Imperial Army started the thrust from Baghdad towards Iran on 15 March 1639, but the flooded River Diyala meant that three days later the army had to halt at the waystation of Çubukköprü, where it would wait for the next twenty days to also have the horses graze on the meadows's fresh spring grass. The commander-in-chief had a floating bridge built with ships. The present commanders, however, shied away from being first to cross over the flood with their troops. Finally, Çiftelerli Osman Pasha, the new governor of Damascus, stepped forward to first lead his troops across, thereby breaking the deadlock. It would take four to five days for all regiments to be transferred over the flooded river. Safavid spies, watching on the other side and seeing the Imperial Army begin to cross, hastened back to give the news to Rustam Xan Saakadze, marshal of Iran.³⁶

The marshal was waiting to see whether the Ottomans could indeed take the war into Iran, because if not, he was planning to wear down the Imperial Army and the Baghdad garrison with scorched-earth tactics. The Imperial Army's crossing over the flood notwithstanding the risk, however, convinced Rustam Saakadze otherwise, and perfected the Safavid court's leaning for peace, as the shah's ambassador to Zuhab would soon admit to the commander-in-chief.³⁷

On 10 April 1639, the shah sent Kütük Mehemmed-kulu Beyg Chagatay³⁸ as envoy to the Ottoman commander-in-chief to strike a peace deal. An Ottoman spy brought news on 17 April to the Imperial Army at Şahriban that the shah's envoy was about to come and ask for peace. The marshal of Iran soon after sent his own letter to the commander-in-chief with a mission of three Safavid functionaries and Topal Mehmed Agha, an officer of the grand vizier who had been taken prisoner during the war. The delegation met the Imperial Army at the waystation of Kızılribat, a township on the Ottoman side of the Baghdad–Kirmanshah border, on 23 April. Deeming it likely that Rustam Saakadze was watching the Imperial Army atop a mountain, Kemankeş Kara Mustafa received the Safavid delegation with a military parade through serried ranks of soldiers stretching the entire distance from the waystation to the encampment, while he also had a mountain near the waystation swarmed with troops to impress likely beholders.[39]

The marshal announced in his letter that the Ottoman envoy Hamzapaşaoğlu Mehmed Agha would soon be sent back to the Imperial Army together with a new envoy from the shah. This legation in turn reached the Imperial Army in Khanki/Haruniya on 29 April. The shah's master-of-the-horse Kütük Mehemmed-kulu Beyg Chagatay, who came as envoy, arguing that he was accredited to the padishah, asked to be forwarded to Murad IV. The commander-in-chief, however, said that he as the padishah's absolute deputy already had Murad IV's answer, and if the shah wished for peace, he should send a *xan* as deputy, otherwise the Imperial Army was there for war and would march on. Kütük Chagatay thereupon handed over Safi's letter, by which the shah accepted the 1555 borders as the principle of peace and that there were no more reasons to keep on fighting because Baghdad, the cause of the war, was back in Ottoman hands, and asked for reconciliation notwithstanding the threat and belittlement by Murad IV. However, the further Safavid request that the Ottomans either tear down the fortress of Kars or hand it over to Iran, and the fact that Kütük Chagatay did not have plenipotentiary powers, angered Kemankeş Kara Mustafa. The commander-in-chief dispatched letters to Rustam Saakadze and Safi, in which he asserted that a bargain on Kars was impossible since the 1555 principle was to apply specifically to the border at Iraq, demanded that the shah send a plenipotentiary ambassador, made known that the Imperial Army marched on, and said that he would not shy away from engaging the Safavid army under Rustam Saakadze's command in battle, giving the marshal a deadline of three days and the shah six days for an answer.[40]

And the commander-in-chief did as he said. The Imperial Army went ahead towards Dartang without awaiting the shah's or the marshal's answer, while Rustam Saakazde withdrew the Safavid army behind the mountain of Darna-Dartang. The news thereof reached the Ottoman encampment on 4 May 1639.[41] On 5 May, the commander-in-chief transferred Küçük Hasan Pasha to the governorate of Van and installed in his stead Bıyıklı Derviş Mehmed Pasha to Baghdad.[42] A veteran of the

Iranian war, Bıyıklı Dervish Mehmed had fought in the Erivan campaign of 1635 as the grand vizier's steward.[43] In the Baghdad campaign of 1638 he had started out as governor of Syria and fought on as governor of Diyarbekr. There he had first commanded the vanguard troops of the Imperial Army through the march from Kurdistan into Iraq, and then, leading a detachment of seven companies and field guns into an outthrusting trench before the fortress of Baghdad, knocked out the Safavid artillery on the Ajam Bastion that had been harassing the Ottoman troops in the main trenchworks.[44]

Bıyıklı Dervish Mehmed took Küçük Hasan's stead as governor of Baghdad on military and disciplinary grounds. In his concern to strengthen the Ottomans' grasp on this newly recaptured land and to wipe out Safavid influence, the commander-in-chief deemed Küçük Hasan's governance too easy-going to eliminate the legacy of the fifteen years of Safavid occupation. By contrast, he regarded Bıyıklı Dervish Mehmed as qualified to fulfil the role of the 'overwhelming ruler' that Baghdad and its garrison of more than 20,000 troops needed[45] for the leadership at the Iranian border. Even after the ratifications were sent out, these measures were not called off right away. Until the end of April 1640, Arnavut Bektaş Agha and the extraordinary Household companies left with him would stand watch against Iran. Constantinople would not lessen the garrison's strength for at least the next eleven years.[46]

The shah soon accepted all Ottoman terms and named Saru Xan Talish his ambassador and plenipotentiary[47] bearing official letters of peace. The embassy set out on 7 May, with Nadr-Ali Beyg Türkman, minister to the head of the royal guard Begdilli Janibek Xan Shamlu, also in attendance. The Imperial Army meanwhile kept marching and on 10 May 1639 reached the plain of Zuhab near Qasr-i Shirin and neighbouring Dartang, where Shah Safi had waited out Murad IV's siege of Baghdad. Only there did Kemankesh Kara Mustafa Pasha halt his advance, for messengers from Iran brought the news of the forthcoming peace embassy, wherefore the commander-in-chief was kindly asked not to march further. The embassy itself reached the encampment on 12 May and was welcomed with less ceremony than the earlier legation, attended to only by the Imperial Council sergeants,[48] feudal colonels, some Rumelian soldiers, and 100 privates from the Egyptian corps. The ambassador duly presented the commander-in-chief with his credentials confirming his plenipotentiary powers to strike a peace deal. He then introduced a thorn into the bargain: the Safavids wanted to keep Darna and Dartang which, according to the 1555 principle, were to end up in Ottoman hands. The commander-in-chief offered in return to forward Saru Xan Talish to the imperial court so that the ambassador could try his luck with Murad IV while the army would march on and engage the Safavids.[49]

Kemankeş Kara Mustafa's ploy worked. Saru Xan Talish communicated with the shah and received orders to pledge for the Safavids to pull out from Darna, Dartang, Kirkuk and the stronghold of Zalim. When the negotiators reached a deal on all conditions, both the Safavid ambassador and envoy joined the Ottoman commander-in-chief's war council together with governors, Janissary generals and Household corps officers on 15 May 1639 and finalised the peace talks. The parties drew up a protocol and Kara Mustafa and Saru Talish signed it as plenipotentiaries on 17 May.[50]

The parties mainly followed the maxim of *uti possidetis*, with small modifications to the good of the Ottomans who bargained from a position of strength. As both parties were willing to make peace with the least entanglement and delay, the plenipotentiaries focused on settling the border, leaving out all other matters that could otherwise be handled in a full-fledged treaty. The resultant border ran upwards from the Persian Gulf through Iraq, Kurdistan, Azerbaijan, Armenia and Georgia as detailed below.[51]

The Ottoman side of the southern border, mostly overlapping (Arabian) Iraq, was made up of the tributary principality of Basra (House of Afrasiyaboğlu), and the provinces of Baghdad (whose borders were marked with posts set up after the finalisation of the peace)[52] and Shahrizor,[53] along with their *banners*[54] and appendages. On the Safavid side of the border were the vassal principality of Huvayza (House of Mushasha), the province of Kirmanshah, and the vassal principality of Ardalan/(easternmost) Kurdistan. Northwards, the Ottomans kept the provinces of Van[55] and Erzurum across the Safavid provinces of Azerbaijan (Tabriz) and Karabakh. In the Caucasus, the province of Kars[56] and fiefdom of Childir (House of Atabegli/Jaqeli) stayed in Ottoman hands facing across the Safavid province of Çukursaᵓd (Erivan). The northernmost frontier at Georgia was split between the Ottoman-tributary lands of Mingrelia (House of Dadiani), Guria (House of Gurieli) and Imereti (House of Bagrationi), and the Safavid-vassal lands of Kartli (the Bagrationis) and Kakheti (the Bagrationis).[57]

Kemankeş Kara Mustafa Pasha, highlighting his powers as Murad IV's plenipotentiary based on specific authorisation, regent by means of commandership-in-chief, and absolute deputy through grand vizierate, had the settlement drawn up as a certificate[58] in his name, and therein pledged, on behalf of the padishah, that as long as the Safavids abided by the deal, so too would the Ottomans.[59] A Safavid functionary, given a three-day deadline, took away this document on 18 May 1639 for the shah to confirm. Safi forthwith sealed and sent it back, together with his own writ of pledge drawn up on 19/20 May, to Kara Mustafa.[60]

In this writ sent to 'grand vizier Mustafa Pasha ... the foremost of the greatest viziers', the shah 'consented' and 'pledged himself' to the articles of the peace. Also thereby Safavid Iran deferred to the Empire, hailing the Ottoman monarch 'his sublimest majesty' as '*shahenshah* (shah of shahs), world-conqueror, supreme sultan, justest khaqan, second Alexander the Great, and God's shadow'.[61] Afterwards the shah wished that the two states thenceforward uphold 'fellowship, mutual love, and union of hearts'.[62] Even if the Safavids may have yearned to become the Ottomans' hierarchical match, they could not claim it, and acknowledged the Ottoman monarch as the highest-ranking sovereign.[63] Maybe as a token thereof that the Ottomans had more weight in shaping the Peace of Zuhab, the Safavids carefully worded the shah's writ of pledge without saying that Safi *gave* or *granted* it. These expressions were otherwise standard in Ottoman writs of pledge.

After the shah's ratification came in, the Safavid delegates and the Ottoman dignitaries on campaign celebrated the peace with two feasts on 22 May, one given by the commander-in-chief in honour of the Safavid mission and the other by the Safavid mission in honour of the Ottoman pashas. On 23 May, Saru Xan Talish headed out towards the shah with a letter of courtesy from the commander-in-chief, and the Imperial Army set out to withdraw. Envoy Kütük Mehemmed-kulu Chagatay was to travel ahead to the imperial court and present the shah's confirmation and writ of pledge to Murad IV.[64]

The commander-in-chief sent out the copy of the peace protocol to Ottoman governors along the Iranian border and ordered them to abide by it, get on well with Safavid authorities across the border, and keep everyone within their provinces in check lest they breach the deal.[65] The Safavids disbanded their troops right away, marshal Rustam Xan Saakadze withdrew from the front to Tabriz, and as soon as Saru Xan Talish came back with Kemankesh Kara Mustafa Pasha's letter, Shah Safi withdrew towards Kazvin, arriving there at the end of May/beginning of June.[66]

Rajab Agha, whom the commander-in-chief sent ahead to rush the news of the peace to Murad IV, reached the imperial court on 4 June 1639. He headed out again for the Imperial Army on the 6th, bearing Murad's written consent to the peace protocol and triumphal regalia for his commander-in-chief. The padishah's dispatch reached Kemankesh Kara Mustafa Pasha at the encampment of Old Mosul on 29 June.[67]

Murad IV had meanwhile wintered in Diyarbekr. In late spring 1639, he marched victoriously through Anatolia and on 8 June reached

1639–1643: Baghdad

Nicomedia, whither the statesmen in the capital travelled to welcome him. He then sailed to Constantinople, and rode into the capital in a procession on 12 June: captured Safavid dignitaries, most notably Mirfattah-oğlu Aka Sadiq Kumshei (shortly known as Mirfattah), Khalaf Beyg/Xan, Naqdi Xan and Aliyar Xan Giraylu,[68] and 100 other prisoner Kızılbaş officers were made to play their trumpets and kettledrums as they were paraded through the crowds that thronged in ranks to watch the conqueror monarch all the way from Bahchekapı up to the Topkapı Palace.

Behind the front, on 16 July, the commander-in-chief set up his headquarters in Diyarbekr, where at the head of a residual group of troops he waited to see whether the Safavids would abide by the deal. Murad IV's decrees consenting to the agreed-upon clauses of the protocol, confirming the appointments to Baghdad, and bestowing vizierate upon Bıyıklı Dervish Mehmed reached from Constantinople to Diyarbekr on 25 July.[69] This bestowal of vizierate is significant in that thenceforward each appointment to the governorship of Baghdad would come along with vizierial rank if the named governor[70] was not already a vizier.[71] Thus, this top deputy of the monarchy in Iraq overlooking Iran would always have the powers of a governor-general,[72] ruling there like a viceroy.

Kütük Mehemmed-kulu Beyg Chagatay and the grand vizier's men travelling beside him reached the capital in August 1639. The marshal of the Imperial Council[73] officially welcomed the envoy in Scutari, escorted him into Constantinople, and took him to Davudpaşa Palace where he was to lodge.[74] Murad IV received Chagatay in audience on 19 September 1639 following an Imperial Council session. The Safavid envoy delivered the confirmation of the border protocol sealed by the shah and the shah's writ of pledge. He, along with Ottoman envoy Hamzapaşaoğlu Mehmed Agha, was entrusted with the padishah's writ of peace to Safi.[75]

While Kütük Chagatay Beyg was waiting in the capital to be given audience, on 20 August 1639, the shah freed high-ranking Ottoman prisoners of war, including a few pashas whom the Safavids had been holding captive since 1636 and whom the shah had recently brought to Kazvin. Ismail Beyg Çepni and Rustam Saakadze's functionary Qasim were to lead this group travelling westwards via Khoy and Khoshab. The Safavids also tore down the stronghold of Kotur (on the border near Khoy, eastwards from Van) as required in the Zuhab protocol. The upholding of the peace set the agenda at the expense of all other subjects for the Shahdom, even the urgency to take back Kandahar from Mughal India.[76]

Diplomacy also went on along the border. An emissary from Kalb-Ali Xan Afşar, the governor of Çukursaʿd, reached the grand vizier in Diyarbekr on 15 September 1639. This representative announced that the shah was in Kazvin, readying gifts to be sent to the padishah[77] with a forthcoming embassy, and thus fully abiding by the agreed-upon terms.

Nevertheless, the commander-in-chief wanted to verify the inflow of news through three separate channels: first, Sarıca Ibrahim Bey the bannerlord[78] of Ergani, who had been the Ottomans' wartime envoy to Shah Safi back in 1636/7,[79] and who was then near Khoy, on the Iranian side of the border to the east of Van, wrote a letter to Kemankeş Kara Mustafa Pasha. Next, from among the freed prisoners, Zulfiqar Agha, former steward to Murtaza Pasha the Ottoman governor of Erivan (who had died amidst the last clashes between the Safavid army and the Ottoman defenders in 1636), sent to the commander-in-chief a list of the names of freed prisoners. The third source was the report by the returning agent of Küçük Hasan Pasha the governor of Van, whom Kara Mustafa had commissioned to send someone across the border to Safavid dignitaries, under the pretext of talking on some border issues but with the real goal of stealthily gathering information. The commander-in-chief then forwarded these letters by Sarıca Ibrahim, Zulfiqar the steward and Küçük Hasan's agent to the imperial court, together with the translation of another paper that Rustam Saakadze had sent to Küçük Hasan by means of the aforesaid agent.[80]

The mission of Ismail Çepni Beyg reached the Imperial Army headquarters in Diyarbekr on 29 October 1639. The commander-in-chief was surprised to find out that, unlike what Sarıca Ibrahim Bey and the agent of Küçük Hasan Pasha had thought, this mission was not a full-fledged legation from the shah with a letter to the padishah, but one bearing a letter from the shah and papers from his *xan*s to the commander-in-chief, thus supplementing the main Safavid legation by Kütük Mehemmed-kulu Beyg Chagatay, which was still busy in Constantinople. Çepni made known that the Safavids had torn down the strongholds of Kotur and Zenjir (on the border near Qasr-i Shirin and Zuhab, between the provinces of Baghdad and Kirmanshah) and smoothed out all border matters. The shah's upcoming full-fledged embassy to the padishah would wait for the envoy Chagatay, still active at the imperial court, to go back to Iran with a letter of answer and gifts of friendship from the padishah, for it was unconventional to send out a second standalone mission while an earlier one was still in business.[81]

The Iranians were worried as to whether Murad IV would confirm the peace agreement, and the fact that the core of the Imperial Army still encamped behind the frontier was furthering these misgivings. Hence, Safi had hurriedly sent Ismail Çepni as emissary without a letter for the padishah and, concerned about Murad IV's wrath, pinned a dispatch rider[82] to the mission to get an urgent update as to whether Murad accepted the peace and what came out from the Chagatay legation. The commander-in-chief wrote back to the shah, saying that the peace was fulfilled and envoy Chagatay would soon be sent back. The dispatch rider rushed this message back to Safi.[83]

At Murad IV's behest, the commander-in-chief set out on 7 November 1639 from Diyarbekr towards the capital. Although the Safavids were abiding by the deal, Kemankeş Kara Mustafa Pasha sent Melek (Tırnakçı Malak) Ahmed Pasha to Mosul as commander-general[84] of the troops that were still not demobilised, against a potential breach from Iran.[85] Melek Ahmed had partaken in the last Iranian campaign as Murad IV's arms-bearer,[86] had been made governor of Diyarbekr after the conquest of Baghdad, and then had joined the Imperial Army's forward thrust towards Iran until the signing of the protocol at Zuhab.[87]

As Kemankeş Kara Mustafa Pasha was faring back to the capital, the outgoing Ottoman envoy, Hamzapaşaoğlu Mehmed Agha, and the returning Safavid envoy, Kütük Mehemmed-kulu Beyg Chagatay, left Constantinople on 13 December 1639. On 17 December they set out from Scutari, and on 29 December they met Kara Mustafa in Göynük (near Bolu).[88] The triumphant commander-in-chief reached the capital on 5 January 1640 and entered Constantinople with a military procession to the Topkapı Palace, reuniting with his lord Murad IV.[89]

Murad IV's writ of peace[90] confirmed the hierarchy of relations hinted at in the shah's earlier pledge. First of all, the ratification steps were not reciprocal. Murad IV sent out his writ of peace only after Safi's pledge reached Constantinople and was looked into by the imperial court. The wording also gives the same message. To put a bold face on, Safi wrote that he himself had spearheaded the reconciliation after Murad IV had made known his willingness for peace. By contrast, in his answer, Murad IV uttered his consent to the peace in words that show how the Ottomans' victory on the battlefield shaped the terms. Murad the 'shah-of-shahs' underscored that he ratified the protocol because the shah had asked for peace, made a pledge, sent the document with his stamp pressed under the text, and 'beseeched [Murad's] august approval'.

After sixty years of fruitless intermittent fighting, both sides took on a pragmatism that shaped the conditions of peace. The agreement itself, which came to be called a peace treaty, was in terms of content nothing more than a border protocol of truce.[91] But this shared willingness to bury the hatchet should not obscure the fact that the Safavids acknowledged defeat. In the same year that they lost Kandahar to Mughal India,[92] they could not afford to fight against the Ottomans whose army had already thrust into Iran. By 1639 Iran's choice troops had been wiped out and Iraq had been lost back to the Ottomans; the Safavids thus had to come to terms with the fact that the Ottomans had prevailed. Peace would make Iran politically steadier, and lessen its financial and military burden, for then the Ottomans would no longer constitute a threat. The Shahdom favoured this scenario over any other adventure.[93]

Though the Ottomans felt satisfied with their gains, they too had become war-weary. Nevertheless, whereas they welcomed the prospect of peace, as conquerors on the ground they could afford waiting for the Shahdom to start overtures with attractive terms. Once the border protocol was ratified into a contract, this setting laid the groundwork of relations up until the downfall of the Safavid monarchy. Iranians could secure lasting peace only by acknowledging Ottoman primacy, and this would perpetually shape Iranian decision-makers' mindset. The Ottomans on the other hand could enforce impositions, or at least they trumped the Safavids' sanction power. This, then, was the background to all interactions between the Empire and Safavid Iran after 1639.

Diplomatic Interregnum and the Protracted State of War

Murad IV's health worsened after his return to Constantinople. One night he drank far too much with Amirguneoğlu (Yusuf Pasha, a.k.a. Tahmaspkulu Xan Akçakoyunlu-Kajar),[94] who was the Iranian second vizier of the Ottoman Imperial Council, and grand-admiral Yekceğiz Bezirganzade Silahdar Mustafa Pasha, who had participated in the campaign of 1638 against the Safavids as governor of Damascus but had stayed beside his friend Murad IV while his troops had fought.[95] Murad became bedridden after this binge, and died on 8 February 1640 at twenty-seven years old. His troubled brother Ibrahim followed him onto the throne while Kemankeş Kara Mustafa Pasha retained the grand vizierate.[96] That the latter remained in office was important for the Safavids, who regarded him as the architect of the Peace of Zuhab and, as we shall see below, saw his continued leadership as assurance that the Ottomans would not call off the deal.

A number of high-ranking Iranian captives living as enforced guests in Constantinople forthwith wrote a letter to Iran telling of Murad IV's death. The dispatch was intercepted in Scutari on 9 February, resulting in the termination of the favourable living conditions that these captives had hitherto enjoyed: the Sublime Porte locked them up at Boğazkesen (Rumelihisarı), the stronghold to the north of Constantinople on the European banks of the Bosphorus.[97]

Kemankeş Kara Mustafa Pasha had the news of Ibrahim's enthronement broadcast with festivities along the Iranian border, and Küçük Hasan

1639–1643: Baghdad

Pasha the governor of Van sent an agent bearing papers to the grand vizierate, reporting that the shah was abiding by the peace. Kara Mustafa briefed his new lord on these papers.[98] Eastwards, the news of Murad IV's death arrived in late February/early March 1640 while the shah was at Mazandaran, and gladdened the Safavid court.[99] It seems that the Safavids still feared him, even after the signing of the peace. His death, in the eyes of Iranians, must have lessened the likelihood of a new war resulting out of the Ottoman monarch's own will.

It was about the same time as the Safavids heard of Murad IV's death, in late February/early March 1640, that Kütük Mehemmed-kulu Beyg Chagatay and Hamzapaşaoğlu Mehmed Agha reached Mazandaran. The shah's court merrily received the two missions and the peace letters they brought.[100] All available reports and the later flow of events indicate that at Mazandaran the shah welcomed Hamzapaşaoğlu Mehmed Agha warmly, but not officially: the Ottoman envoy could not start his diplomatic business, because his credentials had been issued by a sovereign who was no longer alive, making the continued validity of the mission and the missives he brought at best questionable. The diplomatic interregnum had thus begun.

This state of affairs presented an unprecedented situation. Peace treaties in force formally had to be reconfirmed by new Ottoman monarchs upon enthronement. However, the succession of 1640 befell at a time after the peace protocol had been signed, the ratificatory Safavid writ of pledge had been handed over to the imperial court, and the ratificatory Ottoman writ of peace had been sent out, but before the imperial envoy could deliver this document to the shah of Iran and be sent back along with the shah's written acknowledgment. Therefore, the shah might shun meeting with the Ottoman legate, for the delegator was now dead. Likewise, the padishah might declare as invalid both the legation and the letters it bore, on the grounds that Murad IV, their sender, had died before their receipt by the shah.

Likely both to forestall the diplomatic interregnum from undermining the shaky peace and to soothe his own misgivings, Sultan Ibrahim Khan wrote a letter of friendship to Shah Safi, thus establishing contact before uncertainty could grow. In the same dispatch, Kemankesh Kara Mustafa Pasha too sent a letter[101] to the 'augustly-fortunate Shah his sublime Majesty, the sphere of the sun of sultanate with Saturn's portal and Kay-Khusrav's army'.[102] The grand vizier thereby shared with Safi the news of the death of Murad IV 'the supreme sultan, foremost khakan, shadow-caster upon the realms of Arabia and Ajam, shelter of the kings of the Turks and Daylam, the deceased Lord-Sovereign',[103] and of the 'august accession'[104] to the 'Ottoman throne of cosmic-mastership, which is the shelter of the Cyrsus-es and the refuge of the Caesers',[105] by 'the supreme of the sultans of the Earth, the foremost of the khakans, shah-of-shahs, Sultan Ibrahim Khan'.[106]

Next, the grand vizier, underlining that he kept his post and presented to his new lord the terms of the deal struck between Murad IV and Shah Safi, rephrased Ibrahim's spoken answer:

> because Our deceased brother Sultan Murad Khan his Majesty has made peace with the Shah of Ajam, and also because writs-of-pledge from both sides have been given and taken, it is necessary to conform to the dogma *do not violate your oaths after you affirm them*. So long as no violation of the pledge arises from that side, it is appropriate that the path of friendship be open from this side too.

Kara Mustafa thus guaranteed that as long as the Safavids did not go against treaty conditions, the Ottomans would abide by the peace, in the making of which he himself had strived. But in the *sanctio* below, which looks more like a *comminatio*, the grand vizier spelled out for the shah what he truly meant:

> Namely as follows: if Your illustrious party takes insufficient care in safeguarding this treaty, does not observe the peace with heart and soul, and lets arise circumstances indicating the violation of the pledge, then it will be imperative that an unwished-for move also be made by our side. Accordingly, if Your illustrious desire is friendship, You shall please to show diligence to the execution of its necessities, and hurry in the dispatch of missions and missives with gifts worthy of [the shah-of-shah's] august presence.

The grand vizier also sent a letter[107] to the marshal of Iran 'Rustam Xan his sublime Excellency, the administrator of the shahly state, the xan of xans of the shah'.[108] Aside from first Kara Mustafa's mention of his personal 'previous friendship'[109] with Rustam Saakadze, in line with which he also shared the news of the 'soundness of [his own] health',[110] and next the technical as well as rhetorical touch-ups owing to the change of the addressee, this letter was simply a version of the one written to the shah at the same time. And as he did with the shah, the grand vizier demanded from the marshal of Iran too that the Safavid court dismiss envoy Hamzapaşaoğlu Mehmed Agha and send alongside him a reputable ambassador with worthy gifts.[111]

In these letters there is no mention of the name of the diplomatic herald[112] bearing them. The herald must have headed out soon after the enthronement – likely in late February – to hurry the new letters to Hamzapaşaoğlu before his meeting with the shah so that he could hand them over together with the original dispatch. Besides Ibrahim's restlessness, which can be sensed from the documents shuttling inside the Empire (to be seen below), the diplomatic interregnum arising from the death of an Ottoman sovereign after approving a peace but before the fulfilment of the last deed of ratification too had driven the Sublime Porte to announce the imperial succession to the Safavid court. These follow-up letters do not introduce anything new to the set hierarchy, by which the padishah ranked as supreme emperor and the shah as king. Noteworthy is the grand vizier's taking the marshal of Iran, rather than the chief vizier,[113] as his addressee. The grand vizier must have chosen as addressee Iran's marshal Rustam Saakadze instead of chief vizier Mirza Muhammad Saru Taqi because of the lingering state of war and the yet unfulfilled peacemaking. After all, it was the Iranian marshal, and not the chief vizier, who was the wartime absolute deputy of the shah and hence the practical, if not matching, addressee of the padishah's commander-in-chief.

The highlight of these letters is their threatening tone. To ensure that the Ottoman position be understood, it would be enough to let the shah and the marshal of Iran know that as long as the Safavids would abide by the peace, so would the Ottomans. Yet, the Ottoman chancellery inset a *sanctio* into these letters, making an elegant, implicitly worded but explicitly meant threat, like a *comminatio* at that, and included this even in the grand vizier's letter to the shah, a genre which was to reflect the respect that an appointed prime minister had to show towards a reigning king whatever the particularities of their hierarchical relationship and the agenda of the correspondence were. The Sublime Porte wanted to utter, notwithstanding Ibrahim's restlessness, that if Isfahan were to breach the agreed-upon peace, Constantinople would strike back harder. Kemankeş Kara Mustafa openly said 'go farther and fare worse' to the Safavids.

A Self-Confident Empire, a Restless Emperor

Probably in early summer 1640, Bashir, an agent whom Küçük Hasan Pasha at the imperial court's behest had sent to Iran, came back to Van from Tabriz bearing Rustam Saakadze's letters addressed to the governor. Two strongholds had to be torn down in accordance with the treaty and peace was steady, wrote the marshal of Iran. Bashir also brought the news that the envoy – meaning Hamzapaşaoğlu Mehmed Agha – had met with the shah in late May 1640, and was about to be sent back alongside a new ambassador from the shah. These papers were forwarded to the imperial court. In his briefing[114] to the padishah, the grand vizier foresaw that this boded well.[115]

Safi returned to Isfahan on 22 June 1640, with Ottoman envoy Hamzapaşaoğlu Mehmed Agha at the tail of the royal court all the way from Mazandaran. Begdilli Karakhan Beyg Shamlu, brother of Janibek Xan the head of the royal guard, was once again named the envoy-agha's host-officer at the head of military officers and notables leading the legation's procession into the capital. The Ottoman envoy was taken at Safi's behest to the new Royal Grand Mosque[116] of Isfahan to perform the Friday prayer together with the gathered congregation and dignitaries, and after the prayer, Chief-justice Mirza Habibullah Karaki hosted him at an event held in his honour. Safi clothed the padishah's envoy with a robe of honour at the welcome audience and held him in high esteem. On following days, Chief Vizier Saru Taqi and Begdilli Janibek Shamlu hosted him at separate events held again in his honour at the shah's behest.[117]

The missions by Kütük Mehemmed-kulu Beyg Chagatay and Hamzapaşaoğlu Mehmed Agha were far from purely ceremonial; their successful fulfilment was worthy enough to be rewarded. On 15 July 1640, upon the death of Kalb-Ali Xan Afşar while in office, the shah made Chagatay the new governor of Çukursaʿd (Erivan).[118] The Hamzapaşaoğlu legation to Isfahan and the Chagatay legation to Constantinople were indeed not the first diplomatic contacts after the Peace of Zuhab. These two missions were rather a step towards putting the deal of Zuhab into force and starting the reign of peace.

Incoming news from Iraq soon confirmed the above-said good tidings from Azerbaijan. In late September 1640, Bıyıklı Dervish Mehmed Pasha drew up a presentation[119] to the grand vizier: an eyewitness from Isfahan, who had come to Baghdad on 15 September, and Iranian tradesmen likewise coming to Baghdad, verified that the envoy-agha had been warmly received, that the shah had allotted a handsome budget for his forthcoming diplomatic gifts, and that Safi would likely send his chief-of-staff of the musketeers as envoy bearing these gifts.[120] The governor of Baghdad then shared the news that the head of the shah's guard – Begdilli Janibek Xan Shamlu – had strongly counselled Safi to uphold the friendship with the padishah. This was because, first, Iran, already having feuds with India and the Uzbeks, would otherwise become fully encircled and crippled in a war with the Empire. Secondly, the Empire's sovereign was already 'greater' (in strength) than all other monarchs, as Begdilli Janibek had reportedly noted. Thirdly – this must have been spiced up to calm down Ibrahim's misgivings – Begdilli Janibek had said that the new padishah was even 'bolder and more daring than Murad' IV as well as being 'clever and smart'. All in all, the head of the royal guard had underscored that the shah should abide by the peace so that the Safavids could strike back if the

Indians or the Uzbeks were ever to set on. The Iranians were 'extremely weak', wrote the pasha of Baghdad, insomuch that recently 'they wanted to enlist some musketeers, but could not [even carry out the] enlist[ment, let alone the deployment]'. He would soon present more precise news, which he awaited from a few spies he had sent out earlier, who were yet to return.[121]

Bıyıklı Dervish Mehmed also told of the hearsay that Afrasiyaboğlu Ali Pasha of Basra had sent a footman of his to the shah, to whom Safi had not given much heed. Afrasiyaboğlu Ali was a 'double-dealing hypocrite' and 'appealed too much to the shah', remarked the governor of Baghdad. Nevertheless, Bıyıklı Pasha also wrote a letter of friendship to Afrasiyaboğlu: if the foe were to set on Basra, Baghdad would rush any needed amount of troops and munitions to Basra within fifteen days.[122] In other words, if the Afrasiyaboğlus tried to cast off Ottoman overlordship and take on Safavid vassalage, Ottoman forces in Baghdad would show up at the gates of Basra in two weeks. This 'letter of friendship' was nothing other than a threat by the Empire's viceroy in Iraq speaking softly but carrying a big stick.

This presentation from the governor of Baghdad to the grand vizier struck all the right chords to soothe Padishah Ibrahim's misgivings: first, it shared verified information about the shah's warm reception of the Ottoman envoy and about the forthcoming Safavid mission's friendly goal. Next, it underscored that Iran could not pose a threat to the Empire even if it wanted to. Third, it boosted the padishah's feeble mind by assuring him of his perceived might. Yet, neither the Empire's position of strength nor the flattery to his person could comfort Ibrahim.

The diplomatic business went ahead as foreseen. To acknowledge the receipt and validity of Murad IV's writ of peace and wish Ibrahim well on his accession, in mid-October 1640 Shah Safi named Yirmidört Ibrahim Xan Kajar his new ambassador to the padishah.[123] It must have been also in the autumn of 1640 that, after a nine-day trip, a messenger reached Constantinople from the governor of Diyarbekir, Melek Ahmed Pasha, whom the grand vizier had shifted thither as commander-general in case the front were to reopen. The messenger brought papers from Melek Ahmed as well as from the governor of Van: as had been submitted to the imperial court earlier, Safavid troops were indeed gathering, though they were not on the march and their target was not known; the borderlands were yet safe, the pashas held the troops at the Iranian frontier ready.[124] Soon, another messenger from (Küçük) Hasan Pasha reached Constantinople after a sixteen-day trip. The governor of Van let the grand vizier know that contra his former report, there was 'no [military] gathering of the Kızılbaş', peace was steady, the borderlands were safe, and a [Safavid] ambassador was about to arrive. Ibrahim scrawled an *august script* on the grand-vizier's briefing, saying that he awaited good news.[125]

Bıyıklı Dervish Mehmed too sent almost the same news to the imperial court. His first messenger, reaching the capital in fourteen days, reported: 'the borders are safe; and although there is a gathering[126] of the enemy [namely Iranians], mischief[127] has not arisen so far'. The grand vizier briefed this news, together with the update papers coming from Darna, Dartang, Kirkuk, Van and other border localities, to the padishah, and Ibrahim noted his appreciation atop the briefing.[128] Nothing came out of this reported gathering at the Iranian side of the border. Another messenger from Bıyıklı Pasha, reaching the capital from Baghdad in sixteen days, 'brought the news that that frontier was perfectly fine'.[129] This too we learn from the Kemankesh Kara Mustafa's briefing and Ibrahim's script atop.[130] An agent of the grand vizier himself also 'came from Baghdad and reported its wellness and ease'.[131] Ibrahim must have been growing impatient about updates from the Iranian border, for the grand vizier briefed the report for the padishah the same hour as it came in.[132]

Nonetheless worried about the outcome of this business, Ibrahim later wrote another script to his grand vizier: '[the Iranians] used to fear the deceased padishah, I wonder whether they do not fear Us'. To soothe his restless lord, Kemankesh Kara Mustafa answered that the enemy would always fear the Ottoman monarch, whomever he might be, that there was still time for the ambassador to show up, that the Iranian borderlands were safe, that Van, Shahrizor and Baghdad were watched over by the now-twofold troops deployed there with imperial scripts, and that spies had been sent out, who would soon come back with information. Kara Mustafa also assured his lord that any evil to be done by foes would hit back the doer; the Ottoman State was mighty and there was nothing to upset Ibrahim's 'august mind'.[133]

Calming down Ibrahim, who had been traumatised by a constant fear of being put to death throughout his brother Murad IV's reign, was not easy. He assailed his grand vizier with unending enquiries about all kinds of worries that haunted his mind, relations with Iran among these. In one such script, he said: 'that this ambassador has not come ... what is the reason of this? Wherefore do the Kızılbaş halt? I wonder whether they do not take Us seriously. They used to fear the other one [that is Murad IV].'[134]

Ibrahim continued to feel insecure notwithstanding the incoming updates from the agents and spies of frontier governors, because even thereafter he had Kemankeş Kara Mustafa Pasha send further messengers all the way from the capital to the Iranian border. One such commissioner who briefed the grand vizier for Ibrahim was

> Husein the messenger,[135] who had been sent to the border at Van to bring news. He came back in eleven days ... 'Currently there is no mischief, Your servant [Küçük] Hasan Pasha, who is there, said that those borderlands were well and safe and that according to the earlier news coming from other borderlands an ambassador from the Kızılbaş was about to head out.'[136]

Another such messenger rode back from Baghdad to the capital in fifteen days and likewise stated that all was well and safe there.[137] Yet another agent reaching the capital in fifteen days from Kirkuk 'brought the news that those borderlands were safe. As [in] the earlier [report], all is right and orderly.'[138] News that the Iranian border was secure also came from Erzurum.[139]

Ibrahim, helplessly haunted by his misgivings, kept on fretting about Iranian affairs and nagging at his grand vizier. In all likelihood answering the brief on Rustam Xan Saakadze's aforesaid letters from Tabriz to Küçük Hasan Pasha at Van, Ibrahim scribbled the script below to his grand vizier:

> Rustam Xan sent a letter to Hasan Pasha and preached all over. It is not to be trusted, beware! He wants to trick us by saying 'we obey the orders of the two greatly-glorious padishahs, our peace is established, you on that side and we on this side work hard.' It is not to be trusted, keeping an eye out is the only way. Let us prepare [for war, and then] it will not matter if he makes peace or not. God willing, we [the padishah and the grand vizier] will talk this over when I get to the [ceremony for the distribution of the Household corps's] salaries. You shall know so.[140]

Thereupon, the grand vizier felt the need to soothe his lord with even more expressive words than before:

> the enemy will not be trusted just because it preaches and shows obedience. In the age of justice of my mighty padishah, there is no shortcoming in any kind of preparation and measure in any borderland. Care is being taken and attention is being paid. May Your illustrious heart be strong. Henceforward too, so long as the ambassador does not head out and arrive, there will be no shortcoming in preparations and [military] concentration. My imperial padishah, even after the ambassador heads out, our borderlands will not be left vacant, they will still be taken care of and watched over.[141]

The new padishah worried much about how the Shahdom would react to Murad IV's sudden death, and dreaded that others might deem him a monarch weaker than his brother and that this might embolden old foes to start a new war.[142] He seems thus to have become obsessed about what would come out of the Ottoman legation at Isfahan and whether a new Safavid ambassador would be sent, the nonfulfilment of which could forebode a war. Imperial dignitaries, meanwhile, did not share his fear. The news from the pashas at the borderland, the grand vizier's opinion, and the Sublime Porte's diplomatic letters all indicate that Ottoman statesmen neither deemed it likely that the Shahdom would break the peace, nor thought that a war with Iran would jeopardise the Empire's position, because a new confrontation with the Safavids could only bring further gains.

On the other hand, the shah did not know either whether the new padishah would acknowledge Murad IV's deal. So, Safi was no less restless than Ibrahim, insomuch that the Safavids halted their already decided-upon campaign to take back Kandahar from Mughal India until the outcome of their upcoming embassy to Constantinople would become known.[143] And this embassy itself was also belated to start out, for the Shahdom first had to decide about how to react to the diplomatic interregnum stemming from Murad IV's death amidst the consummation of the peace, and then had to let Hamzapaşaoğlu Mehmed Agha fulfil his mission after a lengthy wait owing to the aforesaid uncertainty.[144]

Once the formalities were over, the shah feasted, entertained and honourably discharged the Ottoman envoy. He was to fare back to Constantinople along with Yirmidört Ibrahim Xan Kajar – the governor of Berda (in Karabakh) and now ambassador to the padishah – bearing letters and gifts from the shah.[145] The imperial envoy and the shah's ambassador set out from Isfahan sometime in the winter of 1641.

Back in Constantinople, the aforesaid Safavid captive Mirfattah-oğlu Kumshei and his sons[146] were put to death in late March/early April 1641, on the grounds that their 'elimination was necessary'.[147] Such draconian treatment of these prominent prisoners of war was extremely unusual, as is to be explained by Mirfattah's earlier deeds against the Ottomans. His entanglement with the Ottomans had begun in 1626, when Shah Abbas I had sent him and his troops to Baghdad beleaguered by the Ottomans, where later on he had led the defence. When the Ottomans had beleaguered Erivan in 1635, Shah Safi had likewise sent Mirfattah, then colonel of the Isfahan musketeers,[148] to strengthen the garrison. While the fortress commander, Akçakoyunlu Tahmasp-kulu Xan Kajar, had negotiated the terms of surrender, Mirfattah had opened fire on Ottoman troops amidst the truce, thus sabotaging the deal and gaining notoriety. This notoriety had been further compounded in 1638: as the Ottomans

1639–1643: Baghdad

had besieged Baghdad, he had been promoted to the commandership of the Shahdom's musketeers[149] and entrusted with leading the musketeers manning Baghdad. When Bektaş Xan Mirimanidze, the Safavid governor of Baghdad, had consulted his officers about surrendering, Mirfattah had strongly opposed, knowing that if he fell into Ottoman captivity Murad IV would make him suffer the consequences of his deeds in Erivan three years earlier. Later, after the garrison had yielded, Mirfattah and a few other Safavid generals had hindered the emptying of the fortress, refusing to lay down arms and not disbanding their troops. Ottoman soldiers entering the fortress had made this, together with the breach of truce back in 1635, an excuse to slaughter the defenders, and Mirfattah had fallen captive. Even then, after Ottoman forces had already occupied parts of the fortress, his sons had not given in or left their weapons. This then had triggered another round of slaughter. Only thereafter had Mirfattah's sons ended up alongside other Safavid captives.[150]

The Sublime Porte thus excepted the Mirfattah-oğlus from the ongoing swap of prisoners of war. Even more remarkable is that at the time of execution in the early spring of 1641, the convict's brother was a military general in Safavid Iran: Aka-Tahir Kumshei, brother of Mirfattah-oğlu Aka-Sadiq, was the shah's current commander of musketeers.[151] The execution of the Mirfattahoğlus was thus a blow to the very highest ranks of Safavid officialdom. This notwithstanding, Iranian sources speak of neither the execution nor a reaction thereto from the Shahdom, and Ottoman sources do not give any further clue. We do, however, glean some useful insight from the final relation of Johann Rudolf Schmid, the German emperor's minister-resident at Constantinople. As he reports, Mirfattah-oğlu Kumshei's son and a few other high-ranking prisoners, who had once enjoyed a comfortable captivity because of having surrendered but who following Murad IV's death had been locked up in the Seven Towers, were indeed put to death as part of the deal reached during the latest bargain between the two monarchies. He notes furthermore that the general consensus of Ottoman statesmen was to let these persons live, so as to encourage future defections from Iran; it was considered that if these persons were executed this would motivate potential Safavid defectors to remain loyal unto death to the shah. Evidently, however, such objections were ultimately overruled. The Habsburg minister-resident also remarked that the deal was made between Iran and an Ottoman Empire stronger than it, that neither state would think of starting a war but this could happen only if an uprising in the Ottoman east would lay the groundwork for it, and that Iran's weakness against the Empire was too inbuilt to be deemed temporary or situational.[152]

The Safavid silence about the Ottomans' putting to death the Mirfattahoğlus hints at an embarrassment at having to consent to these belittling executions as part of a diplomatic finessing. As it seems, after the Peace of Zuhab the Safavids had to politically disown the captured Mirfattahoğlus, and shake hands over a deal that also included eliminating them. The bargain was likely made through informal links between courts. By means of these political executions, the two sides did away with likely grounds for strife in the future. As to be seen below in a similar case of even higher profile, it is highly likely that the Safavids firstly asked the Sublime Porte for the repatriation of these commanders, and that upon the Sublime Porte's final refusal to free these persons the Safavid unwillingly requested their execution, which would be a one-time insult, rather than their continued captivity, which would be an ongoing belittlement. The Sublime Porte, on its own part, thus chose to publicly reinforce its superiority by showing off that they could execute two high-ranking commanders of the defeated enemy even after the establishment of peace and business would still continue as usual.

Safavid ambassador Yirmidört Ibrahim Kajar, alongside Ottoman envoy Hamzapaşaoğlu Mehmed, reached Constantinople on 16 June 1641 and entered the city on 17 June, about three months after the executions. The grand vizier, the marshal of the Imperial Council Boynueğri Durak Agha, who on the 1638 campaign had been the first Ottoman officer to step peacefully into Baghdad when the Safavid garrison had asked for quarter,[153] and the privy arms-bearer[154] orchestrated the welcome at the capital, and the embassy was taken to Huseinpaşa Palace near Bayazid Square, chosen to house it. Meeting or communicating with the guests was forbidden for anyone from outside. A Janissary squadron and its captain were pinned to the embassy, both to ensure its safety and control its contacts.[155] The Sublime Porte wanted to oversee the flow of information to the Safavid ambassador. At the same time, Hamzapaşaoğlu Mehmed's second legation, going on since December 1639, also came to an end; he won favour with the padishah and the grand vizier thanks to his service in diplomacy with Iran.[156]

The embassy's welcome pleasantries spanned four weeks. On 14 July 1641, the padishah gave audience to Yirmidört Kajar at Topkapı Palace. The event was conventionally made to coincide with the three-monthly gathering of the Imperial Council where officers of the Household corps received their pay, a symbolic show of might to guest diplomats. The ambassador was outwardly on the brink of quivering upon seeing the splendour, prompting the marshal of the Imperial Council to break the convention and offer him a seat, though this may equally have been a ploy to give the impression that the ambassador was overwhelmed. After the gate-keepers of the Imperial Court took receipt of the shah's gifts, the Imperial Council members proceeded to the audience hall. The grand vizier put beside the pedestals of the throne the shah's letter, which congratulated Ibrahim on his accession and wished their friendship to go on. Given permission, the ambassador neared the padishah and kissed his hand. This was not only a courtly but also a public event: Constantinopolitans had filled the road from Hagia Sophia to the Imperial Gate – the entrance to the outermost courtyard of Topkapı Palace – to see the procession of the Safavid embassy.[157] While there was doubtless much to admire, however, the ambassador's amazement was probably not entirely unfeigned: it was an accepted part of Eastern diplomatic etiquette to profess astonishment and a sense of being tongue-tied when in the presence of a host who was of higher standing than the sender.[158]

The grand vizier received Yirmidört Kajar not long after the padishah's welcome audience.[159] The ambassador could thus deliver Shah Safi's and Rustam Saakzade's letters to Kemankeş Kara Mustafa Pasha, who indeed steered the Empire's Iranian affairs. Yirmidört Kajar was entertained in Constantinople following these official meetings; Imperial Council viziers held feasts of their own in his honour.[160]

In his letter[161] to 'Mustafa Pasha his vizierial, princely, and superb Highness, curator of the Khaqan's Sublime State, reliance of the gorgeously-imposing Ottoman Sultanate, great marshal, the grand vizier',[162] Shah Safi confirmed receipt via envoy Hamzapaşaoğlu Mehmed Agha of the commander-in-chief's 'candid letter', and thereby said 'it has become apparent once again that the goodwill of yours, the sublimely-magnified premier, is true'. As for the grand vizier's words in his last letter that if the Safavids upheld the peace then so would the Ottomans, the shah noted that he himself had started the peace talks with the padishah 'his sublimest Majesty, the supreme of the sultans of the age, the second Alexander the Great, God's shadow'.[163] Therefore, he said, he would uphold the peace with might and main, and expected the grand vizier to do the same. The ambassador was commissioned to raise, in spoken word, further matters for the grand vizier to lay before the padishah. Safi asked Kemankeş Kara Mustafa to keep on doing whatever was needed for the good of the two monarchies, and to let him know of any demand or claim he might have, which the shah would do his best to fulfil.[164]

Likewise, Rustam Saakadze, the marshal of Iran, sent a letter[165] to 'Mustafa Pasha his vizierial, princely, and sublime Majesty, of welkin-dignity, the sponsor of the expediencies of nations, pillar of the Sublime Sultanate, humerus of the elevated Ottoman State, sight of the looks of the Shadow of God, revered marshal, paramount premier'.[166] Rustam acknowledged the grand vizier's 'correspondence of courtesy', which had 'caused complete rejoice over glad-tidings', and wished for Kara Mustafa to long remain in good health.[167] This was rather a correspondence of formality; it was the shah and the Ottoman grand vizier who were doing the real talking.

The Safavids wanted to give the impression that they had taken no offence at the grand vizier's kindly worded threats. Hence, in these answers, they spoke of only the grand vizier's glad-tidings about the imperial enthronement and his readiness to uphold the peace, while they wished away his *sanctio* and *comminatio*. Above all is noteworthy that the shah saw nothing wrong in uttering that he deemed Kemankesh Kara Mustafa his mediator at the imperial court to secure the harmony between the two monarchies, and that he was ready to do anything to contribute to this end in line with whatever the pasha might suggest. Hence, with the letters of 1641, the Safavids emphasised their acknowledgement of Ottoman superiority in hierarchy and in strength. They did not even hide that they needed the peace more than the Ottomans did, and the shah requested – on official record – the grand vizier to intercede with the padishah on the Safavids' behalf.

Even two and a half years after the last battle, the lingering state of war still haunted the relations. The Iranian chancellery retained wartime titles of command in the *inscriptio* it put together for the grand vizier in both letters, and still not the chief vizier but the marshal of Iran corresponded with the padishah's absolute deputy. Furthermore, this Safavid formality came on top of the Ottoman wartime measure that the Janissary chief-of-staff was still standing watch in Baghdad at the head of an army-like garrison of 20,000.

While ambassador Yirmidört Kajar was in business at the Sublime Porte, Rustam Saakadze sent a follow-up letter[168] to the grand vizier: 'from among the evil Kurd[ish tribe]s, who always mean malice and want injury to befall the laws of peace, Baban Suleiman Bey [the elder] repeatedly attacked[169] Budak Soltan Mukri's land,[170] which is within the country of this [Iranian] side in [accordance with] the border-protocol[171] [of Zuhab]', wrote the marshal of Iran. Upon Budak Soltan's report of the breach, Rustam Xan had 'repeatedly written to the former governor of Shahrizor – Jafar Pasha – and the current governor – Hasan Bey – so as to constrain him, and the mentioned Suleiman Bey was not constrained by their constraint, again he was not wasting a moment in stirring sedition'. Rustam claimed that he had neither informed the shah about the matter, nor himself dealt with it, nor entrusted ambassador Yirmidört Kajar to raise the matter at imperial court, 'lest a defect find its way into the pillars of pacification'. Ascribing Kemankesh Mustafa Pasha with the true credit for building the peace, the marshal of Iran requested him to 'discipline [Baban] Suleiman Bey, and if not, authorize this [Iranian] side to set about chastising him'.[172]

That Rustam Saakadze felt compelled to send this follow-up letter hints that the aforesaid breaches were too serious to be dealt with through borderland mechanisms. The gravity of the situation is further highlighted by the fact that the entire letter is devoted to this single problem. The wording of this letter from the marshal of Iran, as well as the two earlier ones, emphasise the extent to which the Safavids had come to deem Kara Mustafa a revered and influential statesman owing to his leadership throughout the fragile and long-drawn-out steps of two and a half years of peacemaking. Thus, outwardly for the good of the Ottoman–Safavid peace and indeed for the good of Iran, the marshal went so far as to claim that he shared with the Ottoman grand vizier information that he had not divulged to the shah. We do not know how this particular case ended up. However, in view of the persons and breaches involved, it foreboded the destructive Baban uprising which would jumble up the Ottoman–Safavid border throughout the 1690s.

At the same time as the Safavid mission to Constantinople, the German emperor too had set about renewing the ongoing treaty with the Turks. An extraordinary Habsburg emissary met with the grand vizier at an audience on 8 July 1641.[173] By then Yirmidört Kajar had been in Constantinople for three weeks; he must have figured out that no 'German campaign' to middle Europe was coming up for the Empire. The Habsburg monarchy was entangled in what would have come to be known as the Thirty Years War, and sought to keep up the peace with its eastern neighbour. That the main Ottoman army would not be tied up in Europe anytime soon, and could thus be fielded against the Safavids if need be, must have informed the ambassador's later report to the shah's court and hardened the Safavids' resolve to uphold their friendship with the Sublime Porte at all costs.

Ambassador Yirmidört Ibrahim Xan Kajar stayed in Constantinople throughout the summer. At the beginning of September 1641[174] the padishah gave him his farewell audience, and after repeating the earlier ceremonies, let him depart. The ambassador left for Iran on 7 September.[175] With him travelled Mutafarriqa Qabil Agha, a 'court patrician' whom Ibrahim appointed as envoy to Shah Safi.[176] Also travelling with Yirmidört Kajar's party were some high- and middle-ranking Iranian commanders who had been taken prisoner at the Ottoman capture of Erivan (1635) and Baghdad

(1638), and whom the Sublime Porte now freed from the dungeon of Seven Towers in return for the Ottoman captives whom Yirmidört Kajar had brought from Iran.[177] But not all Iranians at the Ottoman court were departing. On the day that Yirmidört Kajar set off with his party,[178] the Sublime Porte put to death another high-ranking Iranian, Tahmasp-kulu Xan Akçakoyunlu Kajar, a.k.a. Amirgunaoğlu Yusuf Pasha.[179]

Son of Saru Aslan (Amirguna Xan) Akçakoyunlu Kajar, whom Abbas I had installed as governor of Çukursaʾd in 1604,[180] he had defended the fortress of Erivan against the besieging Ottomans in 1635 and in the end surrendered. Thereupon, Murad IV, himself commanding the army, had let him into the Imperial Marquee, and he had taken up a new name after the audience, becoming Yusuf (his former name Tahmasp-kulu, also adopted, betokens servitude to the House of Safi). Moreover, the padishah had made him a pasha, vizier and governor of Aleppo, while his former steward, also seeking shelter at the Ottoman court, had received the neighbouring governorship of Syrian Tripoli.[181] Not long thereafter, Akçakoyunlu had come to Constantinople and become one of Murad IV's closest courtiers while also holding the Imperial Council post of resident vizier, which he kept until his death. Following the execution, padishah Ibrahim confiscated the pavilion and the gloriette Akçakoyunlu had built in the neighbourhood of Kağıthane.[182] Remarkably, as a member of the Imperial Council he was present both in the welcome and the farewell audiences of Safavid ambassador and his Kajar kinsman Yirmidört Ibrahim Xan.[183]

So why was this formerly Safavid and now Ottoman top-ranking dignitary from Iran executed? The publicised flow of events has it that, at the farewell feast given by the grand vizier, Yirmidört Kajar told his host that he wanted to go back to Iran together with Akçakoyunlu Kajar, as the latter wished to renew his allegiance to the House of Safi and asked for the ambassador's help. But as this former Safavid governor-general was now an Ottoman vizier-pasha, his wish to switch back to the Safavid side would be nothing short of high treason, and the grand vizier thus refused to go ahead on his own initiative. Knowing this well, the ambassador asked whether the padishah would grant the request. The padishah, not liking what he heard, wanted to know whether Akçakoyunlu himself wished to leave or the ambassador made it up. The grand vizier answered that Akçakoyunlu himself had secretly sent word to Yirmidört, asking him to share with the grand vizier his wish to go back to Iran. The padishah, wrathful upon hearing this, said: 'those who do not appreciate Our blessing must be punished. You shall rub out his impure existence from the page of the age!' Akçakoyunlu was then lured into a sham meeting with the grand vizier and put to death on the spot.[184]

1639–1643: Baghdad

This, then, was the tale that the Sublime Porte spread. Other sources, however, suggest differently. Francesco Crasso, a Ragusan physician, remarks in his letter to Alvise Contarini, the Venetian ambassador at Constantinople and the future doge of Venice, that the public opinion swung between believing the official news and giving credit to alternative accounts.[185] The German emperor's minister-resident at Constantinople, Johann Rudolf Schmid, wrote in his final account, for instance, that Yirmidört Kajar himself had requested for Akçakoyunlu Kajar to not be allowed to return to Iran but be put to death, and that Akçakoyunlu had thus met the same end as the dignitaries executed earlier as part of an Ottoman–Safavid deal clinching the Peace of Zuhab.[186]

Yet, the soundest insider information is the padishah's and his grand vizier's confidential communication on the fate of Akçakoyunlu. Correspondence between Ibrahim and Kemankesh Kara Mustafa on this very matter, and involving Ibrahim's own handwriting,[187] does away with any doubts as to what truly happened.

First of all, well before the Yirmidört Kajar embassy, the grand vizier had presented to the padishah a report on 'some circumstances' regarding Akçakoyunlu Kajar, and the two 'had discussed'[188] the matter in a meeting afterwards. Sometime later, the padishah handwrote a note to his grand vizier, asking why he had not been notified of the additional stipend allotted from customs revenues to Akçakoyunlu's 'catering'.[189] The grand vizier, answering that 'the deceased monarch [Murad IV]' had assigned it, advised his lord to 'let [Akçakoyunlu] go on in this manner for some time, and afterwards the august order [of Ibrahim] will be fulfilled nonetheless'.[190] In a later script sent while ambassador Yirmidört was on his way to Constantinople, Ibrahim reminded his grand vizier of the Akçakoyunlu issue. Kara Mustafa wrote back, saying that Akçakoyunlu's fate was sealed, and added:

> he shall remain in this condition until the Ajam ambassador comes, and he will be warned to act properly in absolute accordance with the august decree. Afterwards, that which crosses Your august mind will unfold. It is Your august knowledge that the signal to his downfall is *the ant sprouted wings*.[191] Your august decree will be fulfilled.[192]

In light of what happened afterwards, Ibrahim's order, to which Kemankesh Kara Mustafa twice refers, was that Akçakoyunlu Kajar be put to death. Ibrahim, still troubled by his trauma under his brother Murad IV's reign, seemed keen to rid himself of one of Murad's best friends who still wielded influence as an Imperial Council vizier. The fate of Murad IV's other favourite backs this up further. Vizier Silahdar Mustafa Pasha, courtier and admiral-in-chief at the time of Murad IV's death and alongside Akçakoyunlu intimate enough with Murad to get drunk together, was likewise put to death at Ibrahim's handwritten behest in April 1642. This was undertaken by Koca Sinan Agha, the chief of the palace-guard of Adrianople, and a team of forty palace-guards at the fortress of Temesvar in southeastern Hungary when Silahdar Mustafa was governor thereof, though Silahdar Mustafa's political rivalry with Kemankesh Kara Mustafa also contributed to the former's downfall.[193]

Therefore, Ibrahim had resolved to get rid of Akçakoyunlu at least a few months beforehand. The grand vizier held off the fulfilment of this order for some time, as he saw political expediency in keeping this former Safavid governor-general and now Ottoman Imperial Council vizier as a bargaining chip for the duration of the upcoming embassy from Iran. First the earlier Ottoman–Safavid deal to put to death high-ranking Iranian prisoners-of-war in the Empire, next ambassador Yirmidört Kajar's talks at the Sublime Porte thanks to his credentials to negotiate unwritten agreements, and last but not least Ibrahim's wish to rid himself of Murad IV's friends, all together sealed Akçakoyunlu's fate. And the grand vizier set the timing so as to hit all these targets with a single blow.

For the shah, too, Akçakoyunlu's execution was something to be celebrated. In the eyes of the Safavid court Akçakoyunlu was a top-ranking traitor, and his ongoing high profile at the imperial court only slighted the Shahdom further. Although his star had waned after Ibrahim's accession, he had remained an Imperial Council vizier up until the end. Now that Murad, who had held him so dear, was gone, and given that Ibrahim wished him dead, discarding Akçakoyunlu would come at no cost to the Empire. The Sublime Porte implied to the Safavids that by executing him it was affirming its commitment to the peace. As an added bonus, by putting this former Safavid dignitary of noble stock to death instead of handing him over, the Sublime Porte also signalled that it was interacting with the Shahdom from a position of strength.

Soon after leaving Constantinople on 7 September 1641, ambassador Yirmidört Kajar sent ahead one of his staffers to the shah to herald that Ibrahim acknowledged Murad IV's pledges. This staffer reached Isfahan on 4 October,[194] and only thereupon did Safi embark upon the long-planned Kandahar campaign against Mughal India, which had been put on hold until the finalisation of the peace with the Ottomans.[195] Although the returning Iranian ambassador and the newly appointed Ottoman envoy set out from Constantinople with a plan to fare together, for some reason they split up and followed separate itineraries, reaching the Safavid court more than one month apart from one another. Yirmidört Kajar and the Iranian prisoners of war lately freed by the Sublime Porte arrived in Isfahan at the beginning of December 1641, whereas Qabil Agha showed up at the Iranian capital only at the end of December.[196]

In Iran, Abbas-kulu Beyg, an officer of the royal guard, welcomed and entertained Qabil Agha as host alongside his soldiers. At the audience with the shah in Isfahan, the envoy informed Safi that the new padishah confirmed the peace, and handed over the imperial letter and the gifts.[197] Qabil Agha was held in high esteem throughout his stay at the Safavid court. Iranian officials regularly attended to him while he enjoyed the shah's honours and treats. Chief vizier Saru Taqi, ministers and other dignitaries hosted, feasted and entertained the envoy one by one at the shah's behest. Once the diplomatic business and the courtesy receptions came to an end, Qabil Agha was given leave to depart. Safi, instead of simply entrusting the returning Ottoman envoy with a letter of thanks addressed to Ibrahim, upped the game and named Maqsud Soltan Karadağlu, still the shah's deputy-chieftain of the Kızılbaş Order, his ambassador to Sultan Ibrahim Khan. Karadağlu would go along with Qabil Agha.[198]

Besides the padishah's epistle, the Ottoman envoy had also brought a letter[199] from the grand vizier to 'Rustam Xan [Saakadze] his sublime Excellency, the administrator of the shahly state, the xan of xans of the shah'.[200] The grand vizier wrote that Sultan Ibrahim Khan had 'majestically accepted [Shah Safi's] presents,[201] ... augustly looked at [the shah's letter]', and then decreed that a letter of answer be written to strengthen the friendship between the two dynasties. Kemankeş Kara Mustafa once again highlighted his own agency in building the Peace of Zuhab, and repeated his overlord's words that so long as the Safavids abided by the peace, so would the Ottomans.

Next, the grand vizier brought up two practical issues. Firstly, a place called Shahinqala, which had to end up on the Ottoman side with an eye to its location and distance from the specific areas along the border but was itself not specifically named at the protocol of Zuhab, was still in Safavid hands. If the treaty said so, wrote the grand vizier, that was fine, but otherwise, this went against the peace and had to be set right. Secondly, whereas the Safavids had torn down the strongholds of Zenjir and Kotur and the Ottomans had torn down the strongholds of Maku (on the border, between Bayazid and Nakhchivan) and Magazberd (on the border, between Kars and Erivan) as stipulated in the demarcation, afterwards the Safavids had manned Maku, and thereagainst, the Ottomans had manned Magazberd. Reminding that these issues also went against the treaty, the grand vizier demanded that the Shahdom, in a way worthy of the friendship between the two states, send an answer with envoy Qabil Agha.[202]

The grand vizier's letter, however politely worded, communicated the Ottomans' higher standing against the Safavids. The description that the padishah chose to, but otherwise did not have to, accept the shah's gifts and letter subtly reminded the Safavids how throughout peacetime the Sublime Porte could diplomatically depict such scenes calling forth Ottoman superiority, whereas the Safavid chancellery, when addressing the Ottomans, could not depict the shah in the same standing.

The year 1641 also witnessed action on the Ottoman–Safavid frontier at Iraq. Bıyıklı Dervish Mehmed Pasha went on with the military operations to clinch the Ottoman sway over Iraq's insubordinate tribes, as these could likely trigger a crisis with Iran. In the fiefdoms of Samawat and Khalid, the Khazali and the Bani-Lam tribes, both Ottoman vassals, wanted to defect en masse to the Safavid side, by which the Empire would have lost territory and income. They rose up against Ottoman overlordship and began banditry as a deed of disobedience. Bıyıklı Dervish Pasha sent his steward Ali Agha, leading his choice troops, to crush this pro-Safavid uprising. After a fight of shorter than two hours, most of the Bani-Lam rebels were killed, while the chieftain of the Khazali fled to Iran along with some of his following. The aforesaid fiefdoms were annexed to Baghdad as banners.[203] Shah Safi, although giving Zaydan (on the eastern coast of the Persian Gulf) as fief to the Khazali,[204] did not lay a claim on this tribe's original territory under Ottoman lordship.[205] The Safavids would not let tribal unrest upset relations with the Ottomans.

It was also during Bıyıklı Dervish Mehmed's term as governor-general that a joint committee by the Baghdad governorate and the shah's court demarcated the border at Iraq in the field, spot by spot.[206] Dervish Mehmed Pasha proved to be the subduing governor in reconquered Iraq that the grand vizier hoped him to be. Through pre-emptive and swift strikes, he forestalled large-scale defections to Iran. At a time when the Ottoman–Safavid military withdrawal was still underway and the normalisation had barely begun, conflict could easily break out if such defections were not nipped in the bud.

Shah Safi died on 12 May 1642 at just thirty-one years old, his death, like that of Murad IV, the result of heavy drinking. His nine-year-old son Muhammad, now renamed as Abbas II, took his stead.[207] Safi's legacy was a mixed one. On the one hand, his loss of both Baghdad and Kandahar had dealt heavy blows to his prestige inside Iran and to that of the Safavids abroad. On the other hand, however, the Peace of Zuhab, despite enshrining territorial losses resulting from military defeat, had redressed Safavid Iran's greatest source of instability, namely the Ottoman threat. The kingdom that he bequeathed was thus smaller than what he himself had inherited, but it was also steadier and more wieldable. Safi also bequethed Abbas II a degree of institutional continuity, with Saru Taqi, who had been chief vizier since 1634, remaining at the helm. There were court rivalries, however, and following Safi's death Saru Taqi brought about the execution of Marshal Rustam Xan Saakadze (1643). The threesome of Saru Taqi, Muhammad-Ali Beyg and Begdilli Janibek Xan Shamlu ensured a swift shift, plotting with Queen-mother Anna Khanum until in 1645 Abbas II had Begdilli Shamlu murder Saru Taqi in his own house.[208]

Even as late as three years after the signing of the peace protocol at Zuhab, the peace was still shaky. This in all likelihood was why the Sublime Porte sent 800 further Janissaries from the capital to Baghdad upon learning of Shah Safi's death, in consideration of the upcoming business of renewing the treaty.[209] Notwithstanding this, Abbas II turned his accession into an opportunity to make the peace sounder.

Maqsud Karadağlu, whom Safi had already named ambassador to settle border disputes and talk the Sublime Porte into tearing down the stronghold of Melet on the Van mountain range in line with the terms of peace, received updated instructions and letters to represent the new shah, Abbas II. The 150-man embassy reached Constantinople in early December 1642, and on 30 December, the Imperial Council gathered for the welcome audience. Karadağlu handed over the shah's gifts and was clothed with robes of honour, after which the padishah had him let into audience.[210] The shah's open-handedness with gifts ensured an extraordinarily warm welcome for his ambassador.[211]

The short but precise *expositio* of Abbas II's letter[212] to 'Sultan Ibrahim Khan his most sublime Majesty, the greatest shah-of-shahs, the epitome of creation and genesis, the second Alexander the Great, khaqan born of khaqan, God's shadow'[213] tells how Safi, after sending off his ambassador to the padishah, died while on the road to Khorasan to deal with the Indians, reportedly having bequeathed to Abbas not only the Shahdom but also the 'preservation of the friendship and attachment that have become consolidated with the padishah'. The new shah likewise wrote that he took utmost care to 'consolidate the affection and recovery established between [the two monarchies]'. He asked that Ibrahim too take up these same priorities and that the Ottoman authorities abide by the peace conditions, and noted that Maqsud Karadağlu would share some '[unwritten] further matters' in speech. As it seems, the ambassador handed over the original letter from the late Shah Safi as well.[214] Abbas II also sent a new letter to Grand Vizier Kemankesh Kara Mustafa, telling of Shah Safi's death after having already dispatched the missions of Qabil Agha and the 'princely'[215] Maqsud Soltan to the 'astral court of [the Ottoman] padishah his sublimest majesty the shadow of God',[216] and wishing that peace between the two states continue.[217]

While Abbas II's ambassador was in business at the Ottoman court, (Mutaraffiqa)[218] Yusuf Agha was appointed Ibrahim's forthcoming envoy to bear the letters congratulating the new shah on his accession. This legation was allotted its budget in February.[219] Once diplomatic business was completed, Maqsud Karadağlu was admitted to his farewell audience on 20 February 1643. The Sublime Porte seems to have held the ambassador in high regard. After securing the reconfirmation of the peace, taking receipt of Ibrahim's letter to Abbas II, and getting permission to leave, the embassy set out from Constantinople on 23 February.[220] Once in Iran, envoy Yusuf Agha met the shah's court in Kazvin. Festivities were held in his honour at the halls of the Saadat-abad garden. He handed over the letters and gifts reconfirming the peace at the shah's audience just a few days after this welcome reception.[221]

In his answer,[222] Sultan Ibrahim Khan 'as shah-of-shahs'[223] greeted 'Shah Abbas [II] his sublime Majesty, of Afrasiyab's perception, exalter of Iranian diadem and dignity',[224] and condoled with him on the death of 'Shah Safi, upon him be absolution'. After congratulating Abbas 'on the attainment of the throne and crown', he appreciated the new shah's 'leaning towards concord and union [between the two states]' and 'forewarning the authorities of his domain expressly that they should work painstakingly to consolidate the concurrence and erase disagreement in line with the pledged terms'.[225]

Ibrahim proceeded to state that he happily accepted Abbas's wish to reconfirm the peace, and was therefore sending his 'worldwide-obeyed decree'[226] for the Empire's border authorities to abide by the treaty. He also remarked that Maqsud Karadağlu, after fulfilling his mission, was honourably discharged. Upon which condition he reconfirmed the peace, however, Ibrahim worded as follows:

> Until this moment, Our forefathers, who have reigned on the Ottoman throne, have not wantonly rejected the monarchs who are constant requestors at Their [the Ottoman sovereigns'] Threshold and refuge-seekers under Their shadow, when these [foreign monarchs] opened all around the doors of friendship, prepared the causes of mutual help, and by presenting [their] veracity and designs, knocked the door of manliness and cast down the garments of hostility ... So long as there arises no situation contrary to the pledge and the pact to preoccupy our [celestially-]victorious troops, [peace shall prevail].[227]

In his answer – drawn up by former state secretary Sarı Abdullah Efendi – to the letter that the 'Shah his sublime Majesty, of Jamshid-grandeur,

1639–1643: Baghdad

the unique pearl of crown and dignity'[228] had sent him via ambassador Karadağlu, Kemankeş Kara Mustafa Pasha wished Abbas II well on his 'investiture with the affairs of the sultanate',[229] and condoled with him on the death of Shah Safi 'upon him be God's mercy'. Once '[Ibrahim] the shah-of-shahs his grandiose Majesty, the world's haven, cosmic master, crown-bestower to the reigning sovereigns, supreme of the sultans of the age, God's shadow in Both Worlds'[230] heard of the shah's intention, wrote the grand vizier, his 'seas of majestic beneficence surged, and he pleased to bestow upon the side of [the shah] the friendship-sealed august letter attesting to the alignment of the rites of peace and righteousness'.[231]

Saru Taqi (the chief vizier), Begdilli Janibek Xan Shamlu (the commander of the royal guard), the marshal of the royal court,[232] and Biçerlu Murtaza-kulu Xan Shamlu (the marshal of the royal council)[233] took upon themselves to host and entertain the padishah's envoy at the shah's behest. Throughout his stay at Kazvin, Yusuf Agha impressed his hosts with his diplomatic skills, knowledge of languages and book-lore.[234]

Amidst these diplomatic niceties, neither side deemed border issues worth mentioning in their correspondence, including even the Bani-Lam's failed attempt to defect from Ottoman to Safavid overlordship. The Iranians acknowledged that dealing with such unrest beyond the border was an Ottoman monopoly, even if the uprising was pro-Safavid. In other words, the Shahdom was satisfied with the border as it was, and did not look out for an opportunity to upset it. Small-scale entanglements could be dealt with on the spot, and would at best lead to correspondence between the neighbouring governorates of the Empire and Iran to take coordinated action.

Meanwhile the Safavids were gathering an army for a campaign to eastern Georgia. As soon as the news thereof reached Constantinople, the grand vizier commissioned Mehmed Bey the bannerlord of Arjesh (a banner in the province of Van to the north of the centre) to communicate with envoy Yusuf Agha at the shah's court. The bannerlord of Arjesh then sent a letter to Kazvin with a certain Salih as messenger,[235] and on 10 August 1643, after meeting the messenger, Yusuf Agha wrote from Kazvin to the grand vizier:

> we have men halting night and day at the shah's council and by the side of the chief vizier. But because they had no news to report, nothing has been sent. The shah, the chief vizier, Jani[bek] Xan, and their servants wish so well for You my Sire that words fail. They had campaigned upon Georgia in summer. They were defeated; they intend to enlist more soldiers, make Jani[bek] Xan marshal, and send them to Georgia. Outwardly, they have nothing going on other than this. As to their inner side, [only] God knows.[236]

Salih the messenger came back to Arjesh on 5 September 1643 bearing two sealed letters from envoy Yusuf Agha in Kazvin, one for Mehmed Bey of Arjesh himself and one for the grand vizier. Mehmed Bey dispatched Yusuf Agha's letter to the capital with Salih and sent out a spy to Iran to gather more news about eastern Georgia. As soon as this spy came back, promised the subgovernor of Arjesh, he would forward the report to the imperial court.[237]

The envoy's account of the Ottoman-friendly stance of the Safavids, as he beheld at the shah's court and heard from the northern flank of the borderland, was backed up by a military communication from the southern flank. Dev Kara Murad Agha, who at the siege of Baghdad in 1638 had fought as third general of the Janissary Corps and led forty companies in the grand admiral's column within the trenches dug against the Dark Gate to the west of the fortress,[238] was now the second general of the Corps[239] and commanded the over-8,000-strong Household squadrons extraordinarily posted at Baghdad, which itself had been a measure against the state of war dragging on. Kara Murad Agha, in his letter from Baghdad to the grand vizier, wrote that the frontier was at rest, 'the enemy' did nothing to breach the peace, and the garrison was well-disciplined.[240] Kara Murad was a high-ranking career soldier and currently commander of a border garrison, so his mention of the Safavids as the 'enemy' was evidently nothing more than a hangover from the fifteen years of war and three years of peace ratification. Beyond that, the reports by the Ottomans' Janissary general from Baghdad and imperial envoy from Kazvin in 1643 bear witness to one and the same fact: the Safavids upheld the peace and were willing to keep on doing so.

Yusuf Agha had foreseen in his letter to the grand vizier that the shah would give him leave on 21 or 26 August 1643.[241] In the farewell audience, which then must have been held in late August 1643, the envoy was entrusted with the letters of answer and afterwards he set out for Constantinople.[242] He went back to the Ottoman Empire with an assurance from Abbas II that the Safavids would abide by the peace.[243] In his answer to 'grand vizier Mustafa Pasha his sublime Highness and excellency the humerus of the Khaqan's Sublime State',[244] the shah confirmed that the Safavids had torn down the stronghold of Maku as specified in the peace protocol and also started to demolish Shahinqala, though this spot had not been named in the protocol, stating that if Kemankesh Kara Mustafa Pasha had said so, then doing so was certainly for the good of the peace. Abbas II also asked the grand vizier to inform the 'astral padishah his sublimest majesty the shadow of God'[245] that the fort of Magazberd, already named in the protocol, was still standing and was to be torn down.[246]

1639–1643: Baghdad

In the Safavids' campaign to eastern Georgia in the summer of 1643, nothing happened that concerned relations with the Sublime Porte. Though the grand vizier commissioned the envoy agha in Kazvin to communicate with Ottoman spies sent from the borderland to Iran to see whether the unrest in eastern Georgia would threaten western Georgia or the Ottoman overlordship there, this scenario did not materialise. Iran's Georgian affair did not become an official subject of the diplomacy in 1643. Nor does it seem to have triggered a later Ottoman–Safavid engagement on other platforms. Reports from Georgia, Azerbaijan and Iraq all indicated that the Safavids would not exploit outbreaks of unrest at the borderland to encroach on territory under Ottoman sway.

Notes

1. *Serdengeçti*, also *ölümeri* or *dalkılıç*.
2. Abdülkadir Özcan, 'Tayyar Mehmed Pasha', *Türk Diyanet Vakfı İslam Ansiklopedisi* Ek-2 (2019): 585–6.
3. 'Sen kimsin, niye geldin, adın nedir?'
4. 'Padişahım sağ olsun. Bağdad hakimi olan Bektaş han kulunuzum. Padişahıma Bağdad'ı ve Bağdad kalesini vermeğe geldim.'
5. 'Bunda Kızılbaş kırmağa gelmedim. Bu kale-i Bağdad bize ecdadımızdan mirastır, bunun için geldim. Evvelden kulluk eylesen, bizim ile bu kadar karşılaşmasan olmaz mıydı? Hele sana ve askerinize aman verdim. Sen dahi efendine hizmet ise ancak olur.'
6. Abdülkadir, *Topçular Katibi Abdülkâdir Târihi*, 1099–1101.
7. At the same time, Tezkireci Musa Efendi was installed as judge of Baghdad and Zaynalâbidîn Efendi as mufti. Karaçelebizade, *Ravzatü'l-Ebrâr*, 337; *Tarih-i Naima*, 970, 999; Evliya Çelebi, *Seyahatname*, 4/263.
8. *Topçular Katibi Abdülkâdir Târihi*, 1095.
9. *Kul Kedkhudâsı*.
10. *Zağarcıbaşı*, 'chief hound-keeper'.
11. *Tarih-i Naima*, 813.
12. Katib Çelebi, *Fezleke*, 897; *Tarih-i Naima*, 894. In early March 1640, about a month after Murad IV's death and Ibrahim's enthronement, a large treasury was sent to Baghdad to pay for the accession bonus of the Household soldiers serving there. Topçular Kâtibi Abdülkadir highlights only Baghdad for the accession bonus sent out (*Topçular Katibi Abdülkâdir Târihi*, 1137) whereas all Household troops serving in any province would get this payment. So, this hints at the extraordinarily high number of Janissaries standing watch at Baghdad as a wartime measure.
13. For the sources of these rumours, see Küpeli, *Osmanlı-Safevi Münasebetleri*, 267 (footnote 742).
14. *Sardâr-i akram*, a campaigning grand vizier in wartime whom the monarch

extraordinarily made the unconditional commander of all Ottoman armies and fleets. If so, the grand vizier, who was now also commander-in-chief, then acted not only in his regular capacity as the absolute deputy of the monarch, but also beyond it, as if he himself were the monarch. To mark the commander-in-chief's temporarily unlimited and non-accountable sovereignly powers, the exclusive regalia that distinguished this office from regular grand vizierate included an aigrette (of the type symbolising sovereign monarchy), which the padishah set with his own hands on the commander-in-chief's head. Likewise, the Illustrious Banner (of Prophet Muhammed) was lent out by the imperial court to the company of the commander-in-chief for the span of the campaign. See *Abdurrahman Abdi Paşa Kanunnâmesi*, ed. H. Ahmet Arslantürk (Istanbul: Okur Kitaplığı, 2012), 24; İsmâil Hakkı Uzunçarşılı, *Osmanlı Devletinin Merkez ve Bahriye Teşkilatı* (Ankara: Türk Târih Kurumu, 1998), 158–63; Abdülkadir Özcan, 'Serdâr', *Türkiye Diyânet Vakfı İslam Ansiklopedisi* 36 (2009): 551–2 for further implications of the Ottoman commandership-in-chief. I therefore disagree with Savory's translation of the Safavid *sipahsâlâr* as commander-in-chief (see Roger M. Savory, 'The Office of *Sipahsâlâr* (Commander-in-Chief) in the Safavid State', in *Proceedings of the Second European Conference of Iranian Studies held in Bamberg, 30th September to 4th October 1991*, eds Bert G. Fragner, Christa Fragner, Gherardo Gnoli, Roxane Haag-Higuchi, Mauro Maggi and Paola Orsatti (Roma: Istituto Italiano Per Il Medio Ed Estremo Oriente, 1995), 597–615). The Safavid *sipahsâlâr* was the highest commander of Iran's military, but unlike a commander-in-chief, he still marshalled under the command of a superior, first of all the shah, and on some occasions the chief vizier as well. Therefore, the Safavid *sipahsâlâr*'s office overlapped rather with that of a field marshal/Ottoman *sardâr* or *sipahsâlâr*. See Savory's article also for other historians translating the Safavid *sipahsâlâr* as commander-general/ *Feldmarschall*, which is more accurate. The commander-in-chief, namely the Ottoman *serdâr-ı ekrem*, who temporarily held unrestricted sway over the Empire as its whole, in a way that covered not only the military but also any other thinkable exercise of sovereignty, did not have a matching post in Safavid Iran. Hence, another Ottoman rendering of *sardâr-i akram* was not *sipahsâlâr* but *sipahsâlâr-ı aʾzam*, as can be seen in BOA, *Name-i Humayun Defterleri*, 6, entry 221.

15. The Ottoman terminology for plenipotentiary (*muraxxas*) and plenipotentiary powers (*ruxsat-i kâmila*), which would soon become standard, was not used in this instance. Instead, the grand vizier's inherent capacity as the padishah's 'absolute deputy (*wakîl-i mutlaq*)' was highlighted. Next to this 'general deputation (*wakâlat-i ʿâmma*)', the additional statement that for these talks Kemankeş Kara Mustafa Pasha also held 'absolute regency (*niyâbat-i mutlaqa*)' and 'particular regency (*niyâbat-i xâssa*)' of the padishah especially underscored his case-specific plenipo-

tentiary powers. See BOA, *İbnülemin – Hariciye*, 1/18; Kazvini-Isfahani, *Khuld-i Barîn*, 277–81; Khajagi-Isfahani, *Khulâsatu'ṣ-Siyar*, 271–5; Abdurrahman Hibrî Efendi, *Defter-i Ahbâr*, published in Muhittin Aykun's MA thesis 'Abdurrahman Hibrî Efendi, Defter-i Ahbâr (Transkripsiyon ve Değerlendirme)' (Marmara University, 2004), 76–8 (ff. 37a–38b) for the letter he sent from Zuhab to Shah Safi.

16. *Târîkh-i Safaviyân: Khulâsatu'l-Tavârîkh & Târîkh-i Mullâ Kamâl*, ed. Ibrahim Dehgân (Arâk: Châp-i Farvardîn, HS 1334), 95; *Tarih-i Naima*, 896–8; Seyyid Husein Astarâbâdî, *Târîkh-i Sultânî az Shaykh Safî tâ Shâh Safî*, ed. Ihsân Ishrâqî (Tehran: Intishârât-i 'Ilmî, HS 1366), 257. Before setting out, Murad IV accepted Afrasiyaboğlu Ali's gifts, which betokened that Basra yielded to the Ottomans. Murad reconfirmed Ali as the tributary lord of the Basra-centred principality. The same deal took place with the lords of al-Ahsa (Shafî Xan of Banî Khalid), Oman (Shafî Xan) and the Islands of Hâridât (Shamsaddîn Amîr). The Bedouin chieftains and Kurdish *beg*s too, whose lands now laid within Ottoman borders, themselves came to the Imperial Marquee with gifts. In return for military service to the state by reporting for duty with their troops under the banners of the governor-general of Baghdad whenever called up, they received imperial reconfirmation of their chieftainships and fiefdoms. As a symbolic sign of yielding to Ottoman lordship, aside from gifts, the aforesaid princelings also sent the keys of their main strongholds. The ruler of Basra, for example, sent the keys of Qurna. See Evliya Çelebi, *Seyahatname*, 4/261–2.
17. Karaçelebizade Abdülaziz Efendi, *Zafername*, published in Nermin Yıldırım's MA thesis 'Kara Çelebizâde Abdülaziz Efendi'nin Zafername Adlı Eseri (Tarihçe-i Feth-i Revan ve Bağdad): Tahlil ve Metin' (Mimar Sinan University, 2005), 12, 20, 35–43.
18. *Khalîfatu'l-khulafâ* (mostly shortened to *khulafâ*). See Willem Floor, 'The Khalifeh al-kholafa of the Safavid Sufi Order', *Zeitschrift der Deutschen Morgenländischen Gesellschaft* 153, no. 1 (2003): 51–86.
19. Astarabadi, *Târîkh-i Sultânî*, 254.
20. See Küpeli, *Osmanlı-Safevi Münâsebetleri*, 233–6, 247, 269–70; Kazvini-Isfahani, *Khuld-i Barîn*, 242–3, 255.
21. *mutafarriqa-i Dargâh-ı ᶜÂlî*. See Evoğlu, *Majmaᶜu'l-Inshâ*, f. 277b for the *mutafarriqa*-ship of Mehmed Agha.
22. Karaçelebizade, *Zafername*, 63; Katib Çelebi, *Fezleke*, 879, 899. Two identical edicts (*buyrultu*) from 3 February 1639, to a certain Yaqub Pasha and to Ahmed Agha the *voyvoda* of Mardin, read: 'As of now, the baggage and men of the ambassador of Persia have been sent off to Baghdad. Hence, you shall assign fodder and food sufficient for his fifty men and fifty pack animals and, until they reach Mosul, give [these to them] . . . from the [campaigning Imperial Army's] provisions that are [already] along the way. (Hâlen Acem elçisinin ağırlığı ve adamları Bağdad'a yollanmıştır. İmdi, elli nefer ademisine ve elli davarlarına kifayet miktarı yem ve yemekleri

tayin edip Musul᾿a varınca[ya dek] ... yol üzerinde olan zahirelerden veresi[ni]z.) See Topkapı, *Evrak*, 426/41 for a copy of the edicts.
23. *sipahsâlâr*.
24. *Kurçu-başı*.
25. *Yasavul-başı-yı kur*.
26. Khâjagî Isfahânî, *Khulâsatu᾿s-Siyar*, 264–5; Astarabadi, *Târîkh-i Sultânî*, 257–8.
27. *Majmûᶜa -i Mukâtabat*, 9a–10a (entries IX and X); Hibri, *Defter-i Ahbâr*, 67–9 (34b–35b); Karaçelebizade, *Zafername*, 49–50; Katib Çelebi, *Fezleke*, 899.
28. Küpeli, *Osmanlı-Safevi Münasebetleri*, 270–1.
29. Murad IV allotted the restoration of each section of the fortress to one of the pashas and companies of various Household corps along with the feudal troopers there. Each group put thus together was helped by the campaigning architects, engineers, builders and carpenters. *Topçular Katibi Abdülkâdir Târihi*, 1104; Evliya Çelebi, *Seyahatname*, 4/260.
30. The poems dating and commemorating the conquest were engraved on white marble with pure gold in large and bold letters, so that they could be read even from afar. Evliya Çelebi, *Seyahatname*, 4/260, 263. The kettledrum played by the Baghdad military band was so great that the player needed to climb a few stairs to get set. The fame of this kettledrum had spread to other lands in the Ottoman Empire and Iran. Ibid., 266.
31. Nazmizade, *Gülşen-i Hulefâ*, 235, 239, 241–2, 270, 273, 291, 295 for the celebrations and ceremonies held in Baghdad for the enthronements of Ibrahim (1640) and Mehmed IV (1648), the births of imperial princes Mehmed IV (1642) and Ahmed III (1673), and the conquests of Chania (1645), Rethymo (1646), Varad (1660), Ujvar (1663), Candia (1669) and Kamianets-Podilskyi (1672).
32. The *defterdâr* himself, the new commander of the Janissaries, the battalions of the Household Cavalry Corps, Armourers (*Cebeciler*), Cannoneers (*Topçular*), Artillery Carters (*Top Arabacıları*), the daybooks-master (*rûznâmçe efendisi*), secretaries of the financial department and the Imperial Registry, remaining Janissaries, the pashas of Rumelia, Anatolia, Karaman, Rum (Sivas), Aleppo, Syria, Tripoli, Dulkadir (Marash) and Mosul, the feudal troopers there as a whole, and so on, all participated in this mobilisation to build up the fortifications of Baghdad, which had suffered Ottoman sieges when under Safavid control. Vast numbers of pack animals that the Imperial Army had brought were also put to use. *Topçular Katibi Abdülkâdir Târihi*, 1109.
33. *Yerli Kulu*.
34. This Household Cavalry contingent was left at Baghdad: Karaçelebizade, *Ravzatü᾿l-Ebrâr*, 338; Katib Çelebi, *Fezleke*, 901; *Topçular Katibi Abdülkâdir Târihi*, 1112. Because the local servicemen were being enlisted permanently and all those hired were freshly coming into the governorate's

service, a condensed register showing the breakdown of the corps- and intra-corps divisions was sent to Constantinople: BOA, *İbnülemin – Askeriye*, 267. See also BOA, *Bâb-ı Âsafî Defterhâne-i Âmire Defterleri* vol. 93 for the register of the survey of the houses, shops, inns, gardens and orchards in the city of Baghdad, done in March 1639.

35. About ten years after the war ended, Baghdad would stand as a large fortress-city that concentrated the Ottoman military power and political presence of the southern flank of the Iranian border. The walls, towers and bastions were repaired, upgraded and outfitted with strong, up-to-date artillery. The upkeep of the moat was taken care of as if the Iranians could set on anytime. For the defenders, the moat was to afford a favourable ground to withstand, so as to forestall the shah's army from fully beleaguering the city. A sizable garrison always stood watch on the bulwarks. Even trade caravans had to log themselves in and give up their weapons as they stepped in through the city gates. Baghdad's great breadth, organisation, manning and outfit compensated for the drawbacks that could stem from its lying on low land and the shallowness of the moat that girded it. Those walls that overlooked the land were better fortified, manned and outfitted than those overlooking the Tigris: Jürgen Andersen and Volquard Iversen, *Orientalische Reise-Beschreibungen* (Schleswig: Fürstliche Druckerei durch Johan Holwein, 1669), 166–7; Jean-Baptiste Tavernier, *Tavernier Seyahatnâmesi*, trans. Teoman Tunçdoğan (Istanbul: Kitap Yayınevi, 2010), 236. Aside from the non-garrison military within the walls (such as the pasha's own battalion), the garrison was made up of rotating Household Janissaries, Cannoneers and the Local Service. Above all, the White Gate (east) and the Dark Gate (west), the keep, the Persian Bulwark (south), and the Sultan's Gate (a.k.a. Imamiazam/Muazzam Gate) along with Küçükhasanpaşa Bastion, Melekpaşa Bastion, Musapaşa Bastion, Hasanpaşa Tower, the Flat Tower (*Yassı-kule*) and Zulfikar Bastion were fitted out with artillery more than enough to ward off a beleaguering Iranian army as standalone units even if almost no back-up was to reach from the rest of the fortress. The garrison sternly abided by the night watch, while officers patrolled in disguise for unannounced inspections. The Household corps watched over the keep, where the treasury, stocks and ammunition were held, even more strictly. Evliya Çelebi, *Seyahatname*, 4/263–7. After the garrison was more than filled with Household and Local troops, Kurdish tribal militias were entrusted with the safety of sections of the countryside. Katib Çelebi, *Fezleke*, 900; *Topçular Katibi Abdülkâdir Târihi*, 1127.
36. Topkapı, *Evrak*, 882/40; *Topçular Katibi Abdülkâdir Târihi*, 1113; Karaçelebizade, *Zafername*, 64; Küpeli, *Osmanlı-Safevi Münasebetleri*, 271; Khajagi-Isfahani, *Khulâsatu's-Siyar*, 267.
37. Topkapı, *Evrak*, 556/22.
38. Mirza Naqi Nasiri, *Titles and Emoluments in Safavid Iran: A Third Manual*

of Safavid Administration, ed. Willem Floor (Washington, DC: Mage Publishers, 2008), 172.
39. Karaçelebizade, *Zafername*, 64–5; Katib Çelebi, *Fezleke*, 901; Astarabadi, *Târîkh-i Sultânî*, 257–8 (Astarabadi mistakenly gives the month of Zilqada instead of Zilhijja when dating this mission).
40. Topkapı, *Evrak*, 556/22; Karaçelebizade, *Zafername*, 64–5; Katib Çelebi, *Fezleke*, 901; Küpeli, *Osmanlı-Safevi Münasebetleri*, 272–3.
41. Karaçelebizade, *Zafername*, 65; Katib Çelebi, *Fezleke*, 908.
42. Karaçelebizade, *Zafername*, 65.
43. *Kedkhudâ*.
44. Katib Çelebi, *Fezleke*, 872, 888, 892.
45. At his four-month tenure, Küçük Hasan had made a name for himself as a righteous administrator by holding court to deal out justice. What was expected of Bıyıklı Derviş Mehmed, on the other hand, was to not be as forbearing as his forerunner, and to keep the province's Kurdish and Arab tribes under discipline. Nazmizade, *Gülşen-I Hulefâ*, 232–4.
46. *Topçular Katibi Abdülkâdir Târihi*, 1140, 1160, 1162, 1173. As commander of the Household Janissaries at Baghdad, Bektaş Agha likewise had extraordinarily high-ranking successors, such as Hamza Agha the second general of the Janissaries, and Ibrahim Agha the third general of the Janissaries (*seksoncubaşı*, 'head-mastiffkeeper' of the Corps) who, after serving outstandingly at the siege of Chania, took Arnavut Bektaş's stead in early December 1645. Karaçelebizade, *Ravzatü'l-Ebrâr*, 380. As late as 1651, the Household Janissaries manning Baghdad were still 8,000-strong. İsmail Hakkı Uzunçarşılı, *Osmanlı Devleti Teşkilatlarından Kapıkulu Ocakları I: Acemi Ocağı ve Yeniçeri Ocağı* (Ankara: Türk Tarih Kurumu Basımevi, 1988), 329.
47. Unlike the former Safavid delegate at Zuhab, Saru Xan Talish became named the shah's 'credible deputy (*wakîl-i mu'tamad*)' with reference to his plenipotentiary powers. See BOA, *İbnülemin – Hariciye*, 1/18; Kazvini-Isfahani, *Khuld-i Barîn*, 277–81; Khajagi-Isfahani, *Khulâsatu's-Siyar*, 271–5; Hibri, *Defter-i Ahbâr*, 76–8 (ff. 37a–38b) for the letter that Kemankesh Kara Mustafa Pasha sent from Zuhab to Shah Safi.
48. *Dîvân-i Humâyûn çavuşu*.
49. Topkapı, *Evrak*, 556/22; Karaçelebizade, *Zafername*, 66; Katib Çelebi, *Fezleke*, 908–9; *Târîkh-i Safaviyân: Târîkh-i Mullâ Kamâl*, 95; Küpeli, *Osmanlı-Safevi Münasebetleri*, 274; Türkman, *Zayl*, 220.
50. Topkapı, *Evrak*, 556/22; Karaçelebizade, *Zafername*, 66; Katib Çelebi, *Fezleke*, 909. Two centuries later, the Ottoman Empire and the Kajar Shahdom of Iran would agree, in the Erzurum congresses, to ground their upcoming treaty (of Erzurum) on the 'treaty' of Zuhab. Both sides would produce copies of the ratification given by Murad IV, Kemankesh Kara Mustafa Pasha and Shah Safi. As to the original treaty protocols signed, sealed and exchanged by the two sides, the sides would deem them lost

and even make up separate stories on why and how their respective originals might have gotten lost. See Sabri Ateş, 'Treaty of Zuhab, 1639: Foundational Myth or Foundational Document?', *Iranian Studies* 52, no. 3–4 (2019): 411–20.

51. *Muahedat Mecmuası* II (Ankara: Türk Târih Kurumu, 2008), 308–12; Küpeli, *Osmanlı-Safevi Münasebetleri*, 276; Sawâqib Jahânbakhsh and Tâhira Zakii, 'Tahlîl-i Zamînahâ-yi Muâʿhada-i Zuhâb u Payâmadhâ-yi ân bar Davlat-i Safaviya', *Faslnâma-i Pizhûhishhâ-yi Târîkhî (Muâvanat-i Pizhûhishş u Fannâvârî-yi Dânishgâh-i Isfahân)* 3 (Fall 1395), 15.
52. Jassân, Badrah, Mandaljin, and the plains next to them stayed on the Ottoman side. The border ran from Darna and Dartang, and split up at the border-post (*sarmîl/mil başı*), leaving Darna and Dartang to the Empire. The Iranian territory began from the mountain to the left of the border-post and included Dargazîn, Hamadân, Bâğ-ı Jinân, Mihribân (Marîvân) and Sin, while the land and villages to the east of the mountain by the border-post were left to the Ottomans. In this region, the Ziyâʾaddîn and Hârûnî arms of the Jâf tribe stayed under Ottoman lordship, while the Bîra and Zarduvî branches stayed under Safavid sway. The Iranian stronghold of Zenjir on the aforesaid mountain was to be torn down. Evliya Çelebi, *Seyahatname*, 4/229–49. 'Derteng Boğazı: ... Acem şâhıyla bu Derteng Boğazı'nda hudud kesilip hâlen bu boğaz ağzında bir amûd-ı müntehâya hududnâme yazılmış ve celî hatt ile sikkeyi mermerde kazılmış bir mîl-i mermerdir. Andan içeri cânib-i kıbleye Âl-i Osmanʾın Bağdad hudûdudur, ol amûddan taşra taraf-ı şarka Acem şâhı hudûdudur.' Ibid., 4/249. The translated use of *sarmîl – mil başı* and Evliya Çelebi's description of the erected post by the Dartang pass onto which the border-protocol's text was engraved hint that what is meant by *sarmîl* is indeed a border-post, which seems to have later become the name of that spot too.
53. The stronghold of Zalim and part of the mountain behind it overseeing the stronghold stayed under Ottoman sway. The stronghold of Avraman with the villages pinned thereto stayed in Iran. Along the border, the Ottomans kept Çağangediği, Kızılca, and their pinned territory. Iran kept Marîvân (Mihribân) and its surroundings.
54. *sancak*, Ottoman sub-province.
55. The strongholds of Kotur and Maku were to be torn down.
56. The stronghold of Mağazberd was to be torn down.
57. Sadık Müfit Bilge, *Osmanlı Çağıʾnda Kafkasya 1454–1829* (Istanbul: Kitabevi, 2015), 127, 139–43, 492, 506.
58. *wasîqa*.
59. BOA, *İbnülemin – Hariciye*, 1/18; Kazvini-Isfahani, *Khuld-i Barîn*, 277–81; Khajagi-Isfahani, *Khulâsatuʾs-Siyar*, 271–5; Hibri, *Defter-i Ahbâr*, 76–8 (ff. 37a–38b).
60. Topkapı, *Evrak*, 556/22; Katib Çelebi, *Fezleke*, 909–10.

61. Shâhenshâh, gîtî-sitân, sultân-i aʿzam, khâqân-i aʿdal, sânî-yi Iskandar-i Zulqarnayn, Zillullah.
62. yoldaşlık, sevişmek, gönül birliği.
63. Khajagi-Isfahani, *Khulâsatuʾs-Siyar*, 268–71; Kazvini-Isfahani, *Khuld-i Barîn*, 273–7. The Turki(fied) versions written down in BOA, *İbnülemin – Hariciye* 4/407 and Hibri, *Defter-i Ahbâr*, 78–80 (ff. 38b–40a) hint that Safi's *ahdname* may well have been drafted in Turkish, because, first, the Ottomans then mostly recorded incoming Persian correspondence in the original without a translation, and secondly, (verbatim) translations of incoming diplomatic writs were titled explicity as (verbatim) copies, which is not the case in the two extant Turki(fied) copies of Shah Safi's *ahdname*. Also see Feridun Bey, *Münşeatü's-Selâtîn* vol. 1 ([Istanbul]: Takvimhâne, H 1275), 299–301 (entry: 'İran Şâhı Şah Safi tarafından hudud ve sugûra dâir takdim olunmuş olan nâmenin sûretidir').
64. Topkapı, *Evrak*, 556/22; Karaçelebizade, *Zafername*, 66; Katib Çelebi, *Fezleke*, 909–10; *Topçular Katibi Abdülkâdir Târihi*, 1125; Küpeli, *Osmanlı-Safevi Münasebetleri*, 275.
65. See Topkapı, *Evrak*, 326/32, letter by Nasuhpaşaoğlu Husein Pasha the governor-general of Erzurum to Silahdar Mustafa Pasha the grand admiral, seemingly from summer 1639, speaking of the grand vizier's directives in this regard.
66. Khajagi-Isfahani, *Khulâsatuʾs-Siyar*, 275; Türkman, *Zayl*, 231, 235; Kazvini-Isfahani, *Khuld-i Barîn*, 290.
67. Karaçelebizade, *Zafername*, 57, 69; Katib Çelebi, *Fezleke*, 907; Küpeli, *Osmanlı-Safevi Münasebetleri*, 277–8.
68. Abûlmafâkhir Tafrishî, *Târîkh-i Shâh Safî*, ed. Muhsin Bahrâm-Nijhâd (Tehran: Mîrâs-i Maktûb, HS 1388), 168, 268; *Târîkh-i Mullâ Kamâl*, 94; *Tarih-i Naima*, 814.
69. Karaçelebizade, *Zafername*, 51–2; Katib Çelebi, *Fezleke*, 907–10; *Topçular Katibi Abdülkâdir Târihi*, 1122–3; Küpeli, *Osmanlı-Safevi Münâsebetleri*, 277–8; *Tarih-i Naima*, 929, 936.
70. Ottoman terminology: *beylerbeyi/mîr-i mîrân/amiruʾl-umarâ/vâlî*; Safavid terminology: *hâkim*.
71. A governor with vizierial rank, namely a three-standard pasha, had far more authority and sanction power than a governor without vizierial grade, namely a two-standard pasha. This appointment was made above all for borderlands of strategic weight in foreign dealings, such as Budapest (later Belgrade), Egypt and Baghdad. In urgent developments between states, three-standard pashas, unlike their two-standard colleagues, could themselves take the lead and act forthwith until directives came from the Sublime Porte. With the authority drawn from the Imperial Council affiliation of vizierate, a three-standard pasha could hold the 'padishah's council' and deal out justice, even when he only passed by or was otherwise present in any province governed by a two-standard pasha. Until called off in 1642

by grand vizier Kemankeş Mustafa, vizier-governors could even draw the padishah's monogram, thus issuing their own orders as imperial decrees. See Uzunçarşılı, *Merkez ve Bahriye Teşkilatı*, 206–7; Halil İnalcık, 'Vezir', *Türkiye Diyânet Vakfı İslam Ansiklopedisi* 43 (2013): 90–2; M. Uğur Derman, 'Tuğra', *Türkiye Diyânet Vakfı İslam Ansiklopedisi* 41 (2012): 336–9.

72. Ottoman terminology: *vâlî/beylerbeyi* and *vazîr*; Safavid terminology: *beylerbeyi*.
73. *Dîvân-i Humâyûn çavuşbaşısı/dîvân-beği*.
74. Karaçelebizade, *Zafername*, 57; *Topçular Katibi Abdülkâdir Târihi*, 1125.
75. *Topçular Katibi Abdülkâdir Târihi*, 1126; Katib Çelebi, *Fezleke*, 907; Küpeli, *Osmanlı-Safevi Münasebetleri*, 279.
76. Topkapı, *Evrak*, 465/17; Topkapı, *Evrak*, 730/56; Kazvini-Isfahani, *Khuld-i Barîn*, 291; Karaçelebizade, *Zafername*, 70; Türkman, *Zayl*, 231, 235; Khajagi-Isfahani, *Khulâsatu'ʾs-Siyar*, 277.
77. Topkapı, *Evrak*, 749/13 (letter by Mirahur Husein Pasha the new governor of Anatolia from the grand vizier's headquarters in Diyarbekr to Silahdar Mustafa Pasha the grand admiral in Constantinople, delivered on 26 September 1639); also see Karaçelebizade, *Zafername*, 70; Nasiri, *Titles and Emoluments*, 172.
78. *sancakbeyi*, the appointed chief of a *sancak* (banner, that is, sub-province).
79. Küpeli, *Osmanlı-Safevi Münâsebetleri*, 233.
80. Topkapı, *Evrak*, 465/17.
81. Topkapı, *Evrak*, 730/56; *Bayâz-i Daftarkhâna-i Humâyûnî-yi Davlat-i Îrân-i ʿAsr-i Safavî*, ed. Mansur Sefatgol (Tokyo: Research and Informationm Center for Asian Studies, Institute for Advanced Studies on Asia, University of Tokyo, 2023), 78–9.
82. *çapar*.
83. Topkapı, *Evrak*, 730/56.
84. *sarʿaskar*, a.k.a. *başbuğ*.
85. Karaçelebizade, *Zafername*, 71; *Tarih-i Naima*, 929; Topkapı, *Evrak*, 730/52.
86. *silâhdâr*.
87. *Tarih-i Naima*, 895, 929; Fikret Sarıcaoğlu, 'Melek Ahmed Paşa', *Türk Diyanet Vakfı İslam Ansiklopedisi* 29 (2004): 42–4.
88. Karaçelebizade, *Zafername*, 71; *Topçular Katibi Abdülkâdir Târihi*, 1128; *Tarih-i Naima*, 929; Topkapı, *Evrak*, 730/52.
89. Katib Çelebi, *Fezleke*, 911.
90. BOA, *Hatt-ı Humayun*, 1426/58418; BOA, *Ali Emiri – Murad IV*, 8/767; *Muahedat Mecmuası* II, 308–12. All three copies bear a date (late January/early February 1640) that is about one and a half months later than what must have been in the original, if the original was dated at all.
91. Ernest Tucker, 'From Rhetoric of War to Realities of Peace: The Evolution of Ottoman–Iranian Diplomacy through the Safavid Era', in *Iran and the*

World in the Safavid Age, eds Willem Floor and Edmund Herzig (London: I. B. Tauris, 2012), 86.

92. Jahanbakhsh and Zakii, 'Muâ°hada-i Zuhâb', 12; Hans Robert Roemer, 'The Safavid Period', in *The Cambridge History of Iran* 6, eds Peter Jackson and Laurence Lockhart (Cambridge: Cambridge University Press, 1986), 283; Andrew J. Newman, *Safavid Iran: Rebirth of a Persian Empire* (London: I. B. Tauris, 2006), 73–4. Chief vizier Saru Taqi was to blame for the loss as he had taken a hard line with the governor of Kandahar, who then went over, together with his province, into Mughal lordship.

93. Rudi Matthee, *Persia in Crisis: Safavid Decline and the Fall of Isfahan* (London: I. B. Tauris, 2012), 118–19; Matthee, 'Safavid Iran and the "Turkish Question" or How to Avoid a War on Multiple Fronts', *Iranian Studies* 52, no. 3–4 (2019): 514–15.

94. Faruk Sümer, 'Kaçarlar', *Türkiye Diyânet Vakfı İslâm Ansiklopedisi* ek-1 (2016): 700–1.

95. *Topçular Katibi Abdülkâdir Târihi*, 885; Hibri, *Defter-i Ahbâr*, 105 (f. 53a).

96. Even in his term under Murad IV, he was an outstandingly strong-willed minister, insomuch as he did not even shy away from withholding the fulfilment of some already-issued imperial scripts (*khatt-i humâyûn*, namely an imperial decree with the padishah's own handwriting on top, or an order that the padishah himself wrote down from scratch, which were even more overbearing than an imperial decree) on the grounds that a certain matter was not for the good of the state. He also dared openly to reproach Murad IV at a face-to-face meeting, criticising his lack of knowledge of statecraft. İsmâil Hakkı Uzunçarşılı, *Osmanlı Târihi* vol. 3/1 (Ankara: Türk Târih Kurumu, 3rd edn 1983), 206–7, 209–15.

97. Giorgio Rota, 'The Death of Tahmâspqolî Xân Qâjâr According to a Contemporary Ragusan Source', in *Iran und iranisch geprägte Kulturen. Studien zum 65. Geburtstag von Bert. G. Fragner*, eds Markus Ritter, Ralph Kauz and Birgitt Hoffmann (Wiesbaden: Dr. Ludwig Reichert Verlag, 2008), 56.

98. Topkapı, *Evrak*, z.7022 e.110 [d.794 g.105].

99. Kazvini-Isfahani, *Khuld-i Barîn*, 294; Türkman, *Zayl*, 238; *Târîkh-i Mullâ Kamâl*, 95. The dating in Khajagi-Isfahani, *Khulâsatu'ʾs-Siyar*, 278, is wrong.

100. Türkman, *Zayl*, 242–3, 246; *Târîkh-i Mullâ Kamâl*, 95.

101. Evoğlu, *Majmaʿuʾl-Inşâ*, ff. 276b–277b.

102. 'sipihr-i mihr-i saltanat, ... âlî-hazret ... Kayvân-ayvân ... Kaykhusrav-sipâh ... shah, ... bakht-i humâyûn'.

103. 'sultânuʾl-azam, khâqânuʾl-akram, sâya-andâz-i mamâlikuʾl-Arab waʾl-Ajam, ... maljaʾ-i ... mulûkiʾl-Türk waʾd-Daylam ... marhûm Khudâvandigâr'.

104. 'julûs-i humâyûn'.

1639–1643: Baghdad

105. 'malâz...-i Akâsira wa ... maljaʾ-i ... Qayâsire ... takht-i ... Osmânî ... sâhib-qirânî'.
106. 'azamuʾs-salâtîn-i rûy-i zamîn, akram-i khawâqîn, ... shahinshâh ... Sultan Ibrahim Khan'. Ibid.
107. Evoğlu, *Majmaʿuʾl-Inşâ*, ff. 282ab–283a.
108. 'maâlî-nisâb, ... dawlat-iyâb, ... mudabbir-i ... dawlat-i shâhî, ... xân-ı xanân shâh ... Rustam Xân'.
109. 'muwâlât-i sâlifa'.
110. 'sihhat-i tan-durustî'.
111. Evoğlu, *Majmaʿuʾl-Inşâ*, ff. 282ab–283a.
112. *küçükelçi*, or *nâma-rasân/nâma-bar*, the non-accredited head of a diplomatic mission who ranks below ambassador and envoy, usually picked from among Ottoman Imperial Council sergeants (*çavuş*).
113. *Itimâdu'd-dawla*, but also *vazîr-i/sadr-i aʿzam*, hence grand vizier, which is more common in modern English usage for the Safavid premiers, but is replaced here with 'chief vizier' so as to differentiate from the Ottoman grand vizier.
114. *talkhîs*.
115. Topkapı, *Evrak*, z.7022 e.193 [d.795 g.82]. This undated document and the related series of summations – z.7022 e.244 [d.796 g.27], z.7022 e.249 [d.796 g.32], z.7022 e.315 [d.796 g.97] – are misdated by the archivist to H 18. B. 1058, that is Sultan Ibrahim Khan's death, meaning that the document belongs to Ibrahim's reign without the possibility of a more precise dating. However, any possibility other than that the year should be H 1050 (1640) is ruled out when one bears in mind firstly, the padishah's restlessness about whether the shah would reconfirm the peace by sending an ambassador or restart the war; next, the new padishah's lack of self-confidence as to how he was compared with Murad IV; thirdly, that the padishah was grown up enough to handwrite commands; fourthly, that a Hasan Pasha was the governor-general of Van; fifthly, that an Ahmed Pasha was the governor-general of Diyarbekr; and lastly, that a Rustam Xan in Tabriz oversaw withdrawal after the pacification. See Fikret Sarıcaoğlu, 'Melek Ahmed Paşa', *Türkiye Diyânet Vakfı İslam Ansiklopedisi* 29 (2004): 42–4; Küpeli, *Osmanlı-Safevi Münâsebetleri*, 278.
116. 'masjid-i jâmi-i jadîd-i shâhî'.
117. Kazvini-Isfahani, *Khuld-i Barîn*, 301; Bizhan, *Sahîfa-i Girâmî*, 417; Topkapı, *Evrak*, 640/5 (where the governorate-general chancery of Baghdad titles envoy Hamzapaşaoğlu Mehmed mistakenly as *çavuş* rather than *agha*); Türkman, *Zayl*, 244; Khajagi-Isfahani, *Khulâsatuʾs-Siyar*, 285; also see Küpeli, *Osmanlı-Safevi Münâsebetleri*, 270n, 272, 279 for the cognomen 'Hamzapaşazade' of Mehmed Agha.
118. Khajagi-Isfahani, *Khulâsatuʾs-Siyar*, 285–6. Kütük Mehemmed-kulu Xan Chagatay took up his new post on 21 July 1640. Also see *Târîkh-i Mullâ Kamâl*, 96.

119. ᶜarz.
120. Topkapı, *Evrak*, z.3420 e.1 [d.640 g.5]. The undated document is misdated to H 1058 by the archivist. Firstly, there is a grown-up padishah measuring his reign against that of Murad IV; then there is a Mehmed (Pasha) as (the Ottoman governor-general) of Baghdad; thirdly, there is a Mehmed as Ottoman envoy at Isfahan; fourthly, there is uncertainty as to whether the shah would abide by the peace or choose war; fifthly, there is the Janibek Xan Shamlu as the incumbent head of the Safavid royal guard; and, lastly, there is (Afrasiyaboğlu) Ali Pasha at the helm of Basra. All these at the same time are only possible in the year H 1050 (1640).
121. Ibid.
122. Ibid.
123. Khajagi-Isfahani, *Khulâsatuʾs-Siyar*, 286; Astarabadi, *Târîkh-i Sultânî*, 259. Note that the dating of these events in both sources is blurry.
124. Topkapı, *Evrak*, z.7022 e.249 [d.796 g.32]. See note 59 for the dating of the document.
125. Topkapı, *Evrak*, z.7022 e.244 [d.796 g.27]. See note 59 for the dating of the document.
126. *dernek*.
127. *yaramazlık*.
128. Topkapı, *Evrak*, 796/31.
129. *güzellik*.
130. Topkapı, *Evrak*, 796/36.
131. *iyilik ve ucuzluk*.
132. Topkapı, *Evrak*, 796/38.
133. Topkapı, *Evrak*, z.7022 e.315 [d.796 g.97]. See note 59 for the dating of the document.
134. 'Şu elçinin gelmediği . . . aslı nedir? Kızılbaşʾın . . . ne yüzdendir diretişleri? Yoksa bizden fehm yok mudur? Öbürüsünden havf ederdi.' Topkapı, *Evrak*, 801/3.
135. *ulak*.
136. Topkapı, *Evrak*, 795/49.
137. Topkapı, *Evrak*, 795/50.
138. 'güzellik ve düzenliktir'. Topkapı, *Evrak*, 795/60.
139. Topkapı, *Evrak*, 797/14.
140. 'Rüstem Han Hasan Paşaʾya mektup göndermiş, içinde dünyanın dillerini dökmüş, sakın inan yoktur. "İki azimüşşan padişahın emrime mutiiz ve sulhümüz mukarrerdir" diye "siz bu yandan biz bu yandan çalışırız" diye bize fend etmek ister. İnan yoktur, hemen gene göz kulak tutmaktan ayrısı yoktur. Biz tedariki görelim, ister etsin sulhü i[ster] etmesin. İnşaallah ulufeye vardığım zaman söyleşiriz. Şöyle bilesin.' M. Çağatay Uluçay, 'Sultan İbrahim Deli mi, Hasta mıydı?' *Tarih Dünyası* (series 1) 2, no. 11 (1950): 479–80. I thank Dr Cengiz Babacan for scanning his copy of this work and sending it to me.

1639–1643: Baghdad

141. Topkapı, *Evrak*, 797/62.
142. This is also apparent from further scripts of Ibrahim, some of which too are in all likelihood about the Iranian question, such as the one in Topkapı, *Evrak*, 800/4, where Ibrahim speaks of his misgivings that arise whenever he does not get fresh news from the border, and asks his grand vizier to work as hard as he did in the time of Murad IV.
143. Matthee, *Persia in Crisis*, 123.
144. Türkman, *Zayl*, 245.
145. Kazvini-Isfahani, *Khuld-i Barîn*, 301; Bijan, *Sahîfe-i Girâmî*, 417. Meanwhile, the regnant (*malik*) of Imereti, who had remained an Ottoman vassal after 1639, sent an emissary to Shah Safi bearing gifts: Kazvini-Isfahani, *Khuld-i Barîn*, 299. Imereti had once been vassal to the Safavids amid the last war, so it seems that by this undertaking, its ruler wanted to set up contact with Iran on the groundwork of the new status quo.
146. Rota, 'Death of Tahmâspqolî Xân Qâjâr', 56–7.
147. Katib Çelebi, *Fezleke*, 896, 916; *Tarih-i Vecihi*, f. 20b.
148. *tüfenkçi minbaşısı*.
149. *tüfenkçi akası*.
150. Küpeli, *Osmanlı-Safevi Münâsebetleri*, 153, 159, 212, 214, 248, 259, 263–5; Sawâqib Jahânbakhsh, 'Sâzmân-i Sipâh u Sâhib-mansibân-i Nizâmî-yi ᶜAsr-i Shâh Safî', *Faslnâma-i ᶜIlmî-Pizhûhishî-yi Târîkh-i Islâm u Îrân-i Dânishgâh-i az-Zahrâ*, 23rd year, new period, issue 14 (*payâpay 101*) (Summer HS 1391): 24–5, 31, 33–4; Arakʾel of Tabriz, *Book of History*, trans. George A. Bournoutian (Costa Mesa: Mazda Publishers, 2010), 444.
151. Kazvini-Isfahani, *Khuld-i Barîn*, 332. In the following works, Aka-Tahir is mistaken for his older brother Mir-Fattah, seemingly misled by the Tahir's nickname 'the second Mîr-Fattâh': Kazvini, *ᶜAbbâsnâma*, 56–8; Kathryn Babayan, 'The Waning of the Qizilbash: The Spiritual and the Temporal in the Seventeenth-Century Iran' (PhD diss., Princeton University, 1993), 316. Besides, Aka-Tahir too was put to death after 1643 when he still held the aforesaid post.
152. Schmid, *Finalrelation*, 259–60.
153. *Topçular Katibi Abdülkâdir Târihi*, 1099; Khajagi-Isfahani, *Khulâsatuʾs-Siyar*, 292.
154. *silâhdâr-i shahriyârî*.
155. As was the law, the Central Treasury covered the embassy's costs of travel, housing and food. *Topçular Katibi Abdülkâdir Târihi*, 1153; *Tarih-i Naima*, 951; Murat Uluskan, 'Dîvân-ı Hümâyun Çavuşbaşılığı (XVI. ve XVI. Yüzyıllar)' (MA thesis, Marmara Üniversitesi, 1998), see the list of the marshals of the Imperial Council in the unpaginated appendix.
156. He would go on to be first a master gatekeeper of the Imperial Court, later the marshal of the Imperial Council, and, albeit briefly, commander of the Janissary Corps. Uluskan, 'Divân-ı Hümâyûn Çavuşbaşılığı', section 'Ekler'.

157. *Topçular Katibi Abdülkâdir Târihi*, 1154–5; *Tarih-i Naima*, 951. The grand vizier, Imperial Council viziers, the commander of the Janissary Corps, the *daftardâr*, financial and chancellery staff, Imperial Council sergeants, the two chief justices, and so on, all attended the event. Ceremonies began with the orderly arrival of the Household officers along with the Inner Court officials. This special gathering of the Imperial Council for Yirmidört Ibrahim Kajar's audience happened on a stormy day. Amid the ceremonies, a domed, worn-out building, which stood next to Hagia Sophia and overlooked the Imperial Gate, was struck by lightning when it was swarming with people beholding the procession. Because of the lightning bolt, crash of thunder and consecutive stampede, more than ten people died, while many were wounded.
158. Maria Pia Pedani, 'The Sultan and the Venetian *Bailo*: Ceremonial Diplomatic Protocol in Istanbul', in *Diplomatisches Zeremoniell in Europa und im Mittleren Osten in der Frühen Neuzeit*, eds Ralph Kauz, Giorgio Rota and Jan Paul Niederkorn (Wien: Verlag der Österreichischen Akademie der Wissenschaften, 2009), 296–7.
159. BOA, *Ali Emiri – Ibrahim*, 495. Thirty-nine men from the embassy were clothed with robes of honour according to each one's rank. Although this document giving detailed knowledge about the kind and the worth of the robes of honour given out to each embassy member was drafted on 23 February 1642, it must not have taken long for the embassy to set out. This document was most likely drawn up sometime after the audience.
160. Solakzâde Mehmed Efendi, *Târih* (Istanbul: Mahmud Bey Matbaası, H 1298), 767.
161. Evoğlu, *Majmaᶜuʾl-Inşâ*, ff. 277b–278a.
162. 'Janâb-i vâlâ-nisâb, . . . vazârat u iyâlat-panâh, . . . muʾtaminuʾl-Dawlatiʾl-ᶜAliyyatiʾl . . . Khâqâniya, muᶜtamaduʾs-saltanatiʾl-bahiyyetiʾl-jalîlatiʾl-Osmâniya, . . . sardâr-i muᶜazzam . . . Mustafa Pasha-yi vazîr-i aᶜzam.' *Sardâr-i muᶜazzam* should have technically been *sardâr-i akram* or *-aᶜzam* to demarcate Kemankeş Mustafa Pasha's commandership-in-chief (word for word, 'supreme marshal').
163. 'aᶜzam-ı salâtîn-i rûzgâr, . . . sânî-yi Iskandar-i Zul-qarnayn, . . . aᶜlâ-hazrat . . . Zillullâh'.
164. Evoğlu, *Majmaᶜuʾl-Inşâ*, ff. 277b–278a.
165. Evoğlu, *Majmaᶜuʾl-Inşâ*, ff. 283a–283b.
166. 'ʾâlî-hazrat, sipihr-manzilat, . . . vazârat u iyâlat…-panâh, . . . kâfil-i masâlihuʾl-umam, . . . ruknuʾs-saltanatiʾl-ᶜaliyya, . . . ᶜaduduʾd-Dawlatiʾr-refîʾatiʾl-Osmâniya, . . . manzûr-ı anzâr-i Zillullâhî, sardâr-i mukarram, sadr-i afkham . . . Mustafa Pasha.' *Sardâr-i mukarram* should have technically been *sardâr-i akram* to demarcate Kemankeş Mustafa Pasha's commandership-in-chief.
167. Evoğlu, *Majmaᶜuʾl-Inşâ*, ff. 283a–283b.
168. Evoğlu, *Majmaᶜuʾl-Inşâ*, ff. 284b–285a.

169. *tâkht numûda.*
170. *ulkâ (ülke).*
171. *sinur-nâmche.*
172. Evoğlu, *Majmaʿuʾl-İnşâ*, ff. 284b–285a.
173. Mahmut Halef Cevrioğlu, 'Ottoman Foreign Policy during the Thirty Years War', *Turcica* 49 (2018): 219.
174. Jamâdayilâkhir 1051.
175. *Topçular Katibi Abdülkâdir Târihi*, 1158; Khajagi-Isfahani, *Khulâsatuʾs-Siyar*, 292.
176. Sarı Abdullah (and Cevri), *Dastûrüʾl-İnshâ*, entry heading: 'bâlâda mastûr olan mufassal olmakla gönderilmeyip tekrar mumâ-ileyhe Abdullah Efendi müsveddesiyle ber-vech-i ihtisâr bu nâme tahrîr olunup Sadrazamʾdan Şâh-ı Acemʾe gönderilmiştir'; Kadri Efendi, *Târih* vol. 2, 1158; Khajagi-Isfahani, *Khulâsatuʾs-Siyar*, 292.
177. Müneccimbaşı, *Sahâifüʾl-Ahbâr*, 680; Katib Çelebi, *Fezleke*, 917; *Topçular Katibi Abdülkâdir Târihi*, 1158.
178. Rota, 'Death of Tahmâspqolî Xân Qâjâr', 57.
179. Katib Çelebi, *Fezleke*, 917.
180. *Journal of Zakʾaria of Agulis*, 63; Nasiri, *Titles and Emoluments*, 172.
181. Küpeli, *Osmanlı-Safevi Münâsebetleri*, 215.
182. *Tarih-i Naima*, 951; Katib Çelebi, *Fezleke*, 917.
183. *Topçular Katibi Abdülkâdir Târihi*, 1154, 1158. His brother, Aqçakoyunlu Emirgûneoğlu Abbasqulu Kajar, had stayed back in Iran: *Journal of Zakʾaria of Agulis*, 68, 75.
184. Hacı Halife Mustafa Nihâdî, *Târih-i Nihâdî*, published in Hasine Biga, 'Târih-i Nihâdî (1b–80a) (Transkripsyon ve Değerlendirme)' (MA thesis, Marmara Üniversitesi, 2004); Satiye Büşra Uysal, 'Târih-i Nihâdî (80b–152a) (Transkrispyon ve Değerlendirme)' (MA thesis, Marmara Üniversitesi, 2004); Hande Nalan Özkasap, 'Târih-i Nihâdî (152b–233a) (Transkripsiyon ve Değerlendirme)' (MA thesis, Marmara Üniversitesi, 2004) f. 113a; Solakzade, *Tarih*, 767–8; *Tarih-i Vecihi*, f. 21a; Rota, 'Death of Tahmâspqolî Xân Qâjâr', 57. See ibid. for more details on how the execution was staged.
185. Rota, 'Death of Tahmâspqolî Xân Qâjâr', 57.
186. Schmid, *Finalrelation 4*, 259; Karaçelebizade, *Ravzatüʾl-Ebrâr*, 350.
187. As for Kemankesh Kara Mustafa's words in these exchanges, the handwriting must belong to his confidential secretary, because Mustafa could 'not read or write (*okur-yazar değildi*)' and, notwithstanding his statecraft much appreciated by his contemporaries, he remarked the following on being an illiterate prime minister: 'I do not deserve this office, yet they brought me to it owing to a scarcity of statesmen, whereas the requirement of this post is to read and write. Between the monarch and the minister there are many affairs that pertain to secrets, no scribe should come to know them.' Katib Çelebi, *Fezleke*, 927–8.

188. söyleşilmiş idi.
189. yeme içme.
190. Topkapı, *Evrak*, 794/11, f. 1.
191. 'Karıncanın kanadı bitmesi'.
192. Topkapı, *Evrak*, 794/11, f. 2.
193. *Tarih-i Naima*, 956–8; also see Fındıklılı Mehmed, *Zeyl-i Fezleke*, 80.
194. Khajagi-Isfahani, *Khulâsatuʾs-Siyar*, 292.
195. Matthee, *Persia in Crisis*, 123.
196. Astarabadi, *Târîkh-i Sultânî*, 259–60; Khajagi-Isfahani, *Khulâsatuʾs-Siyar*, 293–4.
197. Khajagi-Isfahani, *Khulâsatuʾs-Siyar*, 294.
198. Türkman, *Zayl*, 250–1; Floor, 'The *Khalifeh al-Kholafa*', 56.
199. Evoğlu, *Majmaʿuʾl-Inşâ*, ff. 283b–284a.
200. 'maâlî-nisâb, ... dawlat-iyâb, ... mudabbir-i ... dawlat-i şhâhî, ... xân-ı xânân-ı shâh'.
201. 'pîsh-kash'.
202. Evoğlu, *Majmaʿuʾl-Inşâ*, ff. 283b–284a.
203. Nazmizade, *Gülşen-i Hulefâ*, 234. Heads of the 600 slain rebels were sent to Baghdad along with a handsome booty. *Tarih-i Naima*, 955.
204. Türkman, *Zayl*, 252.
205. BOA, *Mühimme Defterleri* 89, ent. 57. About a year later, when Bıyıklı Derviş Mehmed was no longer the pasha of Baghdad, his household still held prisoners from the Banî Lâm, most of whom were women and children. On 11 August 1642, the Imperial Council ruled that these prisoners be freed.
206. *Bayâz-i Daftarkhâna-i Safavî*, 87.
207. The briefing and the imperial script at Topkapı, *Evrak*, 794/17, which speaks of the death of the shah, enthronement of the 'son of his son', the Erivan mission to Erzurum announcing this news, and the messenger and papers from Mehmed Pasha the governor of Erzurum to the imperial court reporting on this development, is misdated by the archivist to H 1052 and annotated as to belong to Shah Safi's death and Abbas II's enthronement. The archivist's dating and attribution are wrong, because, firstly, Abbas II was the late Shah Safi's son, not grandson, and, secondly, at the time of Safi's death and Abbas II's enthronement in May 1642, the governor of Erzurum was Nasuhpaşaoğlu Husein Pasha, who held this post from June 1639 to 1643/1644. See Katib Çelebi, *Fezleke*, 907, 925. It seems that this document is from 1629, and about the death of Abbas I followed by the enthronement of Safi, who was Shah Abbas I's grandson, and that the mentioned governor of Erzurum is Tayyar Mehmed Pasha, who held this post from October 1628 to February 1631. See Katib Çelebi, *Fezleke*, 791, 794, 816.
208. Roemer, 'The Safavid Period', 287–8; Matthee, *Persia in Crisis*, 41–3. With the early deaths of Murad IV and Safi on the one hand and the politi-

cal killings of Kemankeş Mustafa Paşa (1644) and Saru Taqi (1645) on the other, the leadership that fought the last Ottoman–Safavid war and then re-established the peace would die out.

209. *Tarih-i Naima*, 958.
210. The embassy was housed at Ferhadpaşa Palace near Bayezid Square, and a certain Dilaver Agha was named host-officer. *Topçular Katibi Abdülkâdir Târihi*, 1169; *Tarih-i Naima*, 961; Sarı Abdullah (and Cevri), *Dastûruʾl-Inshâ*, entry heading: 'Şehinşâh . . . Sultan Ibrahim Han . . . taraf...ına Şah Abbas-ı Sânî cânibinden gelen nâmedir'. In Sarı Abdullah Efendi's correspondence compilation, this letter is misdated to 10 October 1646.
211. Joseph von Hammer-Purgstall, *Geschichte des Osmanischen Reiches* vol. 5 (Graz: Akademische Druck- u. Verlagsanstalt, 1963), 306.
212. Sarı Abdullah (and Cevri), *Dastûruʾl-Inshâ*, entry heading: 'Şehinşah . . . Sultan Ibrahim . . . taraf[ına] . . . Şah Abbas-ı Sânî cânibinden gelen nâmedir'.
213. 'aʿlâ-hazrat . . . shahinshâh-i aʿzam, . . . khulâsa-i îjâd u takwîn, . . . sânî-yi Iskandar-i Zul-Qarnayn, . . . al-Khâqân bin-al-Khâqân, . . . Sultan Ibrahim Khan, . . . Zillullah'.
214. Sarı Abdullah (and Cevri), *Dastûruʾl-Inshâ*, entry heading: 'Şehinşah . . . Sultan Ibrahim . . . taraf[ına] . . . Şah Abbas-ı Sânî cânibinden gelen nâmedir'.
215. 'amârat-panâh'.
216. 'dargâh-i falak-ishtibâh-i aʿlâ-hazrat-i pâdishâh-î-yi zillullâhî'.
217. *Bayâz-i Daftarkhâna-i Safavî*, 80–1.
218. He was likely a *mutafarriqa*. The incomplete titulature in the copy of the letter sent along (see below) is 'qidwatuʾl-amâjid waʾl-akârim' ('model of the glorious and the generous'), the one used for *mutafarriqa*s of the imperial court. See Mübahat Kütükoğlu, *Osmanlı Belgelerinin Dili (Diplomatik)* (Istanbul: Kubbealtı Akademisi Kültür ve Sanʾat Vakfı, 1994), 105.
219. *Topçular Katibi Abdülkâdir Târihi*, 1168; Kazvini, *ᶜAbbâsnâma*, 54.
220. *Topçular Katibi Abdülkâdir Târihi*, 1169; *Tarih-i Naima*, 961. On 22 February, one day before Maqsud Karadağlu set out, all Ottoman civil, military and judicial dignitaries on the highway from Constantinople to the Iranian border were decreed to facilitate the embassy's journey. A host-officer was also sent along as road guide until the caravan left Ottoman territory. See the relevant decree: BOA, *Mühimme d.* 89, ent. 153. 'Mehmed Agha the commissary (*mubâshir*) of the ambassador of Persia', the bookkeeping of whose mission expenses, including those of the Imperial Council sergeants attached to him between the way-stations of Kuruçeşme and Küçükçekmece, were entered into the Central Accounting logs on 19 September 1644 (see BOA, *Başmuhasebe Cebehane-i Amire Kalemi Defterleri*, 40832, page 16/image 7), was in all likelihood the host-officer of Karadağlu on the trip back to Iran. The imperial decree found in BOA, *Cevdet – Hariciye*, 92/4577 should not be mistaken as to belong to

the return journey of Karadağlu: this document is misdated by the archivist to 10 June 1644, however, Mahmud I's (r. 1730–54) monogram atop and the decree's reference to Dervish Mehmed (Agha) as former marshal of the Imperial Council (term: 1738–40) establishes the date as 1741.
221. Kazvini, *Abbâsnâma*, 54.
222. Sarı Abdullah (and Cevri), *Dastûruʾl-Inshâ*, the entry without a heading, following the entry titled 'bu cânipten Şah Abbas-ı Sânî tarafına gönderilmek için sâbıkan reisülküttap olan Abdullah Efendi müsvedde ettiği nâmedir, lâkin bu mektup gönderilmeyip bâdehu yazılan gönderilmiştir'.
223. 'shâhanshâhâna'.
224. "ᶜâlî-hazrat, . . . Afrâsiyâb-farâsat, firâzanda-i dîhîm u gâh-ı Îrânî, . . . Shâh ᶜAbbâs'.
225. Sarı Abdullah (and Cevri), *Dastûruʾl-Inshâ*, the entry without a heading, following the entry titled 'bu cânipten Şah Abbas-ı Sânî tarafına gönderilmek için sâbıkan reisülküttap olan Abdullah Efendi müsvedde ettiği nâmedir, lâkin bu mektup gönderilmeyip bâdehu yazılan gönderilmiştir'.
226. 'farmân-i jihân-mutâᶜ'.
227. Sarı Abdullah (and Cevri), *Dastûruʾl-Inshâ*, the entry without a heading, following the entry titled 'bu cânipten Şah Abbas-ı Sânî tarafına gönderilmek için sâbıkan reisülküttap olan Abdullah Efendi müsvedde ettiği nâmedir, lâkin bu mektup gönderilmeyip bâdehu yazılan gönderilmiştir'.
228. "ᶜâlî-hazrat, . . . Jamshîd-shawkat, . . . durra-i farîda-i afsar u gâh, . . . Shah'.
229. 'taqlîd-i umûr-i saltanat'.
230. 'shawkatlu . . . ᶜâlam-panâh shahenshâh . . . sâhib-qirân, tâj-bakhsh-i khusravân-i avrang-makîn, . . . aᶜzam-i salâtîn-i zamân . . . Zillullah fîʾl-ᶜâlamayn'.
231. Sarı Abdullah (and Cevri), *Dastûruʾl-Inshâ*, letter heading: 'bâlâda mastûr olan mufassal olmakla gönderilmeyip tekrar muma-ileye Abdullah Efendi müsveddesiyle ber-vech-i ihtisar bu nâme tahrir olunup Sadrazamʾdan Şâh-ı Acemʾe gönderilmiştir'; *Bayâz-i Daftarkhâna-i Safavî*, 81–5.
232. *Eşik-akası-başı*.
233. *dîvân beği*.
234. Kazvini, *Abbâsnâma*, 54; Kazvini-Isfahani, *Khuld-i Barîn*, 299–300; Babayan, 'The Waning of the Qizilbash', 316.
235. Topkapı, *Evrak*, 850/9 (letter by Mehmed Bey the governor of Erciş); Topkapı, *Evrak*, 754/64 (letter by envoy Yusuf Agha).
236. Topkapı, *Evrak*, 754/64: 'Şah divanında ve itimadüddevlet yanında gece gündüz durur adamlarımız vardır . . . Ve yazın Gürcistanʾa sefer etmişlerdi. Bozulup, tekrar kul yazıp kışın Canı Xanʾı serdar edip Gürcistanʾa göndermek . . .'
237. Topkapı, *Evrak*, 850/9: letter by Mehmed Bey the subgovernor of Arjesh.
238. Katib Çelebi, *Fezleke*, 891; Abdülkadir Özcan, 'Kara Murad Paşa', *Türk Diyanet Vakfı İslam Ansiklopedisi* 24 (2001): 440–1.

239. Katib Çelebi, *Fezleke*, 935.
240. Topkapı, *Evrak*, 473/25.
241. Topkapı, *Evrak*, 754/64.
242. Kazvini, *ᶜAbbâsnâma*, 45; Babayan, 'The Waning of the Qizilbash', 316.
243. *Târîkh-i Mullâ Kamâl*, 99; Muhammad Hasan Râznihân and Anvar Khâlandî, 'Jihat-gîrî-yi Siyâsat-i Khârijî-yi Safaviyân dar Masʾala-i Munâzaᶜât-i miyân-i Dawlat-i Osmânî vu Uvrupâ (az Muᶜâhada-i Zuhâb tâ Suqût-i Safaviyân)', *Mutâlaᶜât-i Târîkh-i Islâm* 24 (seventh year, spring 1394): 102.
244. 'janâb-i maʾ[â]lî-maʾâb . . . sâhibuʾd-dawla, . . . ᶜaduduʾd-DawlatiʾlʾAliyyetʾiʾ...l-Khaqaniya . . . Mustafa Pasha-i vazîr-i aʾzam'.
245. 'aʾlâ-hazrat falak-rafʾat . . . pâdishâh . . . zillullâh'.
246. *Bayâz-i Daftarkhâna-i Safavî*, 85–7.

3
1644–1660: Armenia and Azerbaijan

Venetian Bids to Ally with Iran against the Ottomans; an Imperial Army in Armenian Highlands

The Ottomans were determined to tighten their grip along the Iranian border. In Baghdad, Küçük Hasan Pasha, now in his second term as governor there, built three additional towers on the Zulfiqar Hill near the Ajam Bastion to strengthen the fortress's defences.[1] The Imperial Council also directed its attention to the northern stretch of the frontier, and on 1 May 1642 gave instructions to Van's governor, Janissary captains, margraves and the governor of Diyarbekr that they together restore the shattered and wrecked sections of the fortress of Van to 'complete steadiness',[2] and in 1645–6 the fortresses of Van and Kars were further repaired.[3] The Ottomans kept an eye on the Iranian borderland even after the treaty had come into full force after the diplomatic business from late 1642 to mid-1643: they carefully watched, for example, the upheavals in eastern Georgia and the Safavid responses thereto in late 1643, mostly through intelligence forwarded to the imperial court by the hereditary governor of Childir, (Atabegli-Jaqeli) Sefer Pasha, who ran spies across the border in Georgia.[4]

The outbreak of hostilities between the Ottoman Empire and the Republic of Venice in 1645 opened a new dimension in relations between Constantinople and Isfahan. In the first year of this Cretan War, the Turks captured Chania, one of the main fortresses of the island. The fight soon spread across the Mediterranean, the Dardanelles, and the whole of island Crete itself. It would demand the entire navy, a large-scale call-up of the army, and all the resources that the Empire could steer towards this engagement, and go on for the next twenty-four years.[5]

Particularly early in the Cretan War, the Venetians strived to squeeze the Empire into a two-front struggle by bringing in the Iranians as an ally. The Republic first sought to do so by the agency of the Polish–Lithuanian Commonwealth, and in 1645 dispatched Giovanni Tiepolo as ambassador to request Polish cooperation in this matter. And thereupon, in 1646, King Wladyslaw IV Vasa of Poland sent to Abbas II his own envoy bearing a letter from Prandota Dzierzek, eastern dragoman of the Crown Chancellery, proposing that the Shahdom and the Commonwealth open war on the Empire in alliance with Venice. Tiepolo also forwarded the Senate's separate letter to the shah by means of Antonio de Fiandra, a Dominican priest who accompanied Jerzy Ilicz, Poland's envoy to Isfahan.[6]

That same year, 1646, a trader named Domenico de Santis set out for the Safavid court as an undercover emissary on behalf of both Venice and Poland. He was bearing a new set of letters from the doge of Venice, the Pope, the German emperor, the king of Poland, and the grand duke of Tuscany to Abbas II, repeating the call that Iran enter the war against the Empire as a Venetian and Polish ally. De Santis linked up with caravans in Aleppo and proceeded over land across northern Mesopotamia in disguise. As he was about to cross into Iran from the border at the province of Shahrizor, a rabbi from his caravan let the Ottoman governor know that de Santis's bales looked odd for a trader and that he was secretly bearing gifts to the shah. The governor rushed troops to detain him, but by the time they arrived the caravan had already crossed the border. Once on Safavid territory, de Santis revealed his true mission. He reached Istafan in the summer/early autumn of 1646, a few months ahead of Jerzy Ilicz, and delivered the aforesaid letters at his audience with the shah. Though he was welcomed warmly, de Santis's mission proved unsuccessful. Abbas II disregarded the Polish and Venetian calls, and de Santis left Isfahan not as warmly as he had been welcomed.[7]

The Polish envoy Jerzy Ilicz, on the other hand, died in Isfahan on 17 October 1647 before he could meet the shah. Antonio de Fiandra, as Ilicz's official designee, handed over to the shah not only the writs he took over but also Dzierzek's letter. In his reply to Dzierzek dated November 1647, which de Fiandra brought to Poland, Abbas II undertook nothing more than to keep up friendly relations with the Polish king.[8]

While these Venetian and Polish attempts to build up an anti-Ottoman alliance with Iran were underway, Marshal Deli Husein Pasha furthered the Turkish footing on Crete, taking among others the fortress-city of Rethymno in 1646, while a full-fledged fleet conflict also unfolded.[9] Deli Husein had won repute in the last Iranian war, standing out first with his artillery skill at the capture of Erivan while grand admiral, and more particularly by his success, as governor of Anatolia, in capturing Baghdad's two bastions, streets in the battle downtown and the Slender Tower[10] within the keep. He had made a name for himself among the soldiery and the public alike for fighting on the front line alongside his men, not only when leading a regiment but even when commanding the Imperial Army itself.[11] He had meanwhile showed up once again at the Iranian borderland in 1644 as Baghdad's governor for about half a year.[12] In 1647, Deli Husein, after expanding the Turkish hold on Crete, ordered more contingents, artillery and ammunition from Constantinople for his next target, Candia (Heraklion), the capital of the island-duchy. The Venetian blockade of the Dardanelles, however, shut away the Imperial Navy laden with these shipments. Thereupon, in 1648, the marshal began beleaguering the heavily fortified and manned Candia with those troops already on Crete, starting trench-and-mine combat.[13]

Iran received the news of the Ottoman advances in Crete and the fall of Chania warily.[14] Safavid dignitaries would have liked the Ottomans to be beaten, or at least bleed over a long-drawn-out war. However, they did not do anything to undermine the Ottoman war effort. Amidst this early phase of the Cretan War and Venice's diplomatic contacts with Iran, tensions rose near the Ottoman–Safavid border at Armenia. In September 1646, Prevezeli Defterdaroğlu Mehmed Pasha, of the same household network as the current grand vizier Nevesinli Salih Pasha,[15] was appointed governor of Erzurum. Unusually, however, he was also created marshal[16] of the Iranian frontier, as if there was an ongoing or upcoming war. Before he headed out, Padishah Ibrahim gave him an audience and said: 'act upon this illustrious script of mine, and if the bad-subsistenced Kızılbaş rebel or run wild, then you are the revered minister[17] drawing the resplendent monogram.[18] All legions in Anatolian provinces as far as Erivan are at your command.'[19] In reaction to the hearsay that Iranian troops were gathering across the border at Armenia, Prevezeli Mehmed was 'encouraged to do whatever [he deem proper] at the Iranian frontier'.[20] Ibrahim saw him off saying 'go get 'em, may you undertake many expeditions at the Ajam frontier'.[21]

The reason for the creation of a marshalship was seemingly the false rumour that Abaza Mehmed Pasha (a former Ottoman Jalali-rebel, sea captain, governor-general, coup-attempter, anti-Janissary figure, and then marshal against Polish-Lithuanian Commonwealth, and who had been put to death in 1634) had in fact escaped execution, and after years of hiding in Iran, showed up in Erzurum to raise an army. Prevezeli Mehmed Pasha's proxy[22] rode in haste to Erzurum and took over the reins while his lord was still in Scutari. There, while Constantinople was still within eyeshot, Prevezeli learned that the hearsay was untrue and that his proxy had everything under control.[23] Nonetheless, as late as about three months after the falsity of the rumours had come out, the governor's marshalship of the Iranian front was still not called off. At his entry procession to Erzurum, the military and administrative officials welcomed him not only as governor-general but also as field marshal, as mark of which the Household corps garrisoning the fortress and feudal troopers greeted him on the road along a march of hours.[24]

This was nothing short of a full military parade, such that a wartime marshal might stage at the waystop of Erzurum[25] on the road to the Iranian combat zone. The showing off was deliberate. As the imperial court deemed authority in Erzurum critical for its grip on the Iranian border, particularly at Georgia and Armenia, even a small likelihood of unrest at this provincial metropolis could trigger immediate intervention from the capital. And the affair of 1646–7 embodies this sensitivity. Erzurum's match across the border was the Iranian province of Çukursaʿd, which was one of Safavid Iran's top-priority provinces, and just as the governors of Erzurum were authorised to correspond, bargain and cooperate with Safavid officials across the border, in turn could the governors of Çukursaʿd also do so with the Ottoman side.[26]

It still remains to be explained why Prevezeli Defterdaroğlu Mehmed Pasha's marshalship did not expire once it became clear that rumours were unfounded. As Ibrahim's words of blessing hint, hearsay about Abaza Mehmed was only part of the reason for Prevezeli Mehmed Pasha's appointment to marshalship. The imperial court was worried less about imposter Abaza Mehmed himself than about how the Safavids, or a borderland vassal from Iran, might try to exploit the situation to attempt a breach; the presence of a marshal at Erzurum could nip in the bud any Iranian plans to encroach westwards. The imperial court thus gave Prevezeli instructions about how to respond to such a breach, namely by gathering troops from Erzurum and further afield and advancing into Iran. Even when the rumours about Abaza Mehmed transpired to be false, the Sublime Porte remained concerned about Safavid troop movements, not only in eastern Armenia and Azerbaijan but also near the Persian Gulf, where in 1645 and 1646 the government of Basra suffered repeated incursions from the Iranian side of the border.[27] Likewise, when the hearsay of a nearing Safavid army had spread in Basra in 1646, its ruler Afrasiyaboğlu Ali Pasha sent a certain Dervish Husein as an emissary bearing gifts to Abbas II to talk him out of an onslaught.[28] Against the background of these tensions, the Ottomans' fielding an army up north at the Iranian frontier was a kind of pre-emptive measure.

Shortly after Prevezeli Defterdaroğlu Mehmed Pasha's entry into Erzurum, a coincidence highlighted the strategic significance of this province in the Empire's dealings with Iran and how the Ottoman strength concentrated there could be put to use. At some point probably in late

1646, Mustafa Bey, Ottoman-vassal margrave of Shushik, a stronghold between Erzurum and the Iranian border,[29] crossed the border and plundered the townships around Erivan. The governor of Çukursaʾd dispatched an emissary bearing a letter and gifts to Prevezeli Defterdaroğlu Mehmed Pasha to report this breach and request Ottoman cooperation. The council of Erzurum resolved to undertake a punitive expedition with an army made up of feudal troopers, half of the Household soldiers posted at the province, and the governor-general's own battalion. Even though the Safavid emissary had requested the Ottomans to field this force, he was disillusioned to see how large it now was, and worried that, far from simply disciplining Mustafa Bey the margrave of Shushik, it would threaten Erivan itself. At Gümüşlükümbet, to the east of the fortress of Erzurum outside the Kars Gate, Prevezeli held a military parade, which alarmed the Iranian scouts, who could allegedly behold the scene from three different directions.[30]

The gathered army besieged Shushik and the garrison gave in the next day. The imperials in part plundered and in part confiscated Margrave Mustafa's palace, estate, herds and arsenal. Mustafa Bey, however, had fled in the dark of the night and sought shelter at the nearby stronghold of Maku, then manned by the Safavids. An Ottoman contingent pursued the runaway margrave, talked Maku's Safavid garrison into handing him over, and brought him to Prevezeli Mehmed Pasha's headquarters. The marshal confiscated his wealth and abrogated his margraveship.[31]

Maku was among the strongholds to be demilitarised and torn down according to the Treaty of Zuhab. The Ottomans had already fulfilled their share of these obligations, and as they had disputed in 1641–2, the Safavids had later manned this wrecked position[32] with musketeers from Mazandaran.[33] The Ottomans had meanwhile re-manned Magazberd, in retaliation to the Safavids at Maku, with a standing company from the Kars Local Servicemen made up of a senior-captain,[34] lieutenant,[35] sergeant,[36] secretary,[37] paymaster,[38] and staff privates. After the Shushik operation, Prevezeli Mehmed Pasha received emissaries from the governors of Çukursaʾd, Karabakh and Azerbaijan. Prevezeli's own emissaries, bearing letters of friendship and gifts, would accompany their three Iranian counterparts on their way back: Evliya Çelebi b. Dervish Mehmed was commissioned to Tabriz, Niksarlı Kilerci Veli Agha to Erivan, and Alacaatlı Hasan Agha to Nakhchivan. However, before the Iranian emissaries set out, Prevezeli reportedly inveighed them:

> In the state of the House of Osman, we do not deem it proper to perpetrate acts contrary to the peace. We have plundered the domain[39] . . . of Mustafa Bey,

1644–1660: Armenia and Azerbaijan

and granted his fort to another bey; as your xan of Erivan – Our brother[40] – had complained from him, he was dealt with. Now, you shall also perpetrate no acts contrary to the peace, shall remove the troops that you put to the fortress of Maku, and demolish it in line with the law of peace. If not, I am currently the monogram-drawing great marshal, I [will] plunder the climes of Erivan and Nakhchivan with a sea of troops.[41]

The marshal did not need so large an army for a punitive expedition; a smaller contingent would have been enough. In mobilising so many troops, therefore, he was also reacting to Safavid military movements across the border. First, by fielding half of the Household soldiers stationed in the fortress, he sent a message: because he was authorised to do so only by virtue of marshalship, not governorship-general. Secondly, the military parade at Gümüşlükümbet was held to impress Iranian onlookers rather than to ensure military discipline. The marshal knew that the Iranians nearby could view that location. Ottoman dignitaries, not knowing the cause of the military movement behind the border, may have therefore chosen not to utter their worries by official means but instead to show strength at the frontier and thus daunt the Safavids without openly targeting them. Prevezeli Mehmed Pasha's reportedly threatening words at the meeting with the emissaries also back up this reading. By pulling off this show without breaching the treaty, he, so to speak, hit the bull's-eye, because formally he undertook the Shushik operation upon the Safavid request to forestall its Ottoman-vassal margrave from raiding into Iran.[42]

The Ottomans must have been aware of the missions shuttling from Venice and Poland to Iran to build an alliance. By staging this show of might in Armenia, which was an edge of the Empire far away from the battlefields of the ongoing Cretan War, the Sublime Porte warned the Iranians, in deed rather than in word, that even when its armies were tied up across the Mediterranean and all available funds were being steered towards to the Venetian campaigns, the Empire could still field another imperial army at the Iranian border which, if need be, was strong enough to fight a standalone war.

Indian Question, Uzbek Revolutions, Escalation at Azerbaijan and Unrest by the Persian Gulf

Ottoman fears that a supposedly resurgent Abaza Mehmed in Armenia might unsettle the relations with the Shahdom proved unfounded. But a similar scenario almost did come true in Iraq. Baghdad's governor at the time was Ibrahim Pasha, a favourite of Grand Vizier Nevesinli Salih. In

September 1647, Grand Admiral (Kapıcıbaşı) Semiz Kara Musa Pasha, having just come back from the Cretan front, almost replaced Nevesinli as grand vizier, but instead, (Tavşantaşlı[43] Tezkireci, posthumously Hezarpare) Ahmed Pasha won the padishah's seal. The new grand vizier warded off his strong rival Semiz Kara Musa by making him governor of Baghdad in early October. At first, Semiz Musa dragged his feet and tried to have his appointment called off, but finally had to comply. Ibrahim Pasha, aware of his patron Nevesinli's downfall, refused to give up the governorate. Baghdad's Local Servicemen, after hearing of what had happened, backed up Ibrahim Pasha and did not let Semiz Musa into the city, asking the imperial court to reconfirm Ibrahim as governor. Nevertheless, knowing only too well that this meant insubordination, the Household companies there took a stand against the Local Service and Ibrahim Pasha, and after they gathered behind their commanding Janissary officer Altıncı Ahmed Agha, a clash broke out. The Household corpsmen shut themselves into the keep and withstood all onslaughts by Ibrahim Pasha and the Locals.[44] This was a crisis: Baghdad, the Empire's foremost bulwark overlooking Iran in the south, was out of operation.

Following the stalemate, Household officers, knowing that Ibrahim Pasha was a 'simpleton', lured him into the keep by feigning capitulation. Ibrahim took the bait, the Household soldiers confined him, and the Locals could not break in notwithstanding all their attempts. This situation dragged on for two or three months during which time the Sublime Porte heard of the uproar. At last, Second Master-of-the-horse[45] Jundi Mehmed Agha came to Baghdad, had Semiz Kara Musa Pasha slip into the city by night aboard a ship, and put to death Ibrahim Pasha, his steward, and those Local officers that had partaken in the disobedience.[46] Some notables and now-decommissioned Local Servicemen whom Semiz Musa persecuted sneaked out of Baghdad, crossed the River Diyala,[47] and fled for their lives to Iran.[48]

The upheaval at Baghdad was a serious one: if it were to grow, it threatened to spill over to Iran, or indeed draw it in. Sound authority in Iraq was essential to the Empire's dealings with Iran. Unlike in its show of might at Armenia, however, the Sublime Porte did not use the 1647 affair of Baghdad to daunt Iran. This is because the state was able to crush the uproar before it could boil over beyond the fortress walls. Thus, a potential entanglement with Iran did not come about. Even the flight of some Local Servicemen to Iran does not seem to have bred tensions, as those who had fled must have only wanted to save themselves, without a further agenda. If strife had arisen, the new grand vizier would have only had himself to

1644–1660: Armenia and Azerbaijan

blame for using Baghdad, so vital a post in relations with Iran, as a chip in a factional rivalry.

Notwithstanding the unrest along the border, the Sublime Porte and the Shahdom continued their friendly exchanges. In 1648, Padishah Ibrahim sent a private letter to Shah Abbas II, asking him to provide two elephants and 500 pieces of *seraser*-type golden cloth.[49] His eagerness to acquire elephants was born out of his fellowship with a courtier and fortune-teller from the district of Eyub, called Voyvoda-kızı, whose tales about Indian monarchs' elephant-riding spellbound him. Ibrahim next developed an obsessive desire for sable furs, in pursuit of which he set about issuing a series of eccentric commands. He ordered that pavilions in Topkapı Palace and other imperial residences in Constantinople should be covered all over with sable fur, and harrassed dignitaries and officials to present him with great loads of sable fur; he furthermore designed a new ceremonial outfit for himself made of sable fur and jewels alone, and sacked the Empire's chief bookkeeper[50] for failing to satisfy his sable fur craze. His quenchless demand for sable fur caused a flow of considerable sums of money from the Empire to Russia, the main source of sable fur, and even a Euroasia-wide rise in the price of this commodity.[51]

Contrary to the diplomatic custom, Ibrahim chose a few palace guards[52] for this private mission to Iran, with one of them leading the team as diplomatic herald. The mission reached Abbas II's encampment at Bastam around July 1648, while the shah was marching east for the Kandahar campaign.[53] Placing an order of elephants and cloth was not the only task of the palace guards though. In his 'epistle for friendship', Ibrahim also wished Abbas II well for the start of his campaign against Mughal India. The shah was more than happy to learn of the padishah's blessing, as he appreciated in his carefully worded answer that spoke of 'preserving the union and observing the necessities of peace'.[54]

Driven by the tensions between the Ottoman Empire and Mughal India, Ibrahim gave his blessing to the Safavid campaign. He would not raise any objections even if the Safavid troops were to march beyond Kandahar towards India proper. The Porte's outward neutrality and low-key consent gave the Iranians free rein in this undertaking (though, as it transpired, having repactured Kandahar in 1649 the Iranians were unable to follow up on this success, and instead spent the next five years defending the city against succesive Indian sieges).[55] It is also noteworthy that the Kandahar campaign, having been decided as early as Safi's last years on the throne, came into the Safavids' agenda only thanks to their assurance that, after the Peace of Zuhab, a feud with the Ottomans was no longer likely.[56]

Thus the Ottoman and Safavid courts quietly reached an understanding on Iran's fight for Kandahar against Mughal India.

Besides the Indian issue, Ibrahim's delegation of palace guards to Iran also fulfilled their private commission: Abbas II appointed Mehemmedkulu Beyg Burun Qasimoğlu[57] as envoy to Ibrahim and sent expensively bedecked elephants, elephant-riders, precious cloths and further gifts. After stepping into Ottoman territory at the province of Baghdad but before reaching Constantinople, however, the envoy would hear of Ibrahim's dethronement; he had to halt his march and get in touch with the shah's court.[58]

On 8 August 1648, a *coup d'état* in the capital enthroned Ibrahim's six-year-old son, Prince Sultan Mehmed (the Hunter). This coup was the outcome of the insecurity for life, office and property felt by the statesmen owing to Ibrahim's arbitrary decrees, odd requests, unreasonable appointments, wasteful spending and high-handed executions throughout his eight-year reign. In the end, a threesome of Janissary generals took on the leadership of the coup, changed the monarch and installed a new grand vizier.[59] Hanafi Mehmed Efendi, a born-Iranian from Nakhchivan who had migrated to the Ottoman Empire amidst his education, played a critical role, as former chief-justice of Asian provinces, in legitimising the dethronement and enthronement for Empress-mother Mahpeyker Kösem Sultan by backing up the opinion that the reign of a sane child was preferable to that of a mad grown-up, and that a regency was lawful.[60]

At the time of the *coup d'état* in Iran's western neighbour, upheavals had also peaked in its eastern neighbour, the Khanate of Bukhara. The Uzbek kingdom had been going through a civil war in the 1640s because of rivalry within the reigning Astrakhanid-Chinggisids dynasty. The Mughal involvement in this struggle had then turned the Uzbek civil war into a Bukharan–Indian conflict, in which the Shahdom had first feigned neutrality following its talks with the 1647 Mughal embassy. However, in the summer of 1648, Abbas II and his chief vizier Alaaddin Husein Khalife-Soltan started the Kandahar campaign against the Mughals.[61] Nadr Muhammad Khan of the Uzbeks, who first had thought that Sultan Ibrahim Khan would not back him up and therefore had not sought Ottoman support for his cause in the Uzbek infighting, had later asked the Sublime Porte for help once the Mughals had occupied Balkh instead of coming to his help. Meanwhile the Safavids, though waging war against the Mughals, did not provide concrete help to the Uzbek khan either. In the letter brought by his ambassador to Constantinople on 30 March 1649, Nadr Muhammad acknowledged having mistakenly believed he could count on the Safavids without seeking Ottoman help, and asked the padishah to step in and cooperate with the shah on his behalf.[62]

Without waiting for the conventional Safavid embassy to congratulate the Ottoman accession, in April 1649 the Sublime Porte sent an imperial letter, in all likelihood via a herald, to 'Shah Abbas [II] . . . his sublime Majesty, befitting the throne of judgment, Khusrav of the realm of Ajam'[63] in the name of the new padishah, and informed the shah of the imperial letters calling on the 'sultanic Nadr Muhammad . . . Khan of the Uzbeks'[64] and his son Abdulaziz Khan to bring an end to the dynastic fight. Reconfirming the peace and referring to the friendship between the Ottomans and the Safavids, the Sublime Porte asked the shah to cooperate in settling the Bukharan conflict and repatriating the Uzbeks that had taken shelter in Iran, and to command Iran's eastern governors to get on well with Nadr Muhammad Khan.[65]

The Sublime Porte took heed of the Bukharan crisis and awaited positive input from Abbas II. The Safavids' congratulatory mission was already on its way to Constantinople, and this issue could well be brought up in the forthcoming imperial letter reconfirming the peace, or discussed amidst the talks with the incoming ambassador. It is highly likely that in the eyes of the Sublime Porte, this letter, although addressed to the shah, concerned Bukhara alone, and did not pertain to the wider subject of Ottoman–Safavid relations. That Mehmed IV's accession was not mentioned in this letter hints that Constantinople had announced it with an earlier mission, either in writing or by spoken word. The Porte must have deemed this message an anomalous one-off, distinct from the conventional correspondence between Constantinople and Isfahan.

In the meantime, Safavid envoy Mehemmed-kulu Beyg Burun Qasimoğlu, upon Ibrahim's overthrow, received from Isfahan updated letters and instructions. He reached Constantinople on 2 June 1649 and, at his audience on 8 June following the customary Imperial Council sitting, handed over Abbas II's letter and lavish gifts. The envoy also delivered the two elephants and golden cloths ordered by the former padishah Ibrahim, the formal goal of his original mission. This legation officially reconfirmed the Peace of Zuhab. On 22 June, the imperial court gave the envoy permission to leave for Iran, after what had been a rather short stay.[66]

It seems that envoy Burun Qasimoğlu did not bargain for or strike any deal with the Sublime Porte other than enshrining the reconfirmation of the peace. The Empire's show of might in 1646 at Armenia had seemingly not embittered the Iranians. The Baghdad affair of 1647 too, which could have triggered a crisis drawing in Iran but was nipped in the bud, had not become a matter of strife either. The same goes also for the correspondence between Isfahan and Venice from 1645 to 1647 and the proposals of an anti-Ottoman alliance that the shah had rejected. Tensions, even if they arose, did not leave behind any written trace. Both parties were satisfied with the state of affairs and did not deem any issue worthy enough to dispute, lest it breed unwished for complications. The Safavids' way of refusing to join the Cretan alliance against the Ottomans seems to have convinced the Sublime Porte that its eastern neighbour did not mean to start a fight. The Safavids likewise feigned ignorance of the Ottomans' daunting show of might in the Armenian borderland.

In the 1650s, the Cretan War became even more exhausting. Marshal Deli Husein Pasha's legions had conquered almost the whole of Crete; however, the Venetian garrison at Candia, the island's capital, withstood.[67] Thanks to the regular fleet support to the Venetians from the Papacy, Spain, Malta and Florence, the sea war turned into a clash between the Turkish Empire and the Mediterranean Catholic coalition.[68]

As the Cretan War went on, news reached Constantinople in Spring 1651 that 'the Kızılbaş [Safavid troops] were on the move' in Azerbaijan, nearing the border. The imperial court sent additional Janissaries to strengthen Van's garrison;[69] however, it soon turned out that this information was not true, or that the Safavid mobilisation targeted elsewhere. Tellingly, though, the Ottoman response to this false alarm highlights the importance of Van, which otherwise was administratively and militarily overshadowed by Erzurum and Baghdad along the Empire's Iranian border. Notwithstanding the heavier investments elsewhere, the Empire was evidently ready to take measures at Van too even upon hearsay of military movement from Iran.[70]

While rumours from Azerbaijan proved for the moment unfounded, tensions did arise on the border at Iraq. On 7 November 1649, the Ottoman customs overseer inspected an incoming Iranian caravan accompanied by some German traders, priests and wayfarers at the customs post of Padishah Bridge, one end of which was Iranian territory and the other end the Empire's. When the overseer wanted to search the German priest more thoroughly than normal because he suspected that the jewelry carried by the priest could be commercial wares rather than personal belongings, the caravan brawled with the customs staff. In the end, all members of the caravan were arrested, while their goods and belongings were put under temporary injunction. The governor of Baghdad suspected Jürgen Andersen, who was travelling with the caravan on his way back to Germany from Iran, of espionage after finding out that he bore a passport drawn up by the Safavids. The pasha guessed that Andersen had acquired the passport in return for his service to the shah, and himself interrogated

Andersen, who said he wanted to go back to Europe and not to visit to Iran again. When this statement was coupled with Andersen's courtly speech befitting the governor's dignity and utterance of his thankfulness in Turkish, the language which he had picked up during his stay at the Safavid court, he was set free, his belongings were given back, and he was furnished with an Ottoman passport, a horse and travel allowance.[71]

Even without concrete evidence, the Ottoman customs overseer had suspected that German–Iranian espionage activity might be underway. Though we do not have more insight as to the Jürgen Andersen incident, it seems unlikely that the customs overseer's sternness was merely accidental. Rather, it probably reflected a general Ottoman policy that applied to any contact, or attempt thereto, between European states and Iran that the Ottomans could uncover.

It soon transpired, meanwhile, that what had the Ottomans gather an imperial army in Armenia upon hearing the news of Safavid mobilisation was not only misgivings. In 1651, a crier-for-help from Baghdad reached Constantinople and warned that Safavid troops were drawing near. As first response, the imperial court posted additional Janissaries from the central squadrons to the fortress of Baghdad. Bosnalı Suleiman Efendi, the former judge of Baghdad who then happened to be in Constantinople, also let the imperial court know that he had urged the governor of Baghdad Shatir Husein Pasha to keep the fortress well-stocked, and had him buy 12,000 thalers' worth of supplies. Bosnalı Suleiman also showed an earlier letter from Janissary colonel[72] Ilyas Agha, commanding officer of the Household corps at Baghdad: three *xan*s along with 3,000 troops were fielded in Huvayza, alongside three other *xan*s with 12,000 troops led by Kur Husein-xanoglu by the neighbouring Kerha Water. Traders coming to Baghdad from across the border were questioned about this call-up, and spies were sent out to glean fresh news. It turned out that the goal of the upcoming expedition was to plunder the outskirts of Baghdad and carry away that year's harvest so as to bring about a dearth in Ottoman Iraq. Moreover, the shah, on the pretext of marching upon Kandahar, was gathering an army and building up his military to set on after 16 September. Therefore, the Baghdad garrison wrote that the grand vizier had to be informed to quickly counter-mobilise and send help.[73]

As soon as Baghdad's new governor (Firari) Kara Mustafa Pasha reached his post in 1651, (Colonel) Mehmed Agha, the new commanding officer of the Household corps at Baghdad, drew up a presentation to the grand vizier, in which, among other issues, he highlighted the following:

The Ottoman Empire and Safavid Iran

> There are successive notifications that the Kızılbaş are gathering in Isfahan under the name of aiding Kandahar, that 10,000 Kızılbaş have gathered in the vicinity of Baghdad in Huvayza and at the site called Kerha Water, that their [numbers] are increasing day by day, and that they are preparing to gather [an army]. But as of now, neither a manner of movement contrary to the peace is known, nor what exactly their idea is. Our troops and ammunition are perfected. There is no fear from or reservation about the enemy. However, our fear is from the matter of state provisions, because the [available] state provisions ... [will] only suffice for six months. It is requested and begged from my sire Your majesty that provisions be purchased for here.[74]

The new judge of Baghdad, Mehmed Efendi, attested to this news with his own presentation.[75]

Unbeknownst to the authorities in Baghdad, the Mughals had beiseged Kandahar,[76] wherefore the Safavids may have mobilised to be ready against the Mughals, not to set on the Ottomans. So, whereas this time the incoming news was not a false alarm, how accurately the Ottomans read the facts is questionable. On the other hand, the English reported that Abbas II was planning to be in Shiraz in May 1651 so as to dispatch an army upon Basra, and that the Afrasiyaboğlus were likely to give in without putting up a fight.[77] By June, Abbas II indeed set out from Isfahan to lead his forces himself against Basra, pledging to start the actual campaign after observing Ramadan (18 August–16 September). If Basra could be taken, the shah would then advance north to attack Baghdad. However, the Safavid march into Iraq had to be called off, because the shah now needed to retaliate against the Mughal onslaught on Kandahar, which forced the mobilised army to march eastwards.[78]

We are are in the dark as to which of these courses of action Abbas II was meaning to take with his projected attack on Iraq. It might have been to open a war against the Ottoman Empire by targeting Baghdad, to present the case as a retaliation to border breaches by an unruly Ottoman vassal, or to claim that Basra, being a freehold-government,[79] in other words a tributary principality, was not necessarily Ottoman territory, so an encroachment upon it would not breach Ottoman lordship rights. Either way, Abbas's projected Iraq campaign did not materialise, but the call-up and build-up made for it did alarm the officials in Baghdad, who in turn updated the imperial court as intelligence came in and asked for reinforcements. The Iranian–Polish traffic of missions and letters, on the other hand, must have only boosted the mistrust in Constantinople towards Abbas II's intentions. Without an actual attack or concrete evidence, the Sublime Porte contented itself with staying on full alert, but did not make the first strike, lest the Iranians deem it a breach in its own right. Since the Peace of Zuhab, the two parties had never come so near to war.

Again in 1651, the Ottomans remarked that 'contrary to usual practice, the Shah sent an emissary to the King of Poland, and a creditable infidel named Pruska also went to the Shah with an epistle from the King'. The Sublime Porte found this exchange odd,[80] but could not dig up its content or the intent behind it. In June 1651, Surkhay II Shamkhal, the Safavid-vassal ruler of Dagestan who had brought the margraves of the land under his sway over the 1640s, sent a mission to the Ottoman-vassal Khan of Crimea and asked for military help against the Russians, who had built a stronghold watching over the road linking Dagestan to Crimea.[81] Nothing notable came from either attempt.

In a letter to the grand vizier in early 1652, (Firari) Kara Mustafa Pasha wrote that 10,000 Kızılbaş (Safavid) troops had indeed gathered near Huvayza and Kerha Water, but only to guard their own land, not to encroach upon Ottoman territory, and that otherwise the Ottoman set-up in Baghdad was confident of being able to fight back against the foe. Baghdad's governor had also sent letters to the Iranian governors of Huvayza and Luristan to forewarn them against sheltering the insubordinate Bani Lam who ran away from his punitive expedition.[82] Musa Pasha the governor of Van too sent spies to the land of the 'Kızılbaş', who returned with the news that the shah was then in Isfahan and that the Safavid troops were to gather near Mashhad with the governor-general of Azerbaijan as their marshal.[83]

It seems then that the Ottomans misread the target of the Iranian mobilisation of 1651, and that the troops gathered not to break into Ottoman Iraq but to strengthen the Safavid defence of Kandahar. This notwithstanding, Ottoman border pashas kept on feeding the imperial court with news from Iran in remarkable detail, insomuch that they forwarded not only their reports but also the raw information or even the original writs upon which they rested their reports. In addition, even after the Ottoman intelligence pickers had found out that the call-up of troops in Iran was steered towards Mughal India, they continued to watch out for troop movements.

Likely in early December 1652, soon after the aforesaid team of spies returned to Van, a mission made up of 'a few Kızılbaş'[84] showed up at Van,[85] bearing a letter from the governor-general of Azerbaijan, Alikulu Xan Saakadze, who was also marshal of Iran,[86] to Governor 'Musa Pasha his princely, sublime majesty'.[87] Mawlana Sheref and Mir-Seyyid, two Ottoman-subject Kurdish princelings, were said to have crossed the border into Iran and raised a stronghold at the spot called Lahan lying within Lahrasp Soltan's land. In abidance with the peace between the two monarchies, the governor of Azerbaijan wanted Musa Pasha to discipline his own underlings and tear down the unlawful stronghold. Ali-kulu Saakadze also asked Musa Pasha to make it known if the Ottomans would not take care of the breach themselves, so that the Safavid side could deal with it. In this latter scenario, highlighted the marshal of Iran, Safavid action against the Ottoman-subject outlaws would not be in breach of the treaty.[88]

Musa Pasha thereupon wrote a letter to the grand vizierate and shared the latest news coming from Azerbaijan. From the Ottoman side, no stronghold had been built, underscored the governor of Van, but the Safavids were using this as a pretext to send a mission for espionage.[89] Beside this own letter of his, he also forwarded the original letter from the governor of Azerbaijan and its partial translation. The dispatch reached the grand vizier's chancellery on 3 January 1653.[90]

Neither the Shahdom nor the Sublime Porte followed up on this correspondence. The Ottoman dignitaries involved must have found out, after all those earlier reports, that the called-up Safavid troops were to march upon Kandahar against Mughal India, and that Iraq was not the target. No news, neither from within nor outside the Empire, confirmed that two Kurdish princelings breached the border from Van towards Tabriz and unlawfully built a stronghold there for themselves. Moreover, even if it had been so, the governor of Van would still not be held answerable, because the alleged outlaws were not regular subjects but vassals, who were not controlled unless they overstepped the mark, so the governor of Van's punishing them would have been enough for the Ottomans to fulfil their contractual obligation to the Safavids. So, if some Kurdish princelings had done as claimed, Musa Pasha would have gained nothing out of telling the grand vizier that Ali-kulu Saakadze's allegations were untrue and that the mission from Tabriz had indeed come to Van for espionage. He could keep up his good standing with the imperial court by disciplining the vassals of his province. What is more likely to have happened in December 1652– January 1653 is, then, that on the eve of setting out eastwards from Tabriz to marshal the Safavid army, Ali-kulu Saakadze made up an agenda for the neighbouring province of Van, so that he could keep the Ottomans across the border a bit busy while he was tied up at Kandahar.

Soon afterwards, Behdinan Ebusaid Bey, the margrave of Imadiya, wrote in his letter to the grand vizier (Tarhuncu Sarı Ahmed Pasha), which reached the chancellery on 4 February 1653: 'there is no trace of the Kızılbaş [troops] hereabout, they are not in motion at all'.[91] In another letter to the grand vizier, which arrived on 9 February, Mehmed Pasha the governor of Mosul likewise told:

earlier the Kızılbaş had gathered for Kandahar, and whereas the xans of the frontier here had also gone [on campaign], it has been heard that they returned to their proper places again.[92] To spy on the said matter deeply, an agent has been sent to Isfahan by [my]self. When he soon comes back, [the news] will be communicated in detail to [Your] esteemed presence.[93]

Another letter to the grand vizierate arrived on 14 March from the bannerlord of Siirt, Zeyneʾl-abidin Bey. As seemingly the least informed of the three, he wrote: 'there is a gathering of the Kızılbaş, their idea is not known.'[94] Even though the *bey* of Siirt lacked the knowledge with which to link this call-up to the defence of Kandahar, he did not speak of any threat to Ottoman lands either. Upon the last Mughal undertaking to win Kandahar in 1653, Abbas II indeed gathered an army.[95] So, the Iranian mobilisations along the border in Azerbaijan, eastern Kurdistan and the east of the Persian Gulf since 1651 were meant to defend Kandahar, but early news had bred a misunderstanding, which then spread and, in the end, but after already having triggered measures on the Ottoman side, came out false, as often happened with hearsay in the borderlands.

In 1653, Abdurrahim Bey, the Basran ruler Afrasiyaboğlu Husein Pasha's relative and emissary, came bearing gifts and a letter to Abbas II in Mazandaran, together with a group of other missions from provincial and sovereign lords, which also included the Ottoman-tributary Georgian rulers of Imereti and Mingrelia.[96] Although we do not know what he told the shah or what Afrasiyaboğlu wrote in his letter, it seems likely that the house of Basra wished to secure Safavid protection, or even overlordship, if it came to a showdown with the Ottomans on the status of the principality. By 1654, the first full-blown Basran crisis had broken out and would keep the Sublime Porte busy for a long time, and also shake its friendship with the Shahdom.

Afrasiyaboğlu Husein had become the ruler of Basra after his father Ali's death. With a letter of endorsement from Mehmed Pasha the governor of al-Ahsa (a land south of Basra on the western coast of the Persian Gulf, stretching along the eastern Arabian Peninsula from what is today Kuwait down to Qatar), Husein's two uncles Ahmed Bey and Fathi Bey went to Baghdad and disputed the succession before governor Kara Murtaza Pasha, pledging as quid pro quo to give certain items from Basra's income over to the Baghdad governorate treasury and also to reward Kara Murtaza himself for his help. The governor of Baghdad readily sent troops upon Basra to unseat Husein and install Ahmed.[97] Husein sent back Kara Murtaza's troops empty-handed, but gave his uncles bannerlordships. Nevertheless, soon after, he tried to have them killed, but failed. When reconcilers stepped in, the uncles' lives were spared on the condition that they be banished to India. The princelings however jumped ship and found shelter once again on the western coast of the Persian Gulf; Al-Ahsa's governor wrote another letter to Kara Murtaza Pasha on their behalf. In his letter to Constantinople, Kara Murtaza Pasha in turn accused Husein of tyrannical behaviour towards the dwellers of Basra, who too had written collective petitions in support of the uncles' claims. He also highlighted which income streams were to be allotted from Basra to the Baghdad Treasury and to the Central Treasury respectively, hinting that for the imperial court and its Baghdad establishment, this centralising dimension of the proposed operation towards the Persian Gulf was also an important factor in decision-making. Satisfied, the grand vizier commanded Kara Murtaza to proceed with his proposal.[98]

When the grand vizier's edict[99] came in, Kara Murtaza Pasha took along the Afrasiyaboğlu princelings and announced the forthcoming Persian Gulf campaign in the late summer of 1654. The gathered division, made up of the governor's own battalion, Baghdad Locals and artillery, encamped at Jewazer on 12 September and Kara Murtaza joined them a few days later at Arja, recently carved out by the governorate of Baghdad from the government of Basra. Daunted by the Baghdad division, and hoping to be rewarded by a new leadership, countryside elders and tribal chieftains of Basra did not withstand the troops marching towards the principality's capital. Afrasiyaboğlu Husein had the fortifications of the city strengthened, and boosted his troops' number and gear. However, seeing that he could not beat off the nearing division, which had been capturing each location on its way (Chaluchiya, Aqara, Mansuriya, Mesopotamian Marshes,[100] Qurna), and that his troops were unwilling to fight against the Ottomans, he took his movable wealth and fled to Iran on 26 September with the help of a friendly tribe. After the 7,000-strong garrison of Basra yielded unconditionally to the Baghdad division on 28 September, Kara Murtaza entered the city with a parade, with Basran elders participating in the procession to show their approval of Afrasiyaboğlu Ahmed's accession. On 30 September, the governor clothed Basra's new ruler in a robe of honour to mark his installation.[101]

Before fleeing to Iran, Afrasiyaboğlu Husein asked Abbas II for military help in return for bringing Basra under Safavid overlordship. The shah, not to breach the peace with the Ottomans, did not answer.[102] From this point onward, however, Kara Murtaza's greed for wealth and power turned the tide against the Ottomans. The governor of Baghdad first made Ahmed and Fathi seize for him the goods stored at the stronghold of Qabban. Next, he set up artillery before the ruler's palace and had

Baghdad's military band play there, while he put to death the dignitaries of Afrasiyaboğlu Husein, who was now hiding in Iran. These offences estranged the Basrans from the new leadership. After the shipments of the goods confiscated for the pasha of Baghdad began to come in, the townsfolk protested the new leadership's high-handed rule. To calm down those opposing the unlawful confiscations, Kara Murtaza this time put to death Ahmed and Fathi, the very Afrasiyaboğlu princelings who legitimised his presence in Basra. He blamed them for what had come to pass, and named his own steward Ramazan Agha the new ruler. This violation further stirred up the Basrans, who were loyal to the House of Afrasiyaboğlu. In the end, the townsfolk teamed up with the tribes from the countryside against Kara Murtaza. The fortified positions of the Marshes, Falluja and Qurna (the main stronghold within the principality standing at the Tigris's confluence with the Euphrates), which had formerly given in to the Ottomans, also rose up.[103]

Seeking investors in Iran interested in restoring him to power, Afrasiyaboğlu Husein proceeded along the east of the Persian Gulf: he first headed eastwards to Huvayza and then southwards to Durak, ending up waiting further east in Bihbehan together with his following. On the eve of setting out for Isfahan with the hope of meeting the shah, he sent ahead his relative Abdurrahim Bey again to Abbas II, with gifts and a letter asking for help.[104]

With the uprising in full swing, the Basrans now sent word to Afrasiyaboğlu Husein asking him to come back from Iran. The runaway ruler readily called off his march to Ishafan and turned back to lead the coalition against Kara Murtaza. He also brought along thousands of hirelings whom he freshly enlisted from among the Safavid-subject Kuhigiyula soldiery and Safavid-vassal Bedouin. The Afrasiyaboğlu faction first set on the Ottoman garrison at Qurna. To help the garrison, Kara Murtaza shipped infantry with a fleet and, overland, sent a 3- or 4,000-strong cavalry force drawn from the Local Service and his own musketeer companies. At the clash near Sharish between Afrasiyaboğlu's Iranian hirelings and the Baghdad's cavalry regiment, which was well outfitted with firearms, the marshy ground determined the outcome to the advantage of the Afrasiyaboğlu–Iranian coalition before the fleet bringing the infantry detachment could arrive. A further group of Afrasiyaboğlu-friendly Bedouins led by Muhammad Rashid also showed up at the battle site and charged, putting the Baghdadi-Ottoman cavalry to flight. Again, before the river-borne infantry had time to arrive, the Bedouins attacked and took the fortress of Qurna, of whose garrison some fled and some were slaughtered.[105]

The shah indirectly helped Afrasiyaboğlu Husein by not hindering his recruitment of fighters in Iran. But as the pasha of Baghdad campaigned against Basra at the grand vizier's behest, a direct Safavid backing to Husein might have led to an Ottoman–Safavid confrontation, because then the Afrasiyaboğlu ruler would have to cast off Ottoman overlordship and become tributary to the Safavids. The shah did not wish the situation to heat up that much, owing to his troth to the peace with the padishah and a foresight that winning over a shifty vassal such as Afrasiyaboğlu Husein would not be worth its consequence of drawing the Empire's armies towards Iran. On the other hand, Kara Murtaza's mistreatment of traders, townsfolk and the Afrasiyaboğlu princelings may have facilitated Abbas II's decision not to hinder Husein from recruiting in Iran, as Kara Murtaza's wrongdoings were at odds with the directives of the grand vizier and had occurred even though the wronged parties had obeyed him.

For Kara Murtaza, meanwhile, things were going from bad to worse. Already on bad terms with their pasha owing to earlier tensions in Baghdad, the Local Service now forsook the campaign. Kara Murtaza had to flee for his life, leaving behind all his belongings and booty. The Basrans did not persecute him, instead giving him and his followers horses to ride back. After all, he was too high-ranking an Ottoman dignitary to harm without imperial orders no matter what he had done. When all the campaigners reached Baghdad, the townsfolk made clear that they had no sympathy for the governor, and the Janissary garrison did not let him into the fortress. Lodging at the Kuşlar stronghold, Kara Murtaza petitioned Constantinople and was accordingly made governor of Aleppo on 8 July 1655. At Basra, Afrasiyaboğlu Husein Pasha sent his tributary gifts to the imperial court and was reappointed to his office.[106]

As the proxy Iranian–Ottoman clash unfolding in the shape of a Baghdadi–Basran fight neared its end, a cross-border theft found its way into official logs. Seydi Murad b. Mirza, an Iranian subject and an international thief, had been caught and Kirmanshah's governor Sheikh-Ali Xan (Zangana) had his right hand chopped off. Even then he stayed true to his trade and a while later showed up on the Ottoman side of the border. When his figure and the 'two stolen small foals along with two grayish mares'[107] he had with him drew people's attention, Hizir Agha the prefect of the Kara Ulus clan became suspicious, and had him brought before the judge. There, Seydi Murad acknowledged his earlier thefts, bodily punishment, and that the horses found with him bore the brand of none other than Sheikh-Ali Zangana, the governor of Kirmanshah. Witnesses[108] from Kızılribat[109] confirmed that Seydi Murad b. Mirza was an Iranian subject, a 'thief son a thief',[110] that he always brought there and sold goods stolen

1644–1660: Armenia and Azerbaijan

from Iran just as he also sold in Iran what he stole in Ottoman territory, and that his right hand had been chopped off at the behest of Sheikh-Ali Xan, the governor of Kirmanshah. Seydi Murad was delivered to Hizir Agha, and judge Abdulhakim of Kara Ulus wrote down the hearing on 2 May 1655.[111] This felony did not have a political dimension and hence did not make it into the diplomatic agenda. It, however, stands out as one of the examples shedding light on criminal prosecutions that involved both Ottoman and Safavid officials. Also remarkable is that this hearing led to what may be the first Ottoman logging of Sheikh-Ali Zangana, who would come to the fore later in the 1680s as Iran's Ottoman-friendly chief vizier advocating for the Shahdom to refuse all calls to team up with Germany, the Papacy, Poland, Russia and Venice against the Ottoman Empire.

Afrasiyaboğlu Husein's restoration, however, did not mean that Basra changed back to its former status. In what one could call the 1655 deal, the imperial court stripped the Basran principality of Qurna, the main fortress of southern Iraq, and brought it under imperial sway as a banner. The principality was also switched from a tributary *freehold-government* to a *hereditary fiefdom*,[112] hence becoming an autonomous province within the Empire. Thenceforward, the governor (no longer *ruler*)[113] of Basra would pay three-monthly taxes to the governorate of Baghdad and yearly taxes to the imperial court, while the state itself would appoint Basra's judge.[114] Basra's conversion from a tributary government to an autonomous province was of direct relevance for Ottoman–Safavid dealings, because the overlordship of this land to the north of the Persian Gulf was a recurring matter of strife between Constantinople and Isfahan.

Less than a year after the Basran affair, the shah sent Afrasiyaboğlu Husein an emissary called Yar-Ali Xan, presumably to affirm the status quo. This mission seems to have been part of a Safavid drive to strengthen friendship with the Ottomans by acknowledging Basra's new status within the Empire, and to the same end the shah sent an extraordinary embassy to Constantinople. The Yar-Ali mission, passing before the Empire's frontline stronghold of Böğürdelen, processionally crossed the Shatt-al-Arab on galleys and boats and entered Basra, where cannon shots greeted the emissary.[115] In the council held, the shah's letter was read aloud and gifts were handed over. Afrasiyaboğlu received the gifts only after examining them one by one. He must have been careful not to do any business with Iran that would go against Basra's tightened ties with the Empire.

Meanwhile the new grand vizier Ibshir Mustafa Pasha (a participant of Murad IV's Iranian campaigns of 1635 and 1638 as his second master-of-the horse),[116] who belatedly had arrived in Scutari on 25 February 1655 to take on the grand vizierate to which he had been appointed a few months earlier, had been keeping an eye on the Iran-related news coming in from around the Persian Gulf. A warlord rather than a prime minister, Ibshir Mustafa was plotting to start a war against the Safavids. He promised rewards to Kurdish margraves so as to embolden them to raid into Iran, the repercussions of which he could then use as a pretext to begin hostilities. The Pinyanishi tribe, from the province of Van, took Ibshir Mustafa's bait, crossed the border from Shahgediği, and looted sheep from the Safavid-subject clans of Afşar and Dunbuli. Ibshir Pasha now proceeded to up the ante: upon receipt of a letter from the shah asking him to explain the reason for this breach, he refused even to answer it. In reaction, then, both to the cross-border raids and Ibshir's non-cooperation, the shah had his sub-governor of Urmia, along with those of Chevlan, Biredos, Dumdumi, Dunbuli and Salmas, raid the Ottoman-subject Pinyanishi, carrying away sheep to Urmia. Seeing that the conditions of his own making were now ripe for the next step, Ibshir Mustafa went ahead to create an Ottoman marshalship at the Iranian border.[117]

While proceeding slowly from Aleppo towards the capital, the unwilling grand vizier had already briefed the padishah about Iranian activity beyond the border. Once at the capital, he appointed former grand vizier Melek Ahmed Pasha as governor-general of Van, alleging that Iranian troop movements near the border necessitated such a weighty figure, who had formerly governed the Empire, to oversee that borderland at this critical time. When Melek Ahmed deemed that the governorship of Van was below him, Mehmed IV handwrote the diploma making him marshal of Iran(ian front). The padishah thereby empowered Melek Ahmed to appoint and unseat officials in all the Asian provinces, and decorated him with marshalship regalia.[118] For all the prestige of this appointment, however, Ibshir Mustafa's real motive for posting Melek Ahmed to Van was to remove a strong rival as far as possible from the capital.[119]

Although the news of Ibshir Mustafa's subsequent fall reached Melek Ahmed before the latter arrived in Van,[120] the marshalship was not called off. On 7 June 1655, at a time when the outcome of the ongoing Basran struggle between Kara Murtaza and the Iranian-supported Afrasiyaboğlu Husein was still uncertain, Melek Ahmed entered Van with a grand procession led by his own battalion[121] and military band, joined by the Van Local Service and the Household corps stationed there. To welcome the marshal, troops from all fiefdoms, banners and tribes presented arms. After a feast by the notables, Melek Ahmed Pasha held the 'padishah's council', exercising his authority as marshal, that is the monarch's absolute deputy in a defined area of jurisdiction, hence as an acting grand vizier. At the council, he had his master-secretary Ghinayizade Ali Efendi read aloud the imperial script empowering him, and thereupon set about wielding the authority stemming from it, commuting one person's death sentence and executing several others previously condemned by the Imperial Council.[122]

The marshal soon turned his attention to the fortifications of this border bulwark across Azerbaijan. The earthen hill at the northern side of the fortress-rock heaped up throughout Iranian sieges over the past centuries could afford a future besieger, namely Iranians, a favourable position to encamp. Melek Ahmed Pasha gathered his own battalion and the Locals, summoned the feudal troopers and the margraves, and mobilised the townsfolk to dump this heap of earth into Lake Van.[123] He then had the tower of the Keep's-Gate[124] rebuilt, strengthened, and set long-range artillery to its crenels. He also upgraded the bulwark of the Tabriz Gate to a sound bastion. The new raisable bridge that gave access to Tabriz Gate over the moat was lifted and chained to the wall every night as a routine security measure at the side of the fortress that overlooked Iran.[125]

Melek Ahmed Pasha's call-up for feudal troopers and margraves was sheer military service. And soon this army was put to use: the marshal's punitive expedition in July 1655 against prince (Rojeki) Koca Abdal-khan (Beğ), lord of Bitlis, who had not obeyed the call-up, ended in the installation of Abdal's son as a biddable replacement.[126] Not long after came Benli Omer Agha, a master-gatekeeper of the Sublime Porte, to Van bearing edicts from the new grand vizier, Dev Kara Murad (now Pasha rather than Agha). Kara Murad highlighted that the former grand vizier Ibshir Mustafa had abused his authority to start a war with Iran, and ordered Melek Ahmed to de-escalate the resultant tensions.[127] This notwithstanding, like the 1654 Basran campaign, the 1655 Bitlis expedition against Koca Abdal-khan would soon lead to new strife between the Ottomans and the Safavids.

This strife unfolded as follows. On 4 September 1655, Melek Ahmed Pasha received a letter from Kara Murtaza Pasha, requesting assistance in securing the rescue of Murtaza's brother Gurji Temres Bey. Gurji Temres had been detained by the Safavid subgovernor[128] of Dunbuli while on his way travelling from Georgia to join his brother Kara Murtaza after fifty years of separation. The marshal soon ordered Ghinayizada Ali Efendi, the master-secretary of his council, who had formerly drafted a letter to the shah when serving in Baghdad's provincial council, to 'draw up a pleasing, eloquent epistle' to the shah, and separate letters to Koca Kayıtmaz Xan (a.k.a. Murtaza-kulu Xan Kajar)[129] the governor of Azerbaijan, Genç-Ali Xan Afşar the governor of Urmia, and to the subgovernors involved. The marshal demanded therein the restitution of the looted sheep to

Pinyanishi, otherwise he threatened his addressees with 'falling in with the troops of Van on the clime of Azerbaijan, and pillaging their provinces [and] dominions'.[130]

Once the letters were drafted, gifts chosen and allowances dealt out, the marshal dispatched two missions to Iran: one led by Sarı Ali Agha to Abbas II in Isfahan, the other by the famed Evliya Çelebi to the governors of Urmia and Tabriz. Aside from the official agenda, Evliya Çelebi was also to ask around whether the governors whom he visited were content with the Safavid regime, and whether they showed any liking for the Ottomans. Melek Ahmed Pasha was particularly keen to know about the governor of Azerbaijan, Kayıtmaz Kajar: the Iranians, said the marshal, were worried that the Bitlis campaign was in fact prompted by other, hidden, motives. Evliya Çelebi was therefore to reassure Kayıtmaz Kajar that the expedition was justified, and to treat him with utmost respect.[131]

The missions headed out from Van on 11 September 1655.[132] Evliya Çelebi soon reached Urmia, and its governor Genç-Ali Xan Afşar welcomed the Ottoman mashal's delegation on the plain outside the town. The guests attended the gathering there fully beweaponed, in ceremonial outfit. The governor and the emissary exchanged words of courtesy on horseback, after which they rode into the stronghold in procession.[133]

Following the feast, Evliya Çelebi handed over the letter. After the council chancellor read it aloud, the governor complained about the Pinyanishi murders and raids. He stated that he had informed the shah, who then had written to the padishah and grand vizier Ibshir Mustafa Pasha, but when the shah's initiative with Ibshir Pasha had not brought forth anything, he had undertaken the expedition. At this point in proceedings, Evliya Çelebi had the grumbling sheep owners from Pinyanishi leave the council room so that he could handle the matter alone with Genç-Ali Afşar.[134] After going over the treaty clauses, the emissary said that the rightful Iranian response to the raids would have been to arrest and deal with the wrongdoers, not to wreck Pinyanishi as a whole with a full-fledged army. Furthermore, he noted, conventions specified that fielding an artillery – even if not fired – and firing the muskets in company of a military band breached the peace. Both sides reached an understanding that the said provision applied to the actual case. When the governor asked what to do to make up for what had happened, Evliya Çelebi, with his well-known fondness for exaggeration, alleges to have answered thus:

> Take no offence, soon enough you see,[135] Melek Ahmed Pasha will get his hands on the Resplendent Monogram and drive 80,000 troops from the provinces of Diyarbekr, Erzurum, Akhaltsikhe, and Van, and devastate these

climes. In particular, the blissful padishah has been saying: 'I shall campaign upon Ajam and conquer the fortress of Erivan which my uncle [Sultan] Murad Khan had taken' and 'Ajam broke the peace and pact by garrisoning troops in the forts of Maku and Kotur, and now hit my domain of Pinyanishi.' The padishah is restless. Hence, my xan, the consequences of this affair will be violent. Immediately collect the sheep, deliver them to the pasha, and renew the peace before all [these] troops strike this clime. Otherwise, when [the Ottomans] will not leave these climes for five to ten years, may the shah not scold you! Consult with provident, unbiased persons.[136]

Evliya Çelebi claims that Genç-Ali Afşar thereupon understood the seriousness of the situation. Khaja Naqdi, one of the master-secretaries of the governor's council, hinted that the Ottomans, who also brought up the Armenia affair of 1646, might be on the lookout for a pretext to start a war, and recommended to give back the looted sheep. After this first round of talks, the mission was quartered in the town with an escort led by a Safavid *dizçöken ağası*. Next day, after taking over Melek Ahmed Pasha's gifts, Genç-Ali Afşar, acknowledging Melek Ahmed's seniority in rank and reportedly calling him 'our vizier-father', agreed to go ahead as advised. The subgovernors who had participated in the Iranian expedition against the Pinyanishi showed up at Urmia on the third day and Evliya Çelebi sent thousands of sheep along with his report to the Ottoman marshal at Van, pledging to send the rest as soon as possible.[137]

After hunting, polo games and feasting together, Genç-Ali Xan Afşar asked Evliya Çelebi about Sarı Ali Agha's mission to Isfahan, worrying that the shah might blame him for harming relations with the Ottomans. The next shipment of thousands of sheep was sent to the complainants along with an additional drove as a gift for Melek Ahmed Pasha himself. The Pinyanishi spokesmen, upon Genç-Ali Afşar's demand, went to the local court of Urmia to get a quittance, a copy of which they handed over to the governor. Evliya Çelebi sent a letter to Sarı Ali Agha to update him on the settlement of the case before his meeting with the shah.[138]

Next, Evliya Çelebi redeemed Gurji Temres Bey, Kara Murtaza Pasha's brother, from detention in Dunbuli. The subgovernor said that he had arrested Temres upon receiving news from the viceroy of Kartli, who had called the detained person a Bagrationi princeling from Imereti fleeing to Baghdad. The subgovernor claimed that he had learned that Temres Bey and Kara Murtaza Pasha were brothers only thereafter. The detainee was handed over to the mission when Evliya Çelebi agreed to draft an official acknowledgement of receipt, to be shown to the shah and the governor of Azerbaijan.[139] As the mission was getting ready to head out from Urmia towards Tabriz, having just received receipts from Melek Ahmed Pasha, an usher[140] of the shah came to unseat and arrest Genç-Ali Xan Afşar, and confiscate his estate. The new governor Taqi Xan showed up at nearby Toprakqale soon afterwards. The marshal's mission left Urmia on 2 October 1655.[141]

Evliya Çelebi entered Tabriz in procession. After handing over the letters and gifts at the council, Evliya Çelebi and governor Kayıtmaz Murtaza-kulu Xan Kajar talked over the Urmia affair. Kayıtmaz Kajar argued that he had warned Genç-Ali Afşar not to stir up the Ottomans, but the latter had been too self-confident owing to his uncle's being at the shah's court. When the emissary showed the quittances and receipts, the governor took no further action against his unseated inferior, and left the issue to the discretion of the shah. Hoping nevertheless to help Genç-Ali Afşar, Evliya Çelebi and Kayıtmaz Kajar wrote letters, with copies of the quittances enclosed, to Abbas II.[142]

On the mission's second day in Tabriz, Kayıtmaz Xan Kajar sent Melek Ahmed Pasha a letter and gifts along with a mission of eighty led by Esed Aka. Next morning, one of Kayıtmaz Kajar's spies, named Gökdolak, rode back in haste from Van to let his lord know that the Ottoman marshal had set up encampment at Gökmeydanı with troops and siege artillery. The spy had no knowledge of the marshal's goal. The Kayıtmaz Kajar diplomatically questioned Evliya Çelebi, remarking the contradiction between the marshal pasha's peace-seeking missions and warlike actions. The emissary tried hard to convince the governor of Azerbaijan that the Ottoman marshal had no intention of threatening Iran, and that the only target of the campaign was Bitlis, whose former lord, Prince Rojeki Koca Abdal, had fled amidst the earlier crackdown. Kayıtmaz Kajar suspected that this answer could be a tactical diversion to take Iran by surprise with an unexpected onslaught. While the governor was pondering how to inform the shah of this news, suspicions died away with the arrival of another spy of his, who told that the target of the marshal's campaign was indeed Rojeki Koca Abdal, who had shown up back in Bitlis. He further reported that, meanwhile, Melek Ahmed Pasha had found out that this man and his partner Khudadad were spies, and that the marshal had left alive him to go back to Tabriz but put his partner Khudadad to death for espionage.[143]

Luckily for everyone involved, the joint updates from Urmia and Tabriz on the Pinyanishi deal reached Isfahan before it was too late. Thereupon the shah met with Sarı Ali Agha and called off the confiscation of Genç-Ali Afşar's estate with a rescript.[144] An usher of the shah arrived from Isfahan in Tabriz on 13 October 1655 to announce the news. After being entertained for a while by the governor of Azerbaijan and the notables of Tabriz, Evliya Çelebi left the city.[145]

1644–1660: Armenia and Azerbaijan

In the end, therefore, the Azerbaijan affair of 1655, which triggered geographically even wider reactions in the shape of military movements and missions from northern Kurdistan all the way up to Isfahan, did not unfold into a conflict between the Ottomans and the Safavids. The episode was significant, however, in illustrating how tensions along one section of the border were connected with tensions in the other flanks: for the Sublime Porte's imposition of extraordinary measures near the border at Azerbaijan was motivated at least in part by its awareness of Abbas II's passive support for Afrasiyaboğlu Husein by the Persian Gulf. This support was discreet enough not to constitute a clear breach of the peace, but it was nevertheless a sufficient threat for the Sublime Porte to respond by creating a marshalship of the Iranian front. The Azerbaijan affair, therefore, was in large part a consequnce of the crisis at the Persian Gulf.

Following Ibshir Mustafa's downfall, his successor as grand vizier, Kara Murad Pasha, set about undoing the entanglements that Ibshir had set in motion. As there was no real reason to break the Peace of Zuhab and as after the Basran affair the Shahdom was working to soothe the Sublime Porte, Melek Ahmed Pasha's marshalship goals became reset now to uphold the peace and assure the Safavids of the Ottomans' steady but friendly stance. Yet, he was still to pull these off with hinted threats sprinkled in between. As Melek Ahmed Pasha's marshalship was soon called off, the near ten-year cycle of Safavid trials of strength and Ottoman shows of might in answer thereto came to an end. Overcoming these challenges made the peace sounder than before.

The governor of Baghdad had undertaken the Basra campaign of 1654 to replace Afrasiyaboğlu Husein Pasha with his uncle Ahmed with the approval of the grand vizier. Kara Murtaza Pasha could not have embarked on a campaign to unseat a ruler and install a new one, strip Basra of its main stronghold along with remarkable income, and convert it from a tributary government into an autonomous province, if he had not borne the decree authorising him to do so. Yet, it was again Kara Murtaza Pasha and the Afrasiyaboğlus Ahmed and Fathi themselves who talked the imperial court into backing their venture. This threesome engineered the imperial decree that they in the end received. The sources hint that the Sublime Porte did not have it in mind to do away with Basra's governing dynasty; the new governor to be installed was still an Afrasiyaboğlu. But it did order a status makeover to tie Basra more tightly to the Empire. For the imperial court, Ahmed the uncle must have seemed a likely more cooperative governor, who would also have Basra chip in more to the Empire's finances. The transfer of certain income streams from Basra's entitlement to the Empire's Central and Baghdad treasuries, and the incorporation of some territory into direct imperial rule were set down from the outset, whereas it seems that the annexation of Qurna was a fait accompli by Kara Murtaza which the imperial court did not want to let go once it had happened. The prospect of more income for the Central Treasury and for an imperial province at the expense of a vassal principality may have been the strongest motive for the imperial court. And except for replacing Afrasiyaboğlu Husein Pasha, it fulfilled its political, administrative and financial goals with the Persian Gulf campaign.

Kara Murtaza's post-conquest misdeeds, which estranged Basran townsfolk and pushed them back to Afrasiyaboğlu Husein's side, seem to have stemmed from Kara Murtaza's hunger for power; there is no evidence that the imperial court endorsed his misdeeds. The limits of the authority bestowed upon the governor of Baghdad and Kara Murtaza's overstepping these limits after entering Basra also help explain Abbas II's course of action in 1654–5 and the Ottomans' reaction thereto. For as long as Kara Murtaza was fulfilling the orders of the imperial court to replace Afrasiyaboğlu Husein with Ahmed the uncle, Abbas II did not give Husein shelter or audience. It was only after Kara Murtaza's high-handed executions and appropriations that Abbas II seems to have surreptitiously helped Husein to raise troops in Iran, or at least connived in it. In doing so, the shah must have calculated that after that stage, the padishah would not deem an Iranian presence on Husein's side a hostility. The business of the upcoming diplomacy between the Ottoman and Safavid monarchs and the Porte's accepting Afrasiyaboğlu Husein's gifts in acknowledgement of his restoration to Basra back this up further.

In all likelihood informed of the situation and Iran's share in it, Shah-Jahan of India sent an embassy to Mehmed IV requesting support in the Mughals' fight against the Safavids. Qaim Beyg, prefect of the Mughal army, set off in autumn 1654, at the height of the Basran crisis, and reached Constantinople on 4 May 1656. Shah-Jahan thereby asked the Ottomans to enter the war.[146] The political setting then was not so unfavourable for a positive answer: in autumn, on top of all that had happened at the Persian Gulf, Surnazen Mustafa Pasha, the governor of Erzurum, reported Iranian troop movements near the border at Armenia. By way of response, in October 1656, the Porte decreed Kara Murtaza Pasha, now governor of Aleppo, to be on full alert and, if need be, march to Baghdad without waiting for another decree.[147] The Mughals wanted to split Iran with the Ottomans. Grand Mufti Khojazade Mesud Efendi, as spokesman of those against such a venture, opposed this. He said that the Empire could deal with Iran anytime it wished, notwithstanding whether the Empire had other military and financial commitments at the

1644–1660: Armenia and Azerbaijan

same time, and that it would benefit from keeping Iran whole as a buffer between itself and Mughal India; if the Safavids were wiped out, India would become a neighbour and the Mughals' claim of dynastic superiority based on Timurid lineage might lead them to challenge the Ottoman overlordship of Mecca and Medina, and hence the Ottoman monarch's supreme standing. The Sublime Porte answered Qaim Beyg in the negative, explaining that the Ottomans were already tied up in their ongoing war with the Republic of Venice and its allies, and that the padishah did not wish to break the peace with the shah.[148]

The Ottomans chose not to embark on an adventure where they could not foresee what it could unfold into. The Shahdom could be cowed by occasional shows of strength, but in the end, the Sublime Porte felt satisfied with the Peace of Zuhab, saw its interest in upholding it, and did not want to resort to war unless the other side broke the peace.

Iranian Diplomacy and Upheavals in Dagestan and Georgia during Wars in the Mediterranean and Transylvania

Throughout the 1655 affair of Azerbaijan, the Empire steered almost all of its resources towards the Cretan War. During the 1650s, the Venetian fleet patrolled the Aegean Sea, otherwise controlled and territorially contained by the Empire. This was a serious blow to the Turks, who had to keep this waterway safely navigable to be able to land their military shipments on Crete. What was more, Venice occasionally blockaded the Dardanelles, further hampering Turkish operations. These setbacks left Marshal Deli Husein Pasha in dire straits while fighting against the Venetian garrison at Candia and its regular reinforcements from the Republic's allies. Kara Murad Pasha, grand admiral in 1654–5, had run the blockade and beaten off the Venetian fleet commanded by Giuseppe Delfino the Admiral of the Ships, but in 1656 the Venetian-Maltese navy commanded by Lorenzo Marcello the Admiral-General of the Sea knocked out the Turkish navy that set sail under Sarı Kenan Pasha the Grand Admiral. The Venetians then occupied Tenedos, fully blockaded the Dardanelles, and thus threatened even the security of Constantinople itself. This crisis was the single most important reason, among and above others, that led to Köprülü Mehmed Pasha's becoming grand vizier with dictatorial powers in 1656.[149]

Both the outgoing and the incoming grand viziers amidst the 1656 crises of the Dardanelles were veterans of the last Iranian war. As grand vizier, Köprülü succeeded Canikli Boynuyaralı Mehmed Pasha, nicknamed for his crooked neck, the result of a poisonous blow amidst Murad

IV's Iranian wars (1635–9).[150] Köprülü himself, while governor of Çorum (in mid-northern Anatolia, within the province of Rûm), had also fought in the Ottomans' retaking of Baghdad from the Safavids back in 1638 and been wounded in trench clashes.

Following the cooling of the Basran crises of 1654–5, Abbas II made Kalb-Ali Soltan/Xan Silsüpür-Afşar[151] ambassador to Mehmed IV to repair relations by declaring that he had refused Afrasiyaboğlu Husein's bid to bring Basra under Safavid overlordship and that he remained committed to upholding the Peace of Zuhab.[152] It seems that this extraordinary embassy set out at the same time as Yar-Ali Xan's aforesaid mission to Basra, and the news of an embassy coming from Iran reached Constantinople a few months ahead. Silsüpür-Afşar, after proceeding even more ceremonially than was the norm and going overboard in feigning reluctance to engage the Ottomans, reached Constantinople with a staff of more than 600 on 21 November 1656, the same day as Hanafi Mehmed Efendi, the Iranian-born grand mufti of the Empire, was unseated due to agedness and loss of hearing. The wait between the arrival and the start of business was rather short. The padishah received the ambassador in audience on the 28 November following a feast at the Imperial Council, after having him clothed in a robe of honour, and Silsüpür-Afşar handed over to Mehmed IV Abbas II's dispatch.[153]

In his letter,[154] the shah once again offered his condolences on Ibrahim's death and his good wishes on the enthronement of the 'Padishah the unrivaled Khusrav'.[155] The shah's earlier letter sent upon Mehmed IV's enthronement had likely not spoken of Ibrahim's fate, out of a sense of delicacy and the circumstances of the accession in 1648. After highlighting the 'union-of-hearts',[156] 'concord' and 'unity'[157] between the two monarchies, Abbas II justified his war against the Mughals by highlighting the defection of some 'ungrateful ones' who had handed his 'patrimony' Kandahar over to [Shah-Jahan] the 'viceroy of India',[158] before Abbas's 'accession to the throne of the sultanate of Iran'.[159] He also put the blame for the prolongation of the war on his foe, who had undertaken successive campaigns to retake Kandahar, which was by then back in Safavid hands. After heralding the then re-established peace with India, the shah said:

> The attainment of favour by those in concordance is the origin of rejoicing for friends. Therefore, and out of affection and honesty, and to fortify the pedestals of recovery and cohesion, [I] found it necessary to dispatch a reliable person to [Your] Superb Banquet and [Your] Exalted Highness. And because sending a trophy from the conquered country was necessary, one elephant has been dispatched as souvenir[160] to [Your] Immortality-Resembling Gathering.

The Sublime Porte wrapped up this embassy rather quickly. On 31 December 1656, Grand Vizier Köprülü Mehmed Pasha hosted Kalb-Ali Silsüpür-Afşar at a feast in the Yusufpasha Garden of Eyub, and on 2 January 1657, Mehmed IV received the ambassador in the farewell audience, having him clothed again in a robe of honour. Silsüpür-Afşar attended the event together with Kose Ismail Agha, chief patrician[161] of the imperial court and the former resident-at-court[162] of the late Kara Murad Pasha, who was now made envoy to forward the imperial letter of answer and gifts to Abbas II. Kose Ismail took these over on 9 January and headed out towards Iran shortly thereafter. He travelled to Isfahan 'with great pomp' along the Baghdad road, leading a staff of about 1,000, unusually large for a legation.[163]

In Isfahan, Kose Ismail Agha was lavishly lodged and feasted at the shah's behest throughout his stay. After a reception by the chief vizier, the shah met with the envoy at the Chehel-Sotun pavilion, and held a ceremony in Naqsh-i Jahan square with cannoneers, musketeers and archers lined up on all four sides and with elephants and lions being exhibited. The shah's feast followed the audience and the handover of the gifts, amidst which Abbas II asked after Mehmed IV's health. Later, the head of the Royal Guard and the head of the Royal Squires[164] hosted Kose Ismail at separate feasts, the protocol of which the chief vizier set down beforehand for these dignitaries. When the envoy, who suffered from syphilis, became bedridden, the shah sent his private physician Savcı Muhammad Sharif to take care of his guest, and the physician succeeded in having the envoy agha get up from his sickbed. At all of these instances, bestowals of gifts and robes of honour accompanied the events.[165]

Such lavish receptions are unlikely to have only been motivated by the Safavids' taste for ceremonial organisation. Kose Ismail Agha's staff amounted to about 1,000 persons, far larger than usual for an Ottoman legation to Iran, and the Safavids were seemingly at pains not to be upstaged by this *coup de théâtre*. After the reception, feast, gift-giving and the handover of the shah's letter of answer at the farewell audience, the envoy was given permission to leave. His illness soon overcame him though, and on his way back he died in Baghdad (1657).[166]

In his counter answer,[167] Abbas II confirmed receipt of the 'cohesion-titled epistle, namely the anthology of the spring-land of unity [and] the selection of the collection of friendship' of Mehmed IV 'his most sublime Majesty, the embroidery of the pillow of world-keeping, embellisher of the superb thrones of sultanate and khaqanship, sultan of the Two Lands and khaqan of the Two Seas, the second Alexander the Great, servant of the Illustrious Sancta'[168] via Kose Ismail Agha the 'linguist of the signs of affinity, cup-bearer of the noblest wine of unity-of-hearts and union'. Formalities aside, the shah also informed the padishah of the death of (Shah-Jahan) the 'viceroy of India' (only later would the Safavids learn that this news was wrong) and of the Safavid military help to Prince Muradbakhsh's quest for the Mughal throne.

From this letter we also learn that upon hearing of Kose Ismail becoming too ill to go on with his journey, when he was likely in Baghdad, Abbas had sent his aide-de-camp Muhammadi-xan Beyg to ask after the envoy agha's health. While the aide-de-camp was on his way, the then-uncertain news of the fight for the Indian throne had spread, because of which the shah halted his aide-de-camp's mission. After sending help for the Safavid-friendly prince Muradbakhsh, the shah had made Muhammadi-xan Beyg go ahead to the 'Superb Sanctuary'.[169] That the shah highlights that his aide-de-camp had travelled light so as to not be a burden to the ill envoy was likely an excuse for the plainness of this low-profile provincial mission, which was now bound for the imperial court. Muhammadi-xan Beyg must have travelled first to Baghdad and then, after Kose Ismail's death, to the Ottoman capital as diplomatic herald to deliver the shah's letter, whose original bearer had just died.

In his earlier letter of 1656, forwarded by ambassador Kalb-Ali Silsüpür-Afşar, Abbas II tried to ensure that the Basran upheaval had not harmed relations; his word choices leave no room for doubt. He must have guessed that his belittlement of the Mughals would not bother the Sublime Porte. By sending Indian 'souvenirs', on the other hand, he meant to show off Iran's might, as these items had come into the shah's grasp by way of military victory. In the later letter of 1657 entrusted to Kose Ismail Agha, Abbas II went even further in highlighting the soundness of the Peace of Zuhab, along with upholding the hierarchical superiority of the padishah by referencing Mehmed IV repeatedly and openly as the supreme-monarch, thus paying lip service to the Ottomans' claimed universal mandate. The Constantinople–Isfahan diplomatic traffic of 1656–7 smoothed over the unwelcome consequences of the first Basran affair before they could threaten the peace.

Shortly after Kose Ismail Agha's departure, some tribesmen from the Kurdish principality[170] of Ardalan came to Isfahan and told Abbas II that Suleiman Xan, the ruler of Ardalan, was planning to defect to the Ottoman side and take with him the wealth he had piled up throughout his rule; the tribesmen, however, had thus far been able to hinder the start of this plot. The shah confirmed this news through Sheikh-Ali Xan Zangana, in all likelihood still the governor of Kirmanshah, and then unseated Suleiman Xan of Ardalan, banishing him to Mashhad. Ardalan's subgovernorships were dealt out to several officials, with Suleiman's sons and brothers among them.[171] That the shah did not put to death Suleiman of Ardalan but instead banished him to the provincial metropolis farthest removed from the Ottoman Empire hints that the shah may have had doubts about the authenticity of the story. He needed to do away with the risk of defection while still leaving room for a later revocation of the sentence. He thus forestalled a potential crisis with the Ottomans, but at the risk of having lost a loyal vassal if the claims were untrue.

In 1657, both the Tigris and the Euphrates burst their banks. Water filled Baghdad's moat, overran the bulwark, brought down the Tower of Conquest near the White Gate, and wrecked 300 ells of the walls around it. The fortress's eastern side overlooking Iran thus became exposed. Governor Haseki Mehmed Pasha oversaw the restoration of the fortifications. The imperial court called up the governors of Diyarbekr, Shahrizor and Mosul to stand guard in the region with their feudal troopers so long as the flood damage rendered the fortress of Baghdad vulnerable.[172] There was no prospect of an onslaught from Iran though, but as with other measures of defence in place since the Peace of Zuhab, the garrison and military works at Baghdad were kept up as if war might break out with Iran at any time.

In the meantime, Köprülü Mehmed Pasha (as commander-in-chief) restored political order and military discipline with harsh methods. He broke the blockade at the Dardanelles, fought off the Venetian fleet on the Aegean, and took back Tenedos, following which Grand Admiral Topal Mehmed Pasha recovered Lemnos. By 1657, the Turks thus regained the upper hand in the Cretan War.[173] In 1658, Hungary claimed Constantinople's main attention. The unruly Ottoman vassal ruler[174] of Transylvania, George II Rakoczi, had defied the Sublime Porte's will and entered the Northern War (1655–60) as a Swedish ally to win the Polish throne. The princes[175] of Wallachia and Moldavia (autonomous governments whose prince-governors were appointed and replaced by the imperial court) had also aligned themselves with their Transylvanian neighbour, while the Turks had fielded the Crimean troops as Polish allies against the Swedish bloc. In 1657, Rakoczi had been beaten and forced into a peace with Poland, after which Khan Mehmed IV Giray's troops had captured almost the whole Transylvanian army. Again, by means of the Crimeans, the Porte had unseated the rebel princes of Wallachia (Constantine Beg II Sherban) and Moldavia (George Beg II Stefan), both of whom then sought shelter with Rakoczi. To crush the insubordination at its source, Köprülü started an imperial campaign into Transylvania.[176]

As the commander-in-chief was campaigning in Transylvania in 1658, Abaza Hasan Pasha, a general from Ibshir Mustafa's team, rose up and called for Köprülü's overthrow. The Household Cavalry, scared by Köprülü's disciplinarian ways, gathered around Abaza Hasan, and a number of governor pashas soon joined the uprising. Moving through Anatolia between Bursa and Iconium, the rebels demanded that Köprülü be put to death. To crush the uprising, the imperial court placed the loyal officials and troops in Anatolia under the command of none other than Kara Murtaza Pasha, but the 30,000-strong rebel army beat the loyalist auxiliaries. This prompted Köprülü to leave the Imperial Army in Transylvania and return to deal with the situation himself. In the end, however, Kara Murtaza made many of the rebels forsake the uprising, and called the remainder to reconciliatory talks while wintering in Aleppo. There, on 16 February 1659, he put to death each and every leader of the uprising.[177] Many mercenaries from among Abaza Hasan's followers fled to Iran, but as the Iranians did not shelter them, they scattered back into Ottoman lands, some ending up getting killed and some going into hiding.[178] One of the mercenaries who had fought in Abaza Hasan's rebel army, had run away to Iran, and afterwards reentered Ottoman service, was Bayburtlu Katırcı Kara Ibrahim,[179] future grand vizier in 1683–5.

While the Ottomans were tied up throughout 1658 in Hungary, in the Mediterranean and across Anatolia, the Shahdom was facing fresh difficulties of its own. The problem this time was the Safavid-vassal Surkhay II Shamkhal of Dagestan, who had become worryingly self-assertive, particularly following his success in driving out the Russians from the northern edges of his land. Abbas II undertook to build a stronghold near Tarku, Dagestan's capital, and another one near Tuzluka, so as to thwart his vassal's ever-growing sway. But Surkhay Shamkhal gathered the grandees of the land, who together decided not only to hinder the construction but also to cast out the Safavids from Dagestan. The Shahdom then brought troops from eastern Georgia, against which the Dagestanis fielded their own fighters, and the two armies met near Velikent. Although the Dagestanis had to pull back to the mountains before the better-equipped troops of the shah, Abbas II called off the campaign with an eye to the unrest in eastern Georgia and the rough terrain of Dagestan. Surkhay II Shamkhal would rule his principality without answering to an overlord until his death ten years later.[180]

Roughly from 1578 to 1632, Dagestan had been an Ottoman vassal, and it had been thrice acknowledged as such by the Safavids in peace agreements, though the Ottomans could not always exercise their overlordship.[181] Now, Dagestan was an independent principality, as the Shamkhalate freed itself from tribute to the Safavids. This overthrow laid

1644–1660: Armenia and Azerbaijan

the groundwork for the Shamkhalate's upcoming re-acknowledgement of the Ottomans as overlord (as to be seen below). Dagestan's sidling up to the Empire would in the end prove to be a matter of life and death for the Safavid monarchy in a way that none of the sides could foresee.

Around the same time, in 1658–9, a threat to the status quo between the Ottoman- and Safavid-tributary halves of Georgia presented itself: Shahnavaz Xan (Vakhtang V Bagration) of Kartli wanted to weld together the fragments of Georgia, including those under Ottoman overlordship, under himself as king by capturing them and installing his sons as prince-governors. Laying a claim to the throne of Imereti, whose rulers hailed from the same Bagrationi dynasty, and to Guria by means of occupation, he began to stage his plans with a 15,000-strong legion. With the strength that would stem from holding sway over the whole of Georgia, he hoped to get rid of Ottoman and Safavid overlordships for good. Atabegli Rustam Pasha Jaqeli, the hereditary governor of Childir, himself of Georgian stock, reported Vakhtang V Bagration (Shahnavaz)'s designs to the Sublime Porte in 1659 and immediately broke into Imereti at the head of his troops to forestall an annexation. However, as Vakhtang V's first strike made the pasha of Childir return empty-handed, he could only report what had come to pass to the imperial court.[182]

The imperial court would not to be able to focus on the unrest across the buffer zone of Georgia between the Empire and Iran until 1662–3, when it would order the governors of Erzurum (Pamuk Mustafa Pasha as commander-general)[183], Kars (Seyyid Yusuf Pasha) and Childir (Atabegli Rustam Pasha Jaqeli) to take the field 'to capture the realm and discipline the Georgians'. The margraves of Ottoman Georgia and Kurdistan were also to help them. This Ottoman army of 40,000 entered Imereti and drove out Archil Bagration, Vakhtang Shahnavaz's son, from the realm.[184] However, a hot pursuit and a punitive campaign into the Safavid-tributary Georgia did not materialise owing to the Empire's unwillingness to trigger a war with Iran while already fighting two wars at the same time, against the Habsburgs in western Hungary and against the Venetian alliance on the Mediterranean.[185] Seizing the opportunity, Archil soon came back to Imereti. Atabegli Arslan Mehmed Pasha Jaqeli, the new governor of Childir, sent letters to the regnant[186] and the notables of Imereti, threatening to overrun the realm if they disobeyed. Archil had the notables reply to the pasha of Childir that nothing could happen in Imereti without the padishah's consent. The imperial court did not acknowledge Archil as regnant, and in turn Archil did not comply with the summons from Constantinople, going instead back to his father's Safavid-vassal realm of Kartli. Because of his reckless behaviour not only in Ottoman but also in

Safavid Georgia, the shah too banished him from his dominions, whereupon Archil took shelter in Russia.[187]

Neither Dagestan's independence in 1658 nor the unrest in Georgia that lasted roughly from 1658 to 1663 begot Ottoman–Safavid strife. The two parties did not attempt to gain territory to the detriment of the other and at the expense of the peace. Constantinople and Isfahan deemed such entanglements in Caucasia a rivalry between and within Georgian dynasties, which should not be allowed to upset Ottoman–Safavid friendship. Thus, neither side interfered in what it acknowledged as the other's territory. As was also the upshot of the Basran upheavals throughout the 1650s, the two states held their status quo too dear to leave it to the mercy of vassal princes.

Notes

1. Nazmizade, *Gülşen-i Hulefâ*, 236.
2. BOA, *Mühimme d.* 89, ent. 14.
3. BOA, *Mühimme d.* 90, ent. 402; Katib Çelebi, *Fezleke*, 992; Evliya Çelebi, *Seyahatname*, 4/128: a severe earthquake wrecked sections of the fortress of Van. Upon the governor's presenting the issue, in 1645–6, the imperial court once again commissioned the Kurdish margraves and certain fiefdoms to rebuild those parts of the fortress. The council chamber in the governor's residence should also have been rebuilt shortly before these repairs. In the same year, the governor of Kars presented to the court a report that there were ruined sections in the keep and in the second-line walls of the fortress of Kars. The decree issued after this report underscored the utmost importance of the good upkeep of the fortress and commissioned the governor to restore it.
4. One such report is to be seen in Topkapı, *Evrak*, 693/33, which reached the grand vizierate on 3 November 1643.
5. A corsair onslaught by the (Hospitaller) Maltese Knights upon an unarmed Ottoman galleon carrying the new judge of Mecca, the deposed chief-eunuch, and the latter's riches, along with 600 other pilgrims, triggered the chain of events that led to the outbreak of the war. After the onset, the Maltese used the island of Crete, Venetian territory, as safe haven in a fait accompli. For details on the outbreak of the Cretan War and the Ottoman conquest of Chania in the same year, see Kenneth M. Setton, *Venice, Austria, and the Turks in the Seventeenth Century* (Philadelphia: The American Philosophical Society, 1991), 110–27, and Uzunçarşılı, *Osmanlı Târihi* vol. 3/1, 216–18.
6. Giorgio Rota, 'Safavid Persia and its Diplomatic Relations with Venice', in *Iran and the World in the Safavid Age*, eds Willem Floor and Edmung Herzig (London: I. B. Tauris, 2012), 151.

7. Tavernier, *Seyahatnâmesi*, 212–21; Jan Reychman and Ananiasz Zajaczkowski, *Handbook of Ottoman-Turkish Diplomatics*, rev. and trans. Andrew S. Ehrenkreutz (The Hague: Mouton, 1968), 181; Dariusz Kołodziejczyk (ed.), *The Relations of the Polish–Lithuanian Commonwealth with Safavid Iran and the Catholicosate of Etcgmiadzin* (Warsaw: Archiwum Glowne Akt Dawnych, 2017), 88; Rota, 'Safavid Persia and its Diplomatic Relations with Venice', 151. Also see Chardin's narration of a Jesuit father, who, in his capacity as the representative of the Pope, the King of France, and several other Christian-European princes, proposed a joint invasion of the eastern Ottoman domains to Abbas II in 1645. Jean Chardin, *Voyages du Chevalier Chardin en Perse, et autres lieux de l'Orient* vol. 8 (Paris: le Normant, Imprimeur-Libraire, 1811), 106–7.
8. Lajos Fekete (ed.), *Einführung in die persische Paläographie: 101 Dokumente*, pub. György Hazai (Budapest: Akademiai Kiado, 1977), 525–7, tables 222–3; Iraj Afshar (ed.), 'Du Farmân-i Safavî Marbût ba Ravâbit-i Îrân u Lahistân', *Râh-namây-i Kitâb* 5 (1962): 581–5. Iraj Afshar's interpretation that Abbas II accepted the proposal to wage war against the Empire and that this did not materialise only due to Wladyslaw IV's death in 1648 is, as expected, backed up neither by the course of events which followed nor by the document he publishes in this article.
9. Setton, *Venice, Austria, and the Turks*, 139–41; Uzunçarşılı, *Osmanlı Târihi* vol. 3/1, 219–20.
10. *Nârîn-qulle*.
11. Mücteba İlgürel, 'Hüseyin Paşa, Deli', in *Türk Diyânet Vakfı İslam Ansiklopedisi* 19 (1999): 4–6.
12. Nazmizade, *Gülşen-i Hulefâ*, entry 'Hukûmet-i el-Vezîr Deli Hüseyin Paşa'.
13. Setton, *Venice, Austria, and the Turks*, 147–50; Uzunçarşılı, *Osmanlı Târihi* vol. 3/1, 220.
14. Evliya Çelebi, *Seyahatname*, 2/157.
15. Evliya Çelebi, *Seyahatname*, 2/185, 189; Mehmed Süreyyâ, *Sicill-i Osmânî* vol. 4 (Istanbul: Târih Vakfı Yurt Yayınları, 1996), 168 (ent. 'Mehmed Paşa (Defterdarzâde)'). Nevesinli Salih Pasha had succeeded Sultanzâde Civankapıcıbaşı Mehmed Pasha in office (1645). Uzunçarşılı, *Osmanlı Târihi* vol. 3/1, 223.
16. Ottoman terminology: *sardâr*, or, seldom and in compound with the former designation, *sipahsâlâr*, a wartime office denoting the supreme command of the Empire's military and paramilitary forces in a given war in the absence of the padishah and the grand vizier on the front. A vizier-marshal had the authority to give out decrees and make appointments (subject to the grand vizier's approval only after the end of the campaign) in the name of the padishah. For this, he was entrusted with a specific number of blank papers with the padishah's monogram drawn on them, enabling him to command

through imperial decrees. If he ran out of monogrammed papers, he also had the authorisation to draw the padishah's monogram on the decrees he issued on the front. In other words, the marshal had grand vizierial powers within the region of his activity. For other extraordinary powers delegated to a marshal, see Uzunçarşılı, *Merkez ve Bahriye Teşkilatı*, 192–4; *Abdurrahman Abdi Paşa Kanunnâmesi*, 24. The office that approximately overlapped this in Safavid Iran was that of the *sipahsâlâr*.

17. *dastûr-i mukarram*, a title reserved for viziers. M. Kütükoğlu, *Osmanlı Belgelerinin Dili*, 102.
18. *tuğra*.
19. Evliya Çelebi, *Seyahatname*, 2/87.
20. 'Acem serhaddinde ne işlerlerse işlesinler deyü istimâletler verilip'.
21. 'göreyim seni. Acem serhaddinde nice gazâlar edersin'. Evliya Çelebi, *Seyahatname*, 2/188.
22. *mutasallim*.
23. Evliya Çelebi, *Seyahatname*, 2/88. Scutari (Üsküdar) is the town overlooking Constantinople across the Bosphorus, the first way-stop eastwards from the capital.
24. Evliya Çelebi, *Seyahatname*, 2/103.
25. A large, rich and strategic province, Erzurum, like Baghdad, was one of the centres of weight in the Ottoman–Safavid borderland. Over the course of the last Iranian war, namely since the 1620s, the imperial court had increased the number of Household troops stationed there, furnished it with strong artillery, and stocked it with supplies. The square-shaped fortress was large and made of stone. Twofold walls and a moat surrounded the well-fortified keep. As of 1646, the artillery build-up was heavy, above all at the side overlooking Iran. Evliya Çelebi, *Seyahatname*, 2/105–6, 108. It was also a site of second-rate gunpowder production since the sixteenth century, and on his Iranian campaign (1635), Murad IV had set up another small foundry to cast siege and fortress guns. Aside from the Household soldiers garrisoning the fortress, the province maintained a sizable cavalry reserve. Gábor Ágoston, *Guns for the Sultan: Military Power and Weapons Industry in the Ottoman Empire* (Cambridge: Cambridge University Press, 2009), 128; Evliya Çelebi, *Seyahatname*, 2/104, 107.
26. By 1646, the single-walled stronghold of Erivan looked sound in its own right, if not in comparison to its Ottoman counterpart of Erzurum. It was encircled in part with moat and in part with crenellation, manned by royal troops, and well-furnished with artillery (left behind by the Ottoman occupation) and ammunition. The governor-general had his own battalion besides the feudals. Erivan's available peacetime military numbered slightly less than that of Erzurum. (Evliya Çelebi, *Seyahatname*, 2/107,143.) A beholder who had toured the whole Ottoman Empire and the Iranian west assessed that if the Ottomans would beleaguer Erivan, it could not withstand for longer than seven days. The blows dealt by artillery fire

1644–1660: Armenia and Azerbaijan

during Murad IV's siege of 1635 were still visible on the bulwarks. (Evliya Çelebi, *Seyahatname*, 2/143.) The walls and towers themselves looked rather irregular as the stronghold lay on a steep cliff, but in return this made its conquest harder. Lacking bastions and battlements, as defence the walls only afforded the artillery set on their terraces. The Keçiqale redoubt, on a hill 1,000-feet to the north, also backed up the stronghold. (Chardin, *Seyahatname*, 257–8.)

27. Matthee, *Persia in Crisis*, 119.
28. Willem Floor, *The Persian Gulf: A Political and Economic History of Five Port Cities 1500–1730* (Washington, DC: Mage Publishers, 2006), 553.
29. Located across the mountains to the south of River Aras. Evliya Çelebi, *Seyahatname*, 2/111.
30. Although Evliya Çelebi's statement that the gathered army numbered 76,000 is in all likelihood an exaggeration, it still hints at the extraordinarily large size of this force. Evliya Çelebi, *Seyahatname*, 2/111. Whenever this book draws on *Seyahatname* as a source, Evliya Çelebi's often-exaggerated figures are ignored for their numeric value and seldom used for their comparative worth against other estimations likewise made by Evliya Çelebi.
31. Evliya Çelebi, *Seyahatname*, 2/114–15.
32. A later document – whose dating 31 December 1699 by the archivist has seemingly no basis – also speaks of two Ottoman agents, sent by a border governor who himself had been commissioned to do so by a vizier, scouting Maku, which they entered and found manned by Safavid soldiers, who said that they were there at the shah's behest to keep the stronghold safe from bandits.
33. According to Evliya Çelebi's habitually exaggerated figures, 2,000. See below.
34. BOA, *Ali Emiri – Mehmed IV*, 31/3499: petition to the grand vizierate by Ali Pasha the governor of Kars, for the appointment in perpetuity as [*kol*] *ağa*[*sı*] of the Magazberd stronghold, subordinated to the fortress of Kars, of Mustafa, whose father Gazi Mehmed had fought in the campaign to recapture the stronghold from the Safavids and then had held the post of [*kol*]*ağa*[*sı*] until his death. The grand vizier gave his edict for the conferral on 26 May 1680. The marginal note fetched on 19 May 1680 from the registry shows that after Gazi Mehmed's death, his son Mustafa had already held this post once: the date of this earlier appointment was 5 June 1679.
35. BOA, *İbnülemin – Tevcihat*, 9/1077: petition to the grand vizierate by Mustafa the [*kol*]*ağa*[*sı*] of Magazberd, for the deposition of Mustafa the steward of the Enlistees' (the *Gönüllüs*') company owing to his not getting on well with the soldiers, and the appointment in his stead of Ahmed, a veteran of the company. The grand vizier commanded the conferral on 21 September 1681. Mustafa the company-steward had been appointed to this post on 23 November 1680, as shown by a registry record fetched on 8 November 1680. BOA, *Ali Emiri – Ahmed III*, 47/4722: petition

to the imperial court by Mehmed the [kol]ağa[sı] of the Enlistees of the Magazberd stronghold, for the deposition of Ismail, who was the steward of the company with a pay of twenty aspers daily, on the grounds that he did not get on well with his fellow soldiers and embezzled from the Local Servicemen's wages, and for the appointment in his stead of another Ismail, a veteran of the corps. The imperial chancellery verified the authenticity of Mehmed's seal on 31 August 1710, the treasury registry fetched the register records of the first Ismail's appointment as the steward of the Enlistee company of the stronghold of Magazberd with twenty aspers daily again on 31 August 1710, and the grand vizier gave the edict for the conferral, with the condition that the claims had to be true, on 17 September 1710.

36. BOA, *Ali Emiri – Mehmed IV*, 38/4314: petition to the imperial court by Abdullah Pasha the governor of Kars, for the appointment, with an imperial decree, of Suleiman, from the Enlistees at Magazberd, as sergeant (*çavuş*) of the company, instead of Khalil, the former sergeant, who had left the stronghold and settled elsewhere. The grand vizier gave his edict for the conferral on 9 June 1675. The marginal note from the registry shows that Khalil had been appointed as sergeant of the Enlistees' company at Magazberd on 6 May 1670, upon the death of his father Qasim and the presentation by Hasan Pasha, the governor of Kars.

37. BOA, *Ali Emiri – Mehmed IV*, 7/723: petition to the grand vizierate by Abubakr, a veteran of the Magazberd corps and a chancellery professional, for his (re-)employment at the secretaryship (*kitâbat*) of the corps at the stronghold of Magazberd, worked up by the grand vizierate on 22 April 1678. Marginal remarks by the registry show that Abubakr had formerly been appointed as the secretary of the corps at Magazberd on 9 June 1671; however, his post had later been given to Mustafa upon presentation by Abdullah the [kol]ağa[sı] of the corps, on 15 May 1676, on the grounds that Abubakr had settled elsewhere and left the stronghold.

38. BOA, *Ali Emiri – Mustafa II*, 46/4582: annotation on 20 September 1700 of an earlier record retrieval on 8 August 1700, that an imperial decree had been written for the employment of Ismail, a veteran of that frontier, with the pay-mastership of the Local Enlistees of the stronghold of Magazberd, upon presentation by Mustafa the [kol]ağa[sı] of the Enlistees.

39. *il*.
40. *karındaşımız*.
41. Evliya Çelebi, *Seyahatname*, 2/115–16.
42. It was also amidst Prevezeli Defterdaroğlu Mehmed Pasha's term at Erzurum that an Iranian emissary named Tokmak Ali came bearing gifts from the governor-general of Çukursaʾd at Erivan. After formalities, emissary Tokmak unsheathed his gilded sword before the marshal and set about praising it. The marshal thereupon spoke to his subordinate Gurji Çalık Deli Dilaver Pasha, who was of Georgian stock from Imereti, a former slave of Kemankeş Kara Mustafa, now subordinated to the marshal and

1644–1660: Armenia and Azerbaijan

well-known for his recklessness and skill at wielding weapons in combat: 'my brother Pasha, can you recognize a good sword', which Deli Dilaver answered: 'a good sword is that which teeth cannot hold onto, let me see this sword'. Then he allegedly crunched Tokmak's sword with his teeth, and says: 'turns out this is nothing', putting it back to the middle of their friendly gathering (. . . 'Paşa karındaşım! Kılıcın yahşisinden tanır mısın?' dedi. Paşa dahi 'kılıcın iyisi diş tutmayandır, göreyim şu kılıcı' dedikte kılıcı paşanın eline verdiklerinde heman kılıcı dişiyle kütür kütür kırıp 'şey değil imiş' deyü . . .). Evliya Çelebi, *Seyahatname*, 2/189. Even after allowing for Evliya Çelebi's well-known leaning towards exaggeration, this story still bears witness to the almost non-stop border diplomacy between neighbouring governors-general of the Ottomans and the Safavids.

43. *Sicill-i Osmânî* I, 212, entry: 'Ahmed Paşa (Hezârpâre)'.
44. Katib Çelebi, *Fezleke*, 1016–17; Nazmizade, *Gülşen-i Hulefâ*, 240; *Tarih-i Naima*, 1114; Ġurabzade Ahmed b. Abdullah Baghdadi, ʿUyûn Akhbâr al-Aʾyân, from the British Library, MS 23309, 268b–269a.
45. *Mîrâkhûr-ı sânî*.
46. Katib Çelebi, *Fezleke*, 1084; *Tarih-i Naima*, 1303–5; Evliya Çelebi, *Seyahatname*, 4/173; Ġurabzade, ʿUyûn Akhbâr, 269a.
47. A tributary of the River Tigris.
48. Nazmizade, *Gülşen-i Hulefâ*, 241; Katib Çelebi, *Fezleke*, 1017; *Tarih-i Naima*, 1115; Ġurabzade, ʿUyûn Akhbâr, 269a. Kara Musa Pasha's persecution of his predecessor's co-factionalists in Baghdad was an extension of the new grand vizier Tavşantaşlı Ahmed Pasha's empire-wide persecution of his own predecessor Nevesinli Salih Pasha's faction. Tavşantaşlı Ahmed was a long-time enemy of Nevesinli, and upon the latter's elimination, he set about rooting out the faction of statesmen associated with the former grand vizier. Ibrahim Pasha was among Nevesinli's closest co-factionalists. In the midst of the Baghdad turmoil, after Nevesinli Salih Pasha's execution, his brother and former governor of Buda, Nevesinli Murtaza Pasha, was first lured with a feigned appointment to Baghdad. However, the concealed decree ordering that he be put to death reached Diyarbekr before him, and was fulfilled. Nevesinli Salih's steward Zulfiqar Agha's estate was confiscated too. Again in 1648, Prevezeli Defterdaroğlu Mehmed Pasha, who was from the same household as Nevesinli Salih, was transferred to the province of Kars as part of the intrigue to execute him. To save his life, he joined insubordinate Varvar Ahmed Pasha's movement. Those members of Nevesinli Salih's faction and household who could flee persecution regrouped at Prevezeli's household. *Tarih-i Naima*,1128; Katib Çelebi, *Fezleke*, 1017, 1032. Andersen and Iversen, *Reise-Beschreibungen*, 156: the subgovernor who 'was dispelled by the Turks' from 'Sangiar' and reached the shah's encampment on 25 December 1648 during the Kandahar campaign must have been one of these exiles. He petitioned through the chief vizier for the right to dwell in Iran, and the shah granted his request.

49. Kazvini-Isfahani, *Khuld-i Barîn*, 454; *Târîkh-i Mullâ Kamâl*, 106; *Tarih-i Naima*, 1144–6.
50. *başdefterdâr*, or *defterdâr-i şıqq-i evvel*, or *Rumeli defterdârı*.
51. *Tarih-i Naima*, 1144–6; Uzunçarşılı, *Osmanlı Târihi* vol. 3/1, 231–3.
52. *bostancı*.
53. Kazvini-Isfahani, *Khuld-i Barîn*, 454; *Târîkh-i Mullâ Kamâl*, 106. A follow-up emissary from Sultan Ibrahim Khan reached Shah Abbas II at Mashhad in late September/early October 1648, sent to make sure that if the first mission could not make it to the shah, this second one would: *Târîkh-i Mullâ Kamâl*, 107.
54. *Târîkh-i Mullâ Kamâl*, 106; Walî-kulu Shamlu, *Qisasuʾl-Khâqânî*, 313; Kazvini-Isfahani, *Khuld-i Barîn*, 454. Kazvini-Isfahani remarks that Ibrahim had sent the letter to make sure that the gathered Iranian army would not target the Empire's territory, and that the order placement for elephants was an excuse to create an occasion for correspondence: Kazvini, *ʿAbbâsnâma*, 97. In light of available sources and facts, Kazvini's claim seems to have been fabricated to gladden his benefactor.
55. Naimur Rahman Farooqi, 'Mughal-Ottoman Relations: A Study of Political and Diplomatic Relations between Mughal India and the Ottoman Empire, 1556–1748' (PhD diss. University of Wisconsin-Madison, 1986), 57–8, 90; Matthee, *Persia in Crisis*, 124.
56. Kazvini-Isfahani, *Khuld-i Barîn*, 305–6.
57. By inference from his name, he must have been the son of Yâdigâr ʿAli Soltân Burun Qâsim, the former head of Mazandaran (musketeers) and thrice Safavid wartime ambassador to the Ottoman Empire in 1615–17, 1618 and 1619. See Küpeli, *Osmanlı-Safevi Münâsebetleri*, 117, 119, 122.
58. *Tarih-i Naima*, 1146; Nazmizade, *Gülşen-i Hulefâ*, 241–2; Karaçelebizade, *Ravzatüʾl-Ebrâr Zeyli*, 26; Kazvini, *ʿAbbâsnâma*, 98.
59. At times through puppet grand viziers and at times by donning this top office themselves, the 'Agha-threesome' would hold sway in Constantinople hand-in-hand with and under the regency of Empress-mother Mâhpaykar Kösem until 1651. For more details, see Halil İnalcık, *Devlet-i Aliyye II – Tagayyür ve Fesad (1603–1656)* (Istanbul: Türkiye İş Bankası Kültür Yayınları, 2014), 251–90; Uzunçarşılı, *Osmanlı Târihi* vol. 3/1, 223–59. For a more recent treatment of Kösem's political weight, see Murat Kocaaslan, *Kösem Sultan. Hayâtı, Vakıfları, Hayır İşleri ve Üsküdarʾdaki Külliyesi* (Istanbul: Okur Kitaplığı, 2014), 25–70.
60. Hanafî Mehmed Efendi first lectured in the seminaries in Istanbul and Adrianople and, transitioning to the judiciary afterwards, became the judge of Medina (1634), Egypt (1641–2), and Adrianople (1646–7) respectively, before moving on to become the chief-justice of Ottoman Asia (1648). In the following decade, he would rise first to the chief-justiceship of Ottoman Europe and in the end become the grand-mufti of the Empire. Mehmet

İpşirli, 'Hanefi Mehmed Efendi', *Türk Diyanet Vakfı İslam Ansiklopedisi* XV (1997): 554.
61. The Safavid troops would capture the city in 1649. Roemer, 'The Safavid Period', 299; Matthee, *Persia in Crisis*, 45, 123–4; Karaçelebi-zade, *Ravzatüʾl-Ebrar Zeyli*, 21. Successive Mughal sieges would keep the Iranian military busy defending this acquisition.
62. J. Audrey Burton, 'Relations between the Khanate of Bukhara and Ottoman Turkey, 1558–1702', *International Journal of Turkish Studies* 5, no. 1–2 (Winter 1990–1), 99–100.
63. "ʿâlî-hazrat, . . . zîbanda-i takht-i dâvarî, . . . Khusrav-i mulk-i Ajam'.
64. 'Özbek hânı . . . saltanat-iyâb Nadr Muhammad'.
65. *Majmûʿa-i Makâtîb*, ff. 68b–70a; *Asnâd u Mukâtabât 1038–1105*, 203–5. For the Porte's attempt to coordinate with India in order to bring an end to the Bukharan civil war, see Farooqi, 'Mughal-Ottoman Relations', 56–7.
66. Abdi Paşa, *Vekâyi-nâme*, 20; Karaçelebi-zade, *Ravzatüʾl-Ebrar Zeyli*, 26; *Tarih-i Vecihi*, f. 44a. Mehemmedqulu Beyg Burun-Qâsimoğlu's departure might have been held up until as late as January 1650. Karaçelebi-zade, *Ravzatüʾl-Ebrar Zeyli*, 31.
67. Uzunçarşılı, *Osmanlı Târihi* vol. 3/1, 327–38.
68. İnalcık, *Devlet-i Aliyye II*, 321.
69. Katib Çelebi, *Fezleke*, 1083; *Tarih-i Naima*, 1289, 1303; Arakʾel, *History*, 385.
70. By the 1650s, following the 1642 and 1646 repairs (see above), the fortress of Van stood as one of the Empire's investment spots along the borderland overlooking Iran. The twofold outer walls of stone surrounded the city and the fortress from three directions, while the fourth was naturally shielded by a hill of giant rocks on which the keep stood. A lower, crenellated bulwark and the moat in turn surrounded the outer wall: Orhan Kılıç, *XVI. ve XVII. Yüzyıllarda Van (1548–1648)* (Van: Van Belediye Başkanlığı Kültür ve Sosyal İşler Müdürlüğü, 1997), 204–5. The rocky hill contained hundreds of caves, which were used for storing cannonballs, gunpowder, various artillery equipment, muskets and musket-parts, grenades, melee weapons, bows and arrows, crossbows, trebuchets, and so on, along with a variety of long-lasting provisions. The artillery set atop the fortifications guarded the fortress against enemies approaching from water and land. For the scenario that the enemy might come to the foot of the hill, holes had been opened in many of the caves, to be used like artillery booths in galleons. Another floor of caves was furnished with stone-firing cannons. Of course, the walls, towers and bastions were also furnished with artillery in consideration of an enemy in trenches. All in all, the fortress was guarded with four layers of artillery sets with specific ranges and targets. The main fortified gate, the four-tier Waterfront Gate (*Yalı Kapısı*) overlooking the pier at Lake Van, stood at the western side of the fortress; the northern side had triple walls garrisoning the Locals. The southern frontage where the Middle Gate

(*Orta Kapı*) and the Stealthy Gate (*Uğrun Kapı*) were, as the best-shielded side thanks to the natural rock, did not have any walls, housing instead the governor, the Janissary commanding-officer, the castellan (*dizdâr*), and council officials, besides the barracks of the Household troops. From atop, a waterway provided the city with abundant fresh water even when beleaguered. The eastern side set against Iran, where the Tabriz Gate and the stronghold Kesikdeveboynu stood, had fivefold walls, was furnished with an extra concentration of artillery, and was watched over by the Local Service. Tunnels inside the rock connected its different sides, granting access between towers to back up bombarded positions amidst a siege. The keep was reserved only for the Household troops and declared an exclusive imperial military zone; the Locals dwelled within the fortress but outside the keep. The garrison constantly kept watch, including at night when disguised sergeants inspected the night duty. The fortress's internal warning mechanism that would trigger a full alert in the event of spotting the enemy was well exercised even sixteen years after the Peace of Zuhab: Evliya Çelebi, *Seyahatname*, 4/115–21. Evliya Çelebi gives the number of the Janissaries garrisoning Van during Melek Ahmed Pasha's term as 3,000 in six squadrons, commanded by Deli Abdi Agha. The Armourers numbered 1,000 in three companies, and the Cannoneers 1,000 in two companies. The Locals, composed of the right-flank (*sağ-kol*) under the command of Husrevpaşayeğeni Suleiman Bey, left-flank (*sol-kol*) under Demircioğlu, Sergeants (*çavuş*), Guards (*mustahfız*), Armourers (*cebeci*), Cannoneers (*topçu*), Bachelors (*ᶜazab*), and Garrisonmen (*hisâr eri*) made up the total figure of 6,000, with a further total of 6,000(!) stationed at the strongholds of Amık, Erciş, Adilcevaz, Ahlat, Tahtıvan and Vestan in the province. Half of this 12,000-strong(!) Local Servicemen force was to be fielded for offensive operations. To this total, Evliya's figures of 3,000(!) feudal troopers and further inflated numbers of fighters coming from the margravates of Hakkari, Mahmudi, Pinyaşi, and the fiefdom-principality of Bitlis should be added. Evliya compares the discipline and perfection of the military class in Van only to Kars in the east and to Egri, Buda and Bosnia in the west: Evliya Çelebi, *Seyahatname*, 4/122–6. Like in other key fortresses, the castellan, to whom the entire Local Service were subordinated, was chosen from among the Household troops serving in the garrison: see BOA, *İbnülemin – Askeriye*, 917 for the presentation to the Porte by Abdullah Pasha the governor of Van, processed on 10 July 1677.

71. He set out on 24 December 1649: Andersen and Iversen, *Reise-Beschreibungen*, 164–6. In Andersen's travelogue, the governor's name is given as Ibrahim, 167–9. However, if the dates he provides are correct, then the actual governor should have been Nogaypaşaoğlu Arslan Pasha. Ibrahim may have been the governor's steward, as suggested by the title of 'agha' used in Andersen's speech in Turkish: 'Ey büyük ağa, Allah-ı Teâlâ seni saklasın ve bir gününü min gün eylesin.' The German transla-

1644–1660: Armenia and Azerbaijan

tion ('Großer Herr/Gott bewahre dich/und mache dir einen Tag zu tausend Tage'), which Andersen himself provides, is accurate (166).
72. *haseki* (khâsse-gî) – corresponding more or less to the modern rank of colonel within the Janissary hierarchy, in which there were four.
73. *Tarih-i Naima*, 1289, 1258; M.
74. Topkapı, *Evrak*, z.4454 e.1 [d.696 g.17]. The chronicle entry in Nazmizade, *Gülşen-i Hulefâ*, 246–7 and this presentation contradict in their dating of exactly when the change of governorship, command of the Household corps, and judgeship of Baghdad took place within the year 1651.
75. Topkapı, *Evrak*, z.4590 e.1 [d.698 g.8].
76. Matthee, *Persia in Crisis*, 124.
77. Floor, *The Persian Gulf*, 554.
78. Willem Floor and Mohammad H. Faghfoory, *The First Dutch-Persian Commercial Conflict: The Attack of Qeshm Island, 1645* (Costa Mesa: Mazda Publishers, 2004), 183–4.
79. *hukûmat-mulkiyyat*.
80. Katib Çelebi, *Fezleke*, 1084; *Tarih-i Naima*, 1374.
81. İsmail Bülbül, 'Başlangıcından Rus Hakimiyetine kadar Kumuk Türkleri ve Tarku Şamhallığı' (PhD diss., University of Sakarya, 2011), 70.
82. Topkapı, *Evrak*, z.6039 e.1 [d.753 g.19]. This undated letter by Mustafa Pasha is misdated by the archivist to H 1073. However, given the context of 10,000 Iranian troops gathered in Huvayza and by the Kerha-Water, and that the only non-vizier governor of Mosul that passed away while in office during the governorate-general of a Mustafa Pasha at Baghdad – mentioned in the letter – took place in early 1652 as far as I could established (see *Tarih-i Naima*, 1384), this letter must have been written and sent immediately in the wake of the 1651 events.
83. Topkapı, *Evrak*, 693/40.
84. 'bir iki Kızılbaş'.
85. Topkapı, *Evrak*, 693/40.
86. Giorgio Rota, 'Caucasians in Safavid Service in the 17th Century', in *Caucasia between the Ottoman Empire and Iran, 1555–1914*, eds Raoul Motika and Michael Ursinus (Wiesbaden: Reichert Verlag, 2000), 107–20; Hirotake Maeda, 'On the Ethno-Social Background of Four Gholâm Families from Georgia in Safavid Iran', *Studia Iranica* 32, no. 2 (2003): 243–78; Willem Floor, *Safavid Government Institutions* (Costa Mesa: Mazda Publishers, 2001), 21, 209; Matthee, *Persia in Crisis*, 39.
87. 'iyâlatuhu ... Musa Pasha, ᶜâlî-hazrat'.
88. Topkapı, *Evrak*, 858/86.
89. Topkapı, *Evrak*, 693/40.
90. Topkapı, *Evrak*, 693/40; 858/86.
91. Topkapı, *Evrak*, d.878 g.39. For the lesser-princely (margravate) rank of the lords of İmâdiye, namely the title 'İmâdiye hâkimi janâb-ı amârat-maâb Abusaid Bey', see BOA, *Mühimme d.* 89, ent. 196 dated 9 Râ 1053.

92. '... gitmiş iken yine geri dönüp yerli yerine geldikleri ...'
93. Topkapı, *Evrak*, d.884 g.3.
94. Topkapı, *Evrak*, d.900 g.13.
95. Matthee, *Persia in Crisis*, 124.
96. Kazvini, *ᶜAbbâsnâma*, 161; Kazvini-Isfahani, *Khuld-i Barîn*, 511.
97. Nazmizade, *Gülşen-i Hulefâ*, 249; Fathullah b. ᶜAlwaan al-Kaᵓbi, *Zâd ul-Musâfir wa Luhnat ul-Muqîm wal-Hâdir* (Baghdad: Matbaᵓat ul-Maᵓârif, 1958), 19; *Tarih-i Naima*, 1626, Floor, *Persian Gulf*, 556–7.
98. Nazmizade, *Gülşen-i Hulefâ*, 249; *Tarih-i Naima*, 1626–7.
99. *buyrultu/farmân-i ᶜâlî*.
100. Jazâyir.
101. Nazmizade, *Gülşen-i Hulefâ*, 250; Rudi Matthee, 'Between Arabs, Turks and Iranians: The Town of Basra, 1600–1700.' *Bulletin of the School of Priental and African Studies, University of London* 69, no. 1 (2006): 65–6; Floor, *Persian Gulf*, 557.
102. Kazvini-Isfahani, *Khuld-i Barîn*, 531; Kazvini, *ᶜAbbâsnâma*, 178.
103. *Tarih-i Naima*, 1627–9; al-Kaᵓbi, *Zâd ul-Musâfir*, 20; Matthee, 'Basra', 66. Due to some inconsistencies, I do not follow the post-capture chronology in Floor's *Persian Gulf*, 559–60. Qabban, named after the weighhouse at its harbour, was a major customs spot for incoming and transit ships: Evliya Çelebi, *Seyahatname*, 4/309.
104. Kazvini, *ᶜAbbâsnâma*, 178–9; al-Kaᵓbi, *Zâd ul-Musâfir*, 20.
105. Nazmizade, *Gülşen-i Hulefâ*, 251–2; *Tarih-i Naima*, 1629; Kazvini-Isfahani, *Khuld-i Barîn*, 532; Matthee, 'Basra', 67; Floor, *Persian Gulf*, 561.
106. Nazmizade, *Gülşen-i Hulefâ*, 248, 252–4; al-Kaᵓbi, *Zâd ul-Musâfir*, 20; Matthee, 'Basra', 67. When Kara Murtaza Pasha's own battalion and the Locals reached the vicinity of Baghdad, they were so mired in mud because of having drunk from muddy ponds not to die of thirst in the desert that their circumstances inspired the following proverb: 'At the battlefield, I will turn your mouth into that of a Murtaza-follower [mahall-i harpte ağzını Murtazalı ağzına döndürürüm]': *Tarih-i Naima*, 1630.
107. 'uğruluk iki küçük tay ile iki dahi kır kısrak'.
108. Witnesses to Seydi Murad b. Mirza's former deeds were Karam Vays b. Shahwali, Adniya b. Shahhasan and Yaqub b. Vaysbeyg, all three from the camp of Kızılribat's subgovernor Haji 'Bey'. Witnesses to the hearing itself were Haji 'Beyg' the 'officer' of Kızılribat, Ali Beyg b. Ahmed, Ali b. Abdullah, Hasan Beyg b. Mehmed, and Sâfî the steward of Ali: Topkapı, *Evrak*, 1043/61.
109. Abdulhakîm, the judge of Kara-Ulus, contradicts himself as he first speaks of Haji Bey as the bannerlord (*sancakbeyi*) of Kızılribat in the main text, but then of Haji Beyg as the officer (*zâbit*) of Kızılribat, hinting at Kızılribat's being instead a township (*nâhiye*), in the signatures of the hearing's witnesses. As Evliya Çelebi remarks, Kızılribat must then have been a

1644–1660: Armenia and Azerbaijan

township. Its tax yield was made into a benefice (*khâss*) and allotted to the funding pool paying the salaries of Baghdad's Local Service. It lay within the banner of Zangâbâd. Evliya Çelebi, *Seyahatname*, 4/f. 329a.

110. 'hırsız oğlu hırsız'.
111. Topkapı, *Evrak*, 1043/61.
112. *yurtluk-ocaklık*. For more information on the dominions and fiefdom administrative units along the Ottoman eastern frontier, see Orhan Kılıç, 'Ocaklık', *Türk Diyânet Vakfı İslam Ansiklopedisi* 33 (2007): 317–18.
113. *hâkim*.
114. Mühürdar Hasan Ağa, *Cevahirü't-Tevarih*, 294; Evliya Çelebi, *Seyahatname*, 1/85, 4/302–5.
115. Böğürdelen was the frontmost point of Ottoman territory bordering the Safavids near Basra. Its name in Turkish means 'flank-piercer' (with flank to be understood here in the anatomical sense), thus alluding to the stronghold's location and function: Evliya Çelebi, *Seyahatname*, 4/312. It should not be confused with the other Ottoman Böğürdelen, also known as Sabac, in the Ottoman province of Bosnia and today's western Serbia.
116. M. Münir Aktepe, 'İpşir Mustafa Paşa', *Türk Diyanet Vakfı İslam Ansiklopedisi* 22 (2000): 375–6.
117. Evliya Çelebi, *Seyahatname*, 4/176; Abdülkadir Özcan, 'Kara Murad Paşa', in *Türkiye Diyânet Vakfı İslam Ansiklopedisi* 24 (2001): 363–5.
118. Evliya Çelebi, *Seyahatname*, 1/133–4.
119. Fındıklılı Mehmed, *Zeyl-i Fezleke*, 11.
120. Evliya Çelebi, *Seyahatname*, 1/134.
121. *Kapı*, composed of *sekban* (infantry) and *sarıca* (cavalry) companies. See İ. Metin Kunt, *Sancaktan Eyalete. 1550–1650 arasında Osmanlı Ümerâsı ve İl İdâresi* (Istanbul: Boğaziçi Üniversitesi Yayınları, 1978), 98–109, and Mehmet İpşirli, 'Kapı Halkı', in *Türkiye Diyânet Vakfı İslam Ansiklopedisi* 24 (2001): 343–4 for more information and further bibliography on pasha contingents.
122. Evliya Çelebi, *Seyahatname*, 4/109–12.
123. Evliya Çelebi, *Seyahatname*, 4/112–13.
124. *İçqale-kapısı qullesi*.
125. Evliya Çelebi, *Seyahatname*, 4/120–1.
126. Evliya Çelebi, *Seyahatname*, 4/132–75. For the full princely rank of the lords of Bitlis, namely the references to their *amârat* as well as *iyâlat*, and that *khan* was part of their given name rather than being the sovereign title *Khan* for the reigning *hâkim* or *beğ*, see BOA, *Name-i Humayun d.* 5, ent. 3; BOA, *Mühimme d.* 120, ent. 826.
127. Evliya Çelebi, *Seyahatname*, 4/176; Abdülkadir Özcan, 'Kara Murad Paşa', in *Türkiye Diyânet Vakfı İslam Ansiklopedisi* 24 (2001): 363–5.
128. *soltân*.
129. Nasiri, *Titles and Emoluments*, 59.
130. Evliya Çelebi, *Seyahatname*, 4/176–7, 201.

131. Master-gatekeeper Benli Omar Agha was sent back to the capital with the assurance for the grand vizier that the collection would be fulfilled: Evliya Çelebi, *Seyahatname*, 4/177–9.
132. Evliya Çelebi, *Seyahatnâme*, 4/179.
133. At the last way station before Urmia, the mission sent a messenger to the *xan*'s steward to announce their arrival, who instructed them to set out early in the morning and sent a welcome letter: Evliya Çelebi, *Seyahatname*, 4/187.
134. Evliya Çelebi, *Seyahatname*, 4/188.
135. 'incinme . . . hemen bir gün görürsün . . .'
136. This private conversation began upon Evliya Çelebi's request. The council members stayed in the room, but they only contributed when addressed. It was also the emissary's proposal to compare the current incident with peace conditions. Master-secretaries Khaja Naqdi and Haji Qurban-kulu produced a certain copy of the Treaty of Zuhab that was kept at the Urmia chancellery's portfolio-desk: Evliya Çelebi, *Seyahatname*, 4/188–9. Reportedly, even copies of earlier, nullified pacts were still kept in provincial chancelleries; Evliya Çelebi tells of having seen a copy of the peace-writ of Nasuhpaşa (1612) in the archives of Sheikh Safi shrine in Ardabil (ibid. 4/214).
137. Evliya Çelebi, *Seyahatname*, 4/189–90.
138. Responding to Genç ᶜAli Xan Afşar's inquiry into İpşir Mustafa Pasha's execution, Evliya Çelebi alleged that the reason behind the execution was that İpşir had stirred up the Pinyanişi to breach the treaty and this had in turn led to the counter-raid from Iran, and that he had tried to talk Mehmed IV into opening war against Iran: Evliya Çelebi, *Seyahatname*, 4/190–2.
139. The governor of Dunbuli, originating from Marash in southeastern Anatolia, welcomed the mission outside the city, and after shaking hands, they together rode inside in procession. Cannon-shots marked their entry. In the council meeting, the governor took over Melek Ahmed Pasha's, Kara Murtaza Pasha's and Genç Ali Xan Afşar's letters, and gave gifts to the delegates: Evliya Çelebi, *Seyahatname*, 4/200–1.
140. *eşik akası*.
141. Before the confiscation, Genç Ali Xan Afşar managed to talk the usher into rewarding Evliya Çelebi with handsome gifts from the estate he was about to lose: Evliya Çelebi, *Seyahatname*, 4/201–3; Kazvini-Isfahani, *Khuld-i Barîn*, 535.
142. It turned out that Kayıtmaz Kajar and Evliya Çelebi knew each other from the latter's travels in the Caucasus when the former was the governor of Gilan: Evliya Çelebi, *Seyahatname*, 4/206–7.
143. Because of his partner Khudadad's fate, this spy refused to go back to Van to pick up further news. For the gifts exchanged and more details on the mission's activities in Tabriz, see Evliya Çelebi, *Seyahatname*, 4/207–10.
144. *raqam*.

1644–1660: Armenia and Azerbaijan

145. Evliya Çelebi, *Seyahatname*, 4/210.
146. Karaçelebi-zade, *Ravzatü'l-Ebrar Zeyli*, 257; [von Reningen] 'Die Hauptrelation des Kaiserlichen Residenten in Constantinopel Simon Reniger von Reningen 1649–1666', ed. Alois Veltze, *Mittheilungen des K. und K. Kriegs-Archivs* N.F. vol. 12, 98; Hammer-Purgstall, *Geschichte* vol. 5, 645.
147. See the summary of the mentioned decree in İsmâil Hakkı Uzunçarşılı, Ibrahim Kemal Baybura and Ülkü Altındağ (eds), *Topkapı Sarayı Müzesi Osmanlı Saray Arşivi Kataloğu: Fermanlar. I. Fasikül* (Ankara: Türk Târih Kurumu, 1985), ent. 367.
148. Claes Ralamb, *İstanbul'a Bir Yolculuk 1657–1658*, trans. Ayda Arel (Istanbul: Kitap Yayınevi, 2008), 92.
149. Setton, *Venice, Austria and the Turks*, 163–85; İnalcık, *Devlet-i Aliyye II*, 326–8, 338.
150. *Anonim Osmanlı Vekayinamesi (H. 1058–1106/M. 1648–1694)*, ed. Ramazan Aktemur as an MA thesis (Istanbul University, 2019), 105.
151. I could not identify whether the Kalb-ᶜAli Xan Afşar, who had been the governor of Urmia in 1633 and partaken in the Van front of the ongoing Ottoman–Safavid War (see Özer Küpeli, 'Osmanlı-Safevi Münasebetleri (1612–1639)' (PhD diss., Ege Üniversitesi, 2009), 139) is the same person as the ambassador in question. The twenty-two-year gap between the two events does not necessarily rule out this possibility. Unat mistakenly provides the name of the Safavid ambassador to the Ottoman court in 1656 (Kalb-ᶜAli Silsüpür-Afşar) as Pir-Ali (see Faik Reşit Unat, *Osmanlı Sefirleri ve Sefaretnameleri*, ed. Bekir Sıtkı Baykal (Ankara: Türk Tarih Kurumu, 1968), 244), without naming a source. In Abdurriza Hushang Mahdavi, *Târîkh-i Ravâbit-ı Khârijî-yi Îrân* (Tehran: Muassasa-i Intisharat-i Amir-i Kabir, HS 1349), 68, Abbas II's sending in 1666 to the Ottoman court an emissary named Pir-Ali Beyg with the agenda of consolidating the peace is mentioned, though again without citation of a source. Presumably, Unat's and Mahdavi's source is Hammer-Purgstall, who in turn uses *Tarih-i Naîmâ* as primary source: Joseph Hammer von Purgstall, *Geschichte des Osmanischen Reiches* vol. 6 (Pest: C. A. Hartleben's Verlag, 1830), 9–10. Mustafa Naima's chronicle, written about half a century after the embassy in question, is the only source providing the name 'Pir-Ali', as opposed to the chronicles of Kazvini, Kazvini-Isfahani and Nazmizade Murtaza that consistently name the ambassador 'Kalb-Ali', which should be taken as correct. In addition, Mahdavi not only reproduces Mustafa Naima's error, likely through Hammer, but also misdates the mission to 1666.
152. Kazvini, *ᶜAbbasnâma*, 222; Kazvini-Isfahani, *Khuld-i Barîn*, 585.
153. *Tarih-i Naima*, 1719; Nazmizade, *Gülşen-i Hulefâ*, 262; *Anonim Osmanlı Vekayinamesi*, 105; Floor, *Persian Gulf*, 562; İpşirli, 'Hanefi Mehmed Efendi', *Türk Diyanet Vakfı İslam Ansiklopedisi* XV (1997): 554. Karaçelebizade notes that the news reporting the coming of an embassy also

spoke of the shah's 'unreasonable proposals': *Ravzatü'l-Ebrar Zeyli*, 292. However, all other sources speak of the letters and assurances exchanged to uphold the peace. Also see *Tarih-i Vecihi*, ff. 70b–71a. Later, the inbound journey and hosting-at-court of the Safavid ambassador (more likely Kalb-Ali Silsüpür-Afşar, less likely Mehemmedkulu Burun-Qasimoğlu) would be mentioned, by mistaking the chronology, in the tales of Köprülü Mehmed Pasha's rise to grand-vizierate: Demetrius Cantemir, *The History of the Growth and Decay of the Othman Empire*, trans. N. Tindal (London: Crown in Ludgate Street, 1734), 255n. For the shah's gifts to the padishah, see [von Reningen] 'Hauptrelation des Kaiserlichen Residenten in Constantinopel Simon Reniger von Reningen 1649–1666', 100.

154. *Asnâd u Mukâtabât, 1038–1105*, 206–8.
155. 'pâdishâh . . . Khusrav-i ʿadîmuʾl-himâl'. The *inscriptio* of Mehmed IV and the titles of Kalb-Ali Afşar are omitted in the surviving copy of this letter.
156. 'yaktâ-dilî'.
157. 'yagânagî'.
158. 'wâlî-yi Hindustân'.
159. 'julûs . . . bar avrang-i saltanat-i Îrân'.
160. 'armağan'.
161. *mutafarriqa-başı*.
162. *Kapı kedkhudâsı*.
163. Nazmizade, *Gülşen-i Hulefâ*, 262; Müneccimbaşı, *Sahâifüʾl-Ahbâr*, vol. 3, 713; Fındıklılı Mehmed, *Zeyl-i Fezleke*, 77. For the list of the gifts picked for the shah and Ismail Agha's being entrusted with them on 9 January 1657 under the oversight of First Master-of-the-horse Abaza Mehmed Agha, see Topkapı, *Evrak*, 448/12 (1491/1). For Ismail Agha's nickname, see Ralamb, *İstanbulʾa Bir Yolculuk*, 92. Kose Ismail and Silsüpür Afşar entered Tokat with a day's distance between each other; Zakaria of Auglis, the Iranian-Armenian merchant trading in Iran and the Ottoman Empire, reports the date of their arrival in Tokat as 14 and 15 February, respectively. However, on the road to Diyarbekr, they set out together. *Journal of Zakʾaria of Agulis*, 59. See also *Tarih-i Vecihi*, f. 71a.
164. *Kullar-akası*.
165. Kazvini, ʿ*Abbasnâma*, 222–3; Kazvini-Isfahani, *Khuld-i Barîn*, 587.
166. Abdi Paşa, *Vekâyi-nâme*, 100–1; *Tarih-i Naima*, 1721; Nazmizade, *Gülşen-i Hulefâ*, 262. The 'one chest of garments, which at the mentioned way-station [Adrianople] came in [to the Imperial Court] from the estate of envoy Zulfiqar Agha who had gone to Persia and passed away' (see Topkapı Sarayı Müzesi Arşivi, *Defter*, 2315, f. 29a/image 28), must have been Kose Ismail Agha's but logged with a mistaken name. This entry is dated 1658 (H 1068), preceded by an entry from June 1658 and followed by one from August 1658, thus safely attributable to summer 1658. Assuming that the Ottoman state sent another envoy to Iran about the same time as Kose Ismail's legation and that this second envoy too died around the same

1644–1660: Armenia and Azerbaijan

time as Kose Ismail, while no other source speaks of or hints at such an event, would be against the ordinary run of things.
167. *Asnâd u Mukâtabât, 1038–1105*, 209–11.
168. "ᶜa'lâ-hazrat, . . . tarâz-i visâda-i . . . jahânbânî, zînat-bakhsh-i arâik-i vâlâ-yi saltanat ve khâqânî, . . . sultânuᵓl-Barrayn u khâqânuᵓl-Bahrayn, sânî-yi Iskandar-i Zul-Qarnayn, khâdimuᵓl-Haramayniᵓ-Sharîfayn'.
169. 'harîm-i vâlâ'.
170. *wilâyat.*
171. Kazvini, ᶜ*Abbâsnâma*, 227; Kazvini-Isfahani, *Khuld-i Barîn*, 593.
172. The two rivers met on the plain of Baghdad, making the fortress of Baghdad look like an island. After the repairs of the wrecked parts of the fortress, Haseki Mehmed Pasha set up camp along with a crowd of dwellers at the spot called Mintiqa, just outside the walls of Baghdad and where the Tigris and the Euphrates had met after the flood. Because of the flood, the ships had begun navigating through there, and overland traffic was facilitated by two bridges. To forestall a later disruption of this kind, the governor-general had two large floodgates built and supported them with a few other dams nearby. Nazmizade, *Gülşen-i Hulefâ*, 262–3; *Tarih-i Naima*, 1765; Ğurabzade, ᶜ*Uyûn Akhbâr*, 270b.
173. Setton, *Venice, Austria, and the Turks*, 185–9; Halil İnalcık, *Devlet-i Aliyye. Osmanlı İmparatorluğu Üzerine Araştırmalar III: Köprülüler Devri* (Istanbul: Türkiye İş Bankası Kültür Yayınları, 2015), 28–34; Uzunçarşılı, *Osmanlı Târihi* vol. 3/1, 375–81.
174. *hâkim, voyvoda.*
175. *Voyvoda, beğ.* Also called *hospodar*, these were Ottoman-appointed princes of these autonomous principalities, which were governments under imperial sovereignty with certain conceded priviledges. The hospodar's rank within Ottoman hierarchy overlapped with that of a two-horsetail-ensign pasha, that is a non-vizier pasha, a governor. See Viorel Panaite, *The Ottoman Law of War and Peace: The Ottoman Empire and Tribute Payers* (Boulder: East European Monographs, 2000), 34. Their additional title *beğ* was not equivalent to that of one-horsetail-ensign *sancakbeyi* (bannerlord): the latter reflected the devalued use in provincial administrative hierarchy, which had evolved during the rise of the Ottomans; however, the Ottomans had not forgotten the true function of this term, which corresponded roughly to duke or prince. This use in original meaning lived on in Ottoman terminology employed for entitling the hospodar-princes of Wallachia and Moldavia, when referring to the era of Anatolian–Turkish principalities in the wake of the Seljuks' downfall, for denoting contemporary independent European principalities or duchies, and in proverbs.
176. After two years of operations, victorious Ottoman forces entered the Transylvanian capital Weissenburg, re-established order, and annexed three strongholds from the realm to the Empire: Hammer von Purgstall, *Geschichte* vol. 6, 30–4, 67–77, 95–8; Gaspar Katko, 'The Redemption of

the Transylvanian Army Captured by the Crimean Tatars in 1657', in *The Crimean Khanate between East and West (15th–18th Century)*, ed. Denis Klein (Wiesbaden: Harrassowitz Verlag, 2012), 91–106; İnalcık, *Devlet-i Aliyye III*, 44–9; Uzunçarşılı, *Osmanlı Târihi* vol. 3/1, 382–7.

177. İnalcık, *Devlet-i Aliyye III*, 49–55; Uzunçarşılı, *Osmanlı Târihi* vol. 3/1, 386–94.
178. *Anonim Osmanlı Vekayinamesi*, 112–13.
179. Fındıklılı Mehmed, *Zeyl-i Fezleke*, 1090; Abdülkadir Özcan, 'Ibrahim Paşa, Kara', *Türkiye Diyânet Vakfı İslam Ansiklopedisi* 21 (2000): 329–30; Uzunçarşılı, *Osmanlı Târihi* vol. 3/2, 423–4.
180. Bülbül, 'Kumuk Türkleri ve Tarku Şamhallığı', 71–4.
181. Bülbül, 'Kumuk Türkleri ve Tarku Şamhallığı', 29, 36–8, 54, 58, 61–4.
182. Fındıklılı Mehmed, *Zeyl-i Fezleke*, 262–3.
183. *sarᶜasker/başbuğ* (Ottoman) (roughly corresponding Safavid *sardâr*), commander of a front in a larger war or of a large-scale military operation.
184. Fındıklılı Mehmed, *Zeyl-i Fezleke*, 263–5.
185. Bilge, *Osmanlı Çağı'nda Kafkasya*, 509.
186. *melik*.
187. Fındıklılı Mehmed, *Zeyl-i Fezleke*, 265–6. Later, coming back to Iran, he became Muslim, entered Safavid service, and was renamed Shahnazar Xan in 1678. He seized the throne of Imereti again in 1679 but had to flee to Russia once more owing to the Georgian nobility's withholding allegiance from him. His claims on Mingrelia, for which he teamed up with Atabegli Arslan Pasha of Childir, also failed. In 1680, Mehmed IV ordered Sheitan Ibrahim Pasha, governor-general of Erzurum, to re-establish authority with a campaign in which Atabeğli Arslan Pasha was beheaded and Mingrelia was overrun. Bilge, *Osmanlı Çağı'nda Kafkasya*, 508–9; *Journal of Zakᵓaria of Agulis*, 156.

4
1660–1682: The Persian Gulf

Iranian-Supported Uprisings in Southern Iraq and the Ottomans' Unmaking of the Principality of Basra

In the years that followed the first Basran crisis, Afrasiyaboğlu Husein took care not to breach the new deal with the imperial court. As noted earlier, he adopted a tone of *froideur* towards the shah's envoy to show that he did not regard himself as beholden to the shah, and regularly sent tributes to Baghdad and Constantinople. At the same time, though, he also fostered ties with the Bedouins of the Basran hinterland, so as to be able to call them up when needed.[1] This was perhaps ominous: within a few years the Empire would have to allot even more resources than before to settle accounts at the Persian Gulf with the Afrasiyaboğlu regime and its Iranian backers.

As first step towards the showdown with the Empire which he had in mind, Afrasiyaboğlu Husein sent a mission to the new Mughal sovereign, Aurangzib. The Basran emissary Qasim Agha set foot in India in January 1661 and the harbourmaster of Surat guided him up to the monarch's court. Qasim Agha handed over his credentials and gifts at the audience in May, and left India in October. Aurangzib then sent his own mission and gifts to the pasha of Basra. Qasim Agha's formal task as envoy was to open up the Indian marker to Basra's Arabian horses, and to secure permission to buy Indian goods without paying customs tolls.[2] However, this mission also served to establish a line of contact between Husein and Aurangzib, a resource that the pasha of Basra would want to draw on if he could neither stay in the Empire nor take shelter in Iran. In the same year, the Venetian Senate sent the shah a diplomatic agent bearing a letter, and once again called on the Safavids to attack the Ottomans. Arakel, Venice's next emissary to Iran in 1663, made the same appeal when meeting with the shah.[3] Neither of these missions, however, yielded the outcome that the Republic wished for. The Shahdom did not turn against its western neighbour.

When in 1663/4 Afrasiyaboğlu Husein sent his yearly tax to the imperial court,[4] he contrived at the same time to also secure for himself appointment as governor of al-Ahsa. He then sent troops, cast out the unseated Mehmed Pasha, and took hold of al-Ahsa after a bloody fight, while his troops raped and robbed the inhabitants. But when Zayd, the sharif of Mecca, let the imperial court know of the atrocities, decrees came out this time to re-install Mehmed Pasha. As Afrasiyaboğlu did not heed Constantinople's behest,[5] the second Basran crisis broke out which, like the first one, would soon spill over to Iran.

When the Ottomans were readying themselves for a new campaign towards the Persian Gulf, a curious diplomatic contact took place between Isfahan and the Sublime Porte. By early April 1664, a mission from Iran was in Ottoman territory, on its way to the imperial court. The emissary was ordered to go ahead to Adrianople where Mehmed IV then was. A decree was issued to all judges, Janissary vice chiefs-of-staff as well as officers, and other governmental agents posted along the road to Adrianople: as the mission proceeded westwards, officials with jurisdiction over wherever it halted were to provide it with food and lodging, and forward it on its way.[6] Aside, however, from this curt instruction that we find contained within a register of Imperial Council decree summaries, no other source mentions a mission from Iran to the Empire in 1664. This Safavid mission seems, therefore, to have been somewhat unofficial. But while we have no attestation to its goal, it is likely that the Shahdom was seeking thereby to assure the Ottomans that it had no intention of siding with Venice or the unbiddable Afrasiyaboğlus.

Afrasiyaboğlu defied the imperial court's directives at a time when the Empire had to mobilise almost all its resources to the Mediterranean and Hungary. When the Habsburgs had breached the borders in 1663 with the pretext of intervening in the uproar in Transylvania, the Sublime Porte had declared an imperial campaign with Köprülü Fazil Ahmed Pasha as commander-in-chief. The talks held in Belgrade failed, the Turkish army advanced forward to besiege Ujvar/Neuhäusel (now Nove Zamky in Slovakia, then northwestern Hungary) on 15 August, and the fortress gave in on 13 September. In the winter of 1664, German–Hungarian troops marched against Szigetvar in southwestern Hungary, but withdrew without much gain. Neither the Turkish gains near Nagykanizsa/ Großkirchen in western Hungary early in this 'German campaign' nor the German victory at St Gotthard on 1 August changed the outcome: the Peace of Vasvar on 10 August sealed the Turkish gains from the last year.[7] Thus, the second Persian Gulf upheaval had arisen when the Empire was already entangled in two full-blown wars, the second of which, here in western Hungary, was about as far removed from Basra as the grand vizier and the Imperial Army could be.

That Afrasiyaboğlu Husein no longer upheld the 1655 settlement came to light at the same time as another earthquake wrecked a tower and a portion of the walls at the fortress of Van in early 1665, triggering another alarm at the border with Iran. Governor Seyyid Yusuf Pasha's report about this came in on 27 May when the imperial court was encamped near Feres in Thrace. Master-gatekeeper Karakaş Ali Agha was sent off to Van as commissary to oversee the repairs.[8] The imperial court felt the need to have this borderland fortress overlooking Azerbaijan sound ahead of the upcoming campaign against Basra and its likely spillover on Iran.

Afrasiyaboğlu Husein did not wait it out at rest. In 1665 he sent another emissary to Aurangzib of India, this time bearing not only gifts but also a petition. The timing of this undertaking was not accidental. The pasha of Basra must have been well aware that the Empire then did not acknowledge Aurangzib's accession.[9] By sending a mission, therefore, he was trying to inveigle himself into the Mughal sovereign's affections. This was a strategic move: with the German–Turkish war, which had taken the pressure off Afrasiyaboğlu, now over, he was worried about the outcomes of his deeds in 1663/4 and was striving to find a haven to shelter. A realm far away from the Empire to the east of Iran and unfriendly towards the Porte was an excellent choice.

Sixteen sixty-five was a busy year in Ottoman–Safavid relations. To top it all, it also witnessed another round of European–Iranian diplomacy about the Ottoman Empire: Antonio Tani, a Dominican father appointed 'Vicar of the East' by the Papacy and created joint envoy by the Grand Duchy of Tuscany and the Republic of Venice, visited Abbas II. The shah welcomed the Italian envoy with great pomp, but refused to meet with him for a private talk. This Italian mission called on Iran once again to wage war against the Ottomans, but could not change the shah's mind. Even Tani himself, to whom the shah's answer must have been communicated in the most polite and delicate way, was under no illusions. As he reported back, the shah would certainly reject the offer.[10]

To discipline the pasha of Basra, the imperial court ruled that an army be gathered. Banyalukalı Kabasakal (Kadirullah) Uzun Ibrahim Pasha, the new governor of Baghdad, was created marshal,[11] while the governors of Diyarbekr (Sheitan Ibrahim Pasha), Aleppo (Sarı Husein Pasha), Shahrizor (Gurji Kenan Pasha), Mosul (Gurji Ibrahim Pasha) and Raqqa (Sarı Mehmed Pasha) became subordinated to him together with their troops.[12] In 1665, shortly after the signing of the Peace of Vasvar, the troops called up for the Basran campaign met outside the walls of

Baghdad. Mehmed Pasha of al-Ahsa was also made to join them from Mecca. The campaign started when Afrasiyaboğlu boldly rejected the marshal's letter calling him to obedience. He also shipped his movable wealth across the border to Iranian territory and seized the former Basran fortress of Qurna, where he locked himself in together with his captain Haji Agha and 4,000 troops, and strengthened its fortifications in readiness for a siege. The 12,000-strong Ottoman division set out from Baghdad in October/November 1665. From his encampment, the marshal sent a follow-up letter to Qurna, again calling on Afrasiyaboğlu to give in, but Basra's lord answered saying 'come what may'. The two forces clashed at Mansuriya. Afrasiyaboğlu's 20,000-strong hireling-Bedouin force was beaten and fled. The Ottomans encamped in the Mesopotamian Marshes, built a floating bridge over the Shatt-al-Arab, and beleaguered Qurna.[13]

Afrasiyaboğlu Husein had manned the fortress with Turkish mercenaries, Bedouins and Iranian musketeers hired by his son. Meanwhile, weary of Husein's appropriations and high-handed governance, the elders of the city of Basra sent a collective letter to the marshal, plighting their troth. Banyalukalı Ibrahim thereupon gave out an edict naming Turkish tradesman Solak Husein (a.k.a. Haji Musallam) the stand-in governor until an appointment be made. Budakoğlu Mehmed, from Afrasiyaboğlu's household, worked to thwart this, but the Basran elders harshly quelled Budakoğlu's undertaking, after which Afrasiyaboğlu Husein's steward and nephew Ibrahim Agha fled the city on 31 December 1665. The coalition of the clergy and elders in Basra made known on 12 January 1666 that the city was unconditionally Ottoman. Afrasiyaboğlu, however, had already sent troops, under Budakoğlu's lead, to take back his metropolis: they entered the city, and set about plundering and killing the dwellers. Those elders who could flee the slaughter went to the marshal's encampment. In the subsequent clash at Kut, the Afrasiyaboğlu-friendly chieftain of the Muntafiq tribe overcame the Ottoman-friendly Emir Reshid's (a.k.a. Ali Shedid) men. Meanwhile the siege of Qurna went on for several months, with the besiegers drawing on fresh reinforcements from Baghdad. But the garrison withstood. The defenders' Bedouin allies kept them well-stocked with supplies from outside, while a dearth of stocks was wearing down the besiegers.[14]

The Basran campaign had begun while the Safavids were busy with their eastern border: awaiting a Mughal onslaught against Kandahar, they were planning a raid into India to strike first.[15] The news that the Sublime Porte had created a marshal and gathered an army in Iraq upset the Shahdom, which now found that it also had to worry about its western borderland. To allay Safavid fears, and to forestall an Ottoman–Safavid clash, Köprülü Ahmed Pasha sent a letter to his Iranian counterpart Mirza Muhammad Mahdi Karaki, which explained the background of the campaign and underscored that the Iranians should not panic, for the campaign's only goal was to wipe out the rebels. Köprülü also assured Karaki that the Ottoman officials at the borderland were warned not to do anything in breach of the treaty, and asked the Safavids to not shelter or help Afrasiyaboğlu, because doing so would break the peace. Abdunnebi Çavuş, an Imperial Council sergeant, set out for Iran bearing this letter in January 1666, amidst the clashes at Basra and Qurna.[16]

Meanwhile Afrasiyaboğlu Husein held out in Qurna against heavy bombardment. Nevertheless, the Empire's investment was too strong to let him get away without a loss. In the end, Sheitan Ibrahim Pasha, the governor of Diyarbekr, contacted the rebel leader, and on 7 March 1666 he struck a bargain: Husein Pasha would forthwith and once only pay 250,000 thalers[17] to the Central Treasury; pledge for the province of Basra to send a yearly lump-sum tax[18] of 100,000 thalers to the Privy Purse; give back to their owners the goods appropriated from trading ships with which he had paid his mercenaries; pull out from the west of the Persian Gulf, namely from al-Ahsa in eastern Arabia; step down on behalf of his son Afrasiyab Bey; and retire to Mecca. Banyalukalı Ibrahim Pasha took the deal and lifted the siege. The marshal's letter telling of the campaign and the settlement reached Grand Vizier Köprülü Ahmed Pasha at the Imperial Army encampment at Timurtaş near Adrianople, on 6 April 1666, and Köprülü approved the agreement. Afrasiyaboğlu Husein's steward and brother-in-law Yahya Agha was to be taken to the imperial court as surety for the deal.[19]

On 2 May 1666, the aforementioned herald Abdunnebi Çavuş arrived back at the Imperial Army encampment by Adrianople bearing Mahdi Karaki's letter of answer: Iran's chief vizier reconfirmed the peace, spoke of Abbas II's recreational journey to Mazandaran, and emphasised that the Ottoman campaign in Iraq did not upset the Shahdom, given that Basra, the target of operations, was Ottoman territory. Karaki also acknowledged Köprülü Ahmed's reminder, but only in the sense that Iran should not back up Afrasiyaboğlu Husein, and made clear that no one could dare to breach the peace, as the Iranian frontier officials were warned with rescripts, and that the Shahdom would never help Afrasiyaboğlu. Köprülü let Mehmed IV know of the incoming answer, that Abdunnebi Çavuş had witnessed the shah's praying for the Ottomans to triumph in the German campaign, and that the herald also spoke of Abbas II's 'renown for light-wittedness and excessive overwhelmedness'.[20] The comment on Abbas II must have stemmed from his worsening health, wherefore a change of air from Isfahan to Mazandaran was felt needful.[21] Also catching syphilis and not being treated very well,[22] Abbas would die shortly after Abdunnebi's visit, to be succeeded by his son[23] Sam (who then chose the regnal name Safi II, but soon held a second coronation and settled on Suleiman). The grand vizier's herald, seemingly not aware of Abbas II's condition, thought of what he witnessed to be an overall weakness rather than a worsening sickness.

The imperial court did not deem Iran an earnest threat. The status quo was already to the Empire's advantage, and Iran could not change it on its own. Right after dealing with Mahdi Karaki's answer, Köprülü Ahmed Pasha was once again made commander-in-chief (on 14 May 1666) to marshal the ongoing siege of Candia, capital of the Venetian Duchy of Crete. He would remain on the island for more than three years and himself command the Imperial Army until the Venetian garrison's capitulation in September 1669.[24]

This 1666 settlement between the imperial court and the Basran establishment, which the Safavids beheld but did not interfere in, would not last long. Contrary to the deal, Husein Pasha did not leave the province, governing on as if he had not stepped down, and his son Afrasiyab Bey's governorship remained only in name. Husein also did not shy away from further meddling in al-Ahsa and thus unsettling the Persian Gulf once again. Basran elders and traders flooded Constantinople with petitions of complaint, asking for compensations against Husein's unlawful high-handedness. He even did not care to pay the yearly lump-sum tax in full. After this last straw breaking the camel's back, his brother-in-law and former steward Yahya Agha, held at the imperial court as surety, offered to take his former lord's stead, claiming that in Basra he wielded enough influence to make the townsfolk and the Bedouin follow his lead. The imperial court named him governor with a decree, and he pledged to lay waste to the House of Afrasiyaboğlu. Mehmed IV gave audience to Yahya on 22 May 1667, had him clothed with a robe of honour, and said: 'hereby I have graciously bestowed the governorship of Basra upon you. If you do not act upon to my august will, you shall not be saved from my sword.' The imperial court also readied itself for a further campaign. Firari Kara Mustafa Pasha was not only made governor of Baghdad once again, but also created marshal to install the new administration in Basra. Kurdish margraves, the governors of Diyarbekr (Sheitan Ibrahim Pasha), Shahrizor (Gurji Kenan Pasha), Mosul (Musa Pasha) and Raqqa (Deli Dilaver Pasha), these pashas' own battalions, feudal troopers, and the Janissaries as well as the Locals of Baghdad were called up to take the field.[25]

An artillery of four bombards[26] and twenty large field-guns[27] from Baghdad's garrison strengthened this secondary Imperial Army.[28] The

Imperial Armory crafted and lent out material too, while further gear was bought as well as manufactured to stock the fortress of Baghdad.[29] Before the campaign's start, Vice Grand Vizier[30] Merzifonlu Kara Mustafa Pasha wrote in a letter[31] that he awaited the marshal to 'regulate the affairs of the province of Basra',[32] hinting therewith that this Imperial Army was not only to quell the insubordination but also do away with the House of Afrasiyaboğlu and set up an imperial governorate. The land of Basra became stripped of its status as hereditary fiefdom; there would no longer be a principality under the name of an autonomous administration. It was to become a regular province of the yearly (lump-sum tax) kind and its governorship a seat of appointment, as had been the case in the sixteenth century. Among his other duties, the marshal was also to take care of the outcomes that this regime change at the Persian Gulf would beget in dealings with Iran.

Seemingly, Yahya (now Pasha, no longer Agha) was not sent to Iraq until the end of the summer, kept instead in Constantinople at least until 18 August 1667.[33] Firari Mustafa meanwhile empowered two commissaries with his decree to shuttle between Baghdad and Constantinople. Then an imperial decree, issued in mid-August 1667 at Adrianople, commanded all districts on the highway from Constantinople to Baghdad to treat these two commissaries as imperial dispatch riders.[34] In critical situations, such as a flare-up in relations with Iran, the marshal could thus communicate quickly with the imperial court and ask about how to proceed.

Although the news of this forthcoming campaign must have scared Afrasiyaboğlu Husein, he was determined to fight for his patrimony. He first had the Basran dwellers' belongings plundered to pay the wages of his Bedouin hirelings, and then tried to shift Basra from Ottoman to Safavid overlordship. But the shah rejected the bid, and on 18 November 1667 Afrasiyaboğlu ordered the city to be emptied and its dwellers to relocate to the Iranian side of the border. As he had done earlier, so too now he shipped his family and movable wealth to Iran. But this time he also set his metropolis on fire and laid waste to even his own palace. Afterwards he first hurried to Qurna to strengthen the defences, then rode out at the head of a contingent, and finally encamped at Sehab, to the east of the Shatt-al-Arab.[35]

By rejecting to take in Basra as vassal, the Safavids upheld their good relations with the Ottomans instead of scoring a quick, but likely unsustainable, gain. The Shahdom had been following this policy since 1639. And now, the Ottomans' military build-up in Iraq, which, according to the hearsay coming from the border, would target Iran as well, also strong-armed the Shahdom.[36]

The campaign kicked off with the gathering of a somewhat well-furnished army and the marshal's coming out to his tent through a military parade next to the stronghold of Kuşlar outside Baghdad on 24 November 1667. The Basran mounted mercenaries,[37] who had been under prosecution, were now forgiven by Mehmed IV's script, and in late October the imperial court decreed the marshal to let this irregular cavalry serve on the campaign.[38] The army set up camp at Arja on 12 December to halt for seven days, and on 5 January 1668, after meeting with the fleet, it processionally walked into Kut, and thus into Basran territory. There, Othman Bey (es-Sadun), chieftain of the Muntafiq, also joined the army together with his 1,000 fighters. The fleet laden with ammunition and heavy weaponry reached the army at Mansuriya.[39] There Yahya Pasha headed out from the army to call the Marsh Arabs to pledge troth to the padishah, bow to his governorship, and join the campaign. The Marsh tribes however did not heed, believing that the marshal would not bother to encroach further and seemingly unaware that this campaign was an imperial undertaking. Nor did they simply refuse to join the Ottoman camp, but instead hampered its progress, laying waste to the bulwarks and tearing down the dwellings in the Mesopotamian Marshes to strip the terrain of anything that could accommodate the Ottoman troops.[40] They would soon find out that they bet on the wrong horse.

The army split into three arms at Mansuriya. The first detachment went ahead through the plain. The second one set sail on the ships laden with ammunition and stocks. The rest entered the Mesopotamian Marshes. As this main body walked through, Firari Kara Mustafa had the marsh jungles on his way cut down in retribution for the Bedouins' hostility. The Bedouin hirelings of Afrasiyaboğlu, led by his nephew Mir-Mahmud, were waiting at the riverside trenches by Dar Beni-Esed to ambush the nearing Ottomans. The marshal, having already heard of this trap from a prisoner taken nearby, arrayed his troops and field guns in anticipation of the ambush. In the clash that broke out on 17 January 1668, the Ottomans overran Afrasiyaboğlu's Bedouin. Afterwards, the Imperial Army advanced rather slowly until it reached the stronghold of Suveyb on 17 February 1668, two hours' march away from Qurna,[41] the Basran territory's main stronghold.

To beleaguer Qurna, one Janissary company, the governorate troops of Shahrizor and Raqqa, Baghdad Locals' right-flank Enlistees,[42] and five companies from the marshal's own infantry[43] dug themselves into trenches overlooking the keep. A floating bridge was built on the Shatt-al-Arab's Zakiya stream to help the rest of the army to cross. The army then encamped, guarded by Mosul governorate troops. The rest of the Janissary companies, Firari Mustafa's own infantry and cavalry,[44] and Baghdad Locals entrenched themselves against the ditch and the fortress gate. With the batteries set up, bombardment began from all four sides. Relief troops headed by Afrasiyaboğlu Husein wanted to hit the Ottomans, but a detachment led by the governor of Diyarbekr crossed the Zakiya stream and scattered them. Afrasiyaboğlu then fled into Iran towards Huvayza, on 23 February 1668. Meanwhile the Ottomans drove the trenches forward and reached the ditch. The marshal gathered all Household, Local and mercenary captains to order an assault on 24 February. Once it began, the defenders in Qurna lost all hope. They forsook the fortress on 1 March and ran away into Iran towards Huvayza, following in the footsteps of their fallen leader. A few thousand died during the fight, 1,500 drowned in the stream, and over 1,000 fell prisoner, while those that Afrasiyaboğlu had forcibly brought to Qurna were freed. The marshal rode victoriously into the fortress.[45]

With Basra's main stronghold taken, the pashas and officers in the army gathered to bear witness to an attestation[46] drafted by the judge of the Imperial Army and underwritten by eleven elders of Basra:

> The domain of Basra was conferred upon you [, Yahya Pasha,] by the sublime padishah and we were ordered to make you seize it ... After the conquest and capture of the Marshes, of Qurna, and of other fortresses materialized by the stroke of blade, we have handed over to Yahya Pasha and made him wholly seize the aforesaid province, which the transgressor Husein [Afrasiyaboğlu] had possessed.

Yahya then confirmed that his authority stemmed from the imperial script that appointed him.[47] The city of Basra too yielded in March 1668 to the marshal's besieging troops. With Yahya installed as governor, there now began a restoration drive, calling upon the townsfolk to return home.[48]

At the same time as Basra came under imperial sway, a remarkable Iranian–Ottoman contact took place across the Caspian Sea and Thrace: an emissary of the Shamkhal of Dagestan, who had cast off Safavid overlordship, set out from Derbend[49] and showed up in Adrianople. Vice Grand Vizier Merzifonlu Kara Mustafa Pasha let him into audience and clothed him with a 'high'[50] grade robe of honour in mid-March 1668.[51] The emissary dwelt at the Empire's co-capital at least from 21 March to 1 June.[52] When the time came for him to leave, he was entrusted with 'elite'[53] robes of honour sent for the 'governors of the Shamkhal'.[54]

Surkhay II had died in 1667/8 and Buday had followed him as the new lord of Dagestan,[55] which must have been the occasion for the Derbend mission to the Empire in the spring of 1668: Dagestan, now under a new ruler, quietly got in touch with the Sublime Porte. The new Shamkhal likely wanted not only to uphold Dagestan's independence from Iran but also to win over the Ottomans by acknowledging them, more in name than in deed, as overlord. The Empire's heartland on the one hand lay too far away from Dagestan to let the imperial court meddle in Dagestan's affairs, but at the same time the Ottomans could field troops as far as the western shores of the Caspian Sea if a war broke out with Iran or Russia. Dagestan's Ottoman diplomacy in 1668 seems to be the first of its kind since the Peace of Zuhab.

The Sublime Porte not only clothed the emissary of Dagestan with a robe of honour, which was conventional, but also sent robes of honour for the Shamkhal and the lesser lords of Dagestan to wear. If this had been an uncalled-for move, the Sublime Porte would have likely not done so at a time when it was not only on friendly terms but also needed to cooperate with the Safavids. Therefore, the new Shamkhal seems to have acknowledged the padishah as his overlord through this mission. Not in a full-fledged vassalage though, for otherwise the occasion would not have ended up buried only in a few financial transactions between the Ottoman subsidiary government and the Central Treasury, as there is seemingly no extant decree facilitating the emissary's trip, no diplomatic correspondence, or no log in chronicles about the mission's business. So, the Shamkhal must have acknowledged the padishah as overlord just in case, without meaning any concrete service. And the Sublime Porte must have accepted it just in case, without shouting it out or awaiting its fulfilment, lest the Ottoman–Safavid friendship be harmed. Dagestan, a principality that had formerly stood in vassalage at times to the Empire and at times to Iran, and since 1658 an independent land, flirted as of 1668 with the Ottomans and shunned an entanglement with the Safavids. The Shamkhal must have planned to play the two monarchies off against one another in time of need or, if one day it came to a showdown between the two states, he could make the most out of it for his principality. The Sublime Porte, on the other hand, must have liked to keep a friendly principality at Iran's northwestern rim. Through Dagestan, the Ottomans were effortlessly pulling off in eastern Caucasia what Iran had strived for at the Persian Gulf by means of Basra but failed.

Meanwhile the Persian Gulf did not calm down even after Yahya's installment as Basra's governor. Afrasiyaboğlu Husein had already shipped his movable wealth to the trusteeship of Navruz Xan, the Iranian subgovernor of Durak at the north of the Gulf. Afrasiyaboğlu himself fled thither after losing the showdown. The marshal's messengers followed him up to not only Durak but also Huvayza and Bihbehan at the northeastern nook of the Gulf, demanding that Afrasiyaboğlu and his belongings be handed over. The Mushasha ruler of Huvayza answered the marshal's letter: Afrasiyaboğlu, his small following, and some Basran dwellers were indeed at Durak, he himself had reported the situation to the shah, and would get in touch with the marshal as soon as the shah's orders reached him. Firari Mustafa had Yahya broadcast an official pardon to hearten those who had left Basra for Iran now to return. He also wrote a letter to the commander-in-chief putting himself forward as candidate if the padishah wished to send an ambassador to the shah to take over Afrasiyaboğlu and his belongings. Heedful of the marshal's threat that the Ottoman army would cross the border to punish anyone sheltering Afrasiyaboğlu, the Iranians did not let him stay. Leaving his family and household in Durak, he fared further east. By July 1668, together with his 2,000 followers, he was in Shiraz, on his way for the shah's court where he hoped to talk the shah into helping him. But the shah now bade him to stop there. The marshal, as the padishah's absolute deputy, had sent an emissary to the shah to demand Afrasiyaboğlu's handover.[56]

This Ottoman mission stirred up conflict among Safavid statesmen: one group leaned towards handing over Afrasiyaboğlu while the other lobbied for sheltering him, and maybe even backing him up militarily. The shah also sent troops to Huvayza just in case, but not wanting to start a war with the Ottomans, he did not let Afrasiyaboğlu Husein dwell in Iran. In the end, the overthrown prince of Basra fled to India.[57]

Basra, at the southeastern edge of the Empire bordering Iran, was no longer a special territory.[58] The marshal left 1,500 Janissaries to garrison Qurna, with a further enlistment of a 3,000-strong Basran Local Service[59] alongside artillery, ammunition and stocks. Specified income streams of the province were allotted for the salaries of the Local Service. He then disbanded the army and sent a messenger to the imperial court[60] bearing victory-letters[61] along with the campaign report. A bookkeeper, a surveyor, a judge and a harbourmaster, all appointed by the state, soon reached Basra to take over the administration, finances and trade, but first of all to survey the land, its output and income streams.[62] The register showing the newly set-up garrisons of the province was also forwarded to the grand vizierate.[63]

The Ottomans' uprooting the House of Afrasiyaboğlu from the Persian Gulf had consequences for Iran. No longer was there in southern Iraq a principality with which the Safavids could bargain, deal with, or under favourable circumstances, team up with against the Ottomans. The former principality, once a tributary freehold-government and more recently an autonomous hereditary-fiefdom, was swallowed and became a governorate. The Ottomans thus happened to deal a twofold blow to the Safavids within one year, by wiping out a duplicitous regime at the Empire's southernmost flank bordering Iran and receiving homage from the once-Safavid-vassal and now-independent Dagestan. The Safavids found themselves weakened both at the Persian Gulf, where they had tacitly been backing up local challenges to Ottoman sway since 1638, and in the Caucasus, where they had now lost a footing to the east of Georgia.

To the north of the Persian Gulf, the reorganisation of the former vassal principality into an imperial province needed work. The padishah decreed in late July 1668 that the villages, croplands, grazing grounds, harbours, customs, tithe tax, non-canonical taxes and other income streams of Basra, his 'patrimony' at the farthest spot of the Iranian border, be surveyed and logged anew.[64] Another decree sent out at the same time enacted Firari Mustafa's bid to set up a Basran Local Service and enlist men for it. The Basran Locals numbered between 2,000 and 3,000.[65] Haji Ebubekr Bey, the Empire's former Jidda-based governor of Ethiopia, was appointed as land surveyor, and Ahmed Efendi, former bookkeeper of Nagykanizsa/ Großkirchen in western Hungary, came in as survey secretary.[66] The Ottomans were incorporating the north of the Persian Gulf, and the Iranians could only watch it happen.

It soon turned out, though, that Yahya Pasha was not a tame servant to fulfil the imperial court's will in the province. In a letter probably dating from late 1668 amidst an ongoing correspondence, Vice Grand Vizier Merzifonlu Kara Mustafa already spoke of a new, upcoming 'Basran campaign'. He reminded the governor of Baghdad to forward the latest news to the imperial court, because some hearsay had spread, though no trustworthy source had verified it. The decision to undertake yet another campaign seems to have been taken following Firari Mustafa's report of new unrest near the Persian Gulf.[67] And soon enough, at the beginning of 1669, Yahya openly undermined the bookkeeping and the survey. The province's available income could already keep up the Local Service, he said, and claimed that the imperial court had not set a precondition for him to let in a state-appointed bookkeeper or surveyor. The Local Servicemen, whose pay was withheld, together with the Janissaries, then beset Yahya, and drove him out of the city in March 1669.[68]

The military, administrative, financial and provincial officials in Basra had judge Abdulhalim b. Abdullah[69] Efendi draft a collective petition, signed it, and therein informed: on 8 March 1669, Yahya Pasha showed up at the feast that his steward Abdulkadir Agha gave; by nightfall, Yahya, his steward, his treasurer, his cousin Osman, Ali b. Abdan (chieftain of the tribe Khalt) and about fifty horsemen crossed the Shatt-al-Arab; in

Gürdelen, where he made a stop, Yahya slaughtered about 150 inhabitants and recruited further allies; and thereafter he went over into Iran like his former lord Afrasiyaboğlu Husein. Basra's dignitaries disclaimed responsibility for the governor's flight, as the province had been obedient and they had not hindered Yahya's governance. The officials chose land-surveyor Haji Ebubekr Bey as stand-in governor to forestall an upheaval until a new governor was appointed with a decree.[70]

Though Yahya had sided with the imperial court to overthrow Afrasiyaboğlu Husein, he proved to have been too good a learner to forget his former lord's fallback plans. After gathering more Bedouin from the north of the Mesopotamian Marshes and from the Iranian territories of Huvayza and Durak, and thus reaching a strength of 15–20,000, Yahya sprang back in the countryside on the Ottoman side of the border on 20 March 1669, nestling first in the stronghold of Suveyb,[71] and next showing up near the city of Basra at the head of this Bedouin-Iranian force. He cut off the riverway between Basra and Qurna, and began to appropriate goods from incoming ships. He also killed two Janissaries and one Basran Local Serviceman, while also capturing three other Locals. Yahya, now at the head of a throng of recruits from Iran, made known that he would not set foot in Basra unless the surveyor, the bookkeeper, the Household companies and the Local Service left the city. The officials in Basra sent to the imperial court on 24 March a collective petition accusing the outlaw governor of having hindered the land and income survey so as to rule Basra as if it were his principality, and they asked what to do next.[72]

Upon request of eleven Basran elders, judge Abdulhalim Efendi b. Abdullah drew up another attestation on 26 March 1669: Yahya was committing banditry in the countryside; he had killed Fathi Beşe the Janissary and his servant, and wounded the Basran Local Serviceman Musabey b. Abdullah. It thus became logged that Yahya had indeed risen up against Ottoman authority. Abdullah b. Ahmed, the mufti of Basra, then gave the ruling[73] that the pasha should be put to death.[74] Surveyor Haji Abubekr Bey and bookkeeper Husein Efendi also wrote their own presentation to the grand vizier within the same days: Yahya Pasha, who had run away notwithstanding the officials' proper behaviour towards him, was now blockading Basra.[75]

An officer from the Qurna garrison, Mustafa Agha, confirmed on 2 April 1669 in a letter to Commander-in-chief Köprülü Ahmed Pasha that Yahya had risen up, gathered an army, and blockaded Basra as well as Qurna. Mustafa Agha also gave the names of a few state officials captured by the rebels.[76] Another letter between the same correspondents logs that Yahya's forces included both Basran and Iranian-Huvayzan

Bedouins, and that the Qurna garrison had so far withstood steadfastly against onslaughts. They had run out of food, however, and neither Basra nor Baghdad had sent backup notwithstanding the messages from Qurna asking for supplies.[77] Yahya's blockade was taking its toll; the garrison of Qurna was asking for help from the grand vizier who was marshalling the siege of Candia on Crete.

Yahya laid siege to Basra on 18 April 1669, and on 29 April, he captured the not-so-well fortified city. He then set about killing both the non-Basran Ottomans and the Ottoman-friendly Basrans in town. The land surveyor, the bookkeeper, Local officers, and other officials all fled to Baghdad without even taking their belongings.[78] Once Yahya's troops, made up of Marsh Arabs and the Banu Ka'b from Iran-Huvayza were done with their slaughter and plunder, a certain Hidayat sent word from within the town to the Afrasiyaboğlu-friendly Basrans who had fled into Iran amidst earlier uprisings: 'the opportunity is ours, immediately come to Basra!'[79]

Yahya's blockade of Qurna soon grew into a full-blown siege, but the garrison kept up the defence. The Bedouin-Iranian force besieging Qurna numbered 10,000 and wielded four cannons. The defenders had been sitting in trenches since the first day, yet no news of the awaited help had come. The besiegers heavily guarded their rear at Zakiya, where they had cut off the ship traffic. They had taken hold of the provisions from seven ships in transit and from three further ships sent to Qurna from Baghdad. The Safavid-vassal ruler of Huvayza, Afrasiyaboğlu Husein's long-time fellow in Iran, also helped Yahya by sending 400 further musketeers along with enough supplies to a force already made up mostly of Iranian subjects. Yahya's mounted patrol had also intercepted earlier papers coming from Basra, besides killing two captains and capturing five,[80] while another group on horseback ambushed the provision train earmarked for the Janissaries. On 30 April 1669, two months after the beginning of the clashes, the Qurna garrison's Local and Household captains wrote another letter, this time most likely to the governor-general of Baghdad: they had almost run out of stocks, even though a Bedouin chieftain had somehow been smuggling in some supplies.[81]

Firari Mustafa Pasha sent the Local Service along with the Beyat and Bajilan tribal warriors and a few of his own infantry companies to relieve the garrison. This detachment first overcame the Bedouin musketeers guarding the besiegers' rear between the Zakiya stream and the fortress, and then broke its way through the siege into Qurna. Yahya, probably fearing that more reinforcements might reach them soon, ordered an all-out onslaught. Qurna's garrison and the auxiliary cavalry waiting outside the fortress thwarted this with a counterattack, and in the battle on 25 May 1669, Yahya's forces were shattered. When the news of Yahya's definite uprising reached the imperial court on 6 August at the Kartalkayası highlands near Larissa, in Thessaly (Greece), Master-gatekeeper Mustafa Agha (thenceforward Kapıcıbaşı Mustafa Pasha) was appointed Basra's new governor and hurriedly sent off to Iraq. Firari Mustafa, still governing at Baghdad, was once again created marshal so as to install Kapıcıbaşı Mustafa to his governorate and quell any disobedience. Mindful that the rebels might regroup and again attack Qurna, the marshal and Basra's new governor led their own battalions along with Baghdad Locals to strike first, without even waiting for the troops from Diyarbekr, Mosul and Shahrizor called up to serve under the marshal. When this first-strike contingent showed up before Qurna at the end of August, Yahya deemed his cause lost. He pulled back across the Zakiya stream on 5 September and headed towards Basra with his leftover forces. Kapıcıbaşı Mustafa, however, sent a 2,000-strong detachment led by his stand-in to pursue the fleeing foe. Yahya, frightened by this, gave up the thought of re-entrenching himself in Basra, and crossed over to Iran on 6 September.[82]

Yahya first abided in the stronghold of Durak, but would soon be thrown out of Iran and find shelter in India.[83] Some of his scattered hirelings fled towards Basra and plundered it on their way out. Before heading out from Qurna for Basra, the marshal filled up the garrison to full strength, paid the soldiers' salaries for the next three months, stocked enough provisions for six months, and left abundant artillery as well as ammunition.[84]

The final defeat and flight of Yahya, who had been backed-up by Iranian subjects, happened at the same time as a Safavid officer defected to the Ottoman side. Muhammad Beyg from the Safavid military class, who was the chief of an unnamed clan most likely from the Kızılbaş, fled from Iran, sought shelter in the Empire together with his clansmen, and sought admission into Ottoman service. He was appointed governor of Trebizond, a remarkably high post that must have outmatched his rank in the Safavid hierarchy. Mehmed IV granted him an audience on 20 July 1669, and clothing him with a robe of honour for his new post, said: 'if you act uprightly, you will enjoy even more of my august grace'.[85] Muhammad Beyg, now (Ajam Mehmed) Pasha, would go on to hold various governorships with the Empire.[86]

Back by the Persian Gulf, the marshal entered Basra in early October 1669 and gathered the dignitaries on the same day. Judge Abdulhalim Efendi b. Abdullah officialised with an attestation that the marshal handed over the province to the new governor. Kapıcıbaşı Mustafa Pasha, together with the troops to man the garrisons, pledged to find out and prosecute any leftover cliques that had sided with Yahya, and hence with the Afrasiyaboğlus, as these had strong ties with Safavid vassals in Iran. The rest of the campaigning bannerlords, stewards, administrators, chancellors, officials, officers and Basran chieftains bore witness to the sitting.[87] This document, which also logged a full campaign report, was given to the marshal to acknowledge that he had fulfilled his commission.[88] The leftovers of the former principality thus were wiped out, and the land became an imperial province once again. The establishment of direct Ottoman rule in southern Iraq reshaped the power structure in the Persian Gulf, which would beget consequences in dealings with the Safavids.

Mehmed IV congratulated Firari Mustafa with his script: 'you shall prosper! You served worthily of my monarchy's reputation, honour shall be yours! You as well as my servants with you have attained my blessings. My bread is rightfully yours!' The padishah gifted the marshal one of his own swords and one of his own Privy sable furs overspread with a robe of honour. Firari Mustafa was now to take care of Baghdad, which the padishah called Iraq's bulwark against Iran. The governor was to keep an eye on the Household as well as Local garrison troops, and on the 'newly conquered'[89] Basra. He was also to run trustworthy spies in Iran, and let the imperial court know whenever something came up.[90]

The overthrown Afrasiyaboğlu establishment in Basra had been drawing on a hinterland that stretched over onto the Iranian side of the border. At each showdown with the Ottomans, the first measure that each uprising leader took had been to ship their family and movable wealth to the safekeeping of their Safavid-subject friends in Iran. The Afrasiyaboğlu's foremost confederate across the border had been the Mushasha rulers of Huvayza, but other dignitaries to the east of the Persian Gulf had been involved too. Safavid vassals in Iran had been available to the Afrasiyaboğlu establishment in Basra as a mercenary recruitment pool as well.

Nothing, however, hints that the shah had let the Afrasiyaboğlu regime hire men from among Safavid vassals. The Sublime Porte's downgrading Basra from tributary government to a hereditary fiefdom in 1655 seems to have been enough for the Safavids to accept that southern Iraq was now more tightly linked to the Empire, and that intervention in the region thenceforth was much more likely to trigger hostilities between Constantinople and Isfahan. That the Safavids forbade Afrasiyaboğlu Husein and Yahya to abide in Iran means that the Shahdom was aware of the new setting around the Persian Gulf. And Basra's becoming a regular governorate over 1667–9 must have cleared any doubts that may have lingered. The Shahdom would no longer foster uprisings against the Ottomans in southern Iraq.

Renewed Calls for the Safavids to join anti-Ottoman Alliances, False Alarms at the Border, Wasted Mobilisations

The last round of the Persian Gulf showdowns unfolded amidst the final and maybe the toughest phase of the siege of Candia. Strengthened each year with fresh troops, the sides fought on with trench ambushes, mine bursts, onslaughts, and on-and-off bargaining. Mehmed IV wintered in Larissa, mainland Greece, to oversee military shipments to the Imperial Army on Crete. Candia gave in at the same time as Firari Mustafa was about to enter Basra. The Turks thus completed the conquest of Crete from the Republic of Venice on 27 September 1669.[91]

Thereupon, most likely with a diplomatic herald,[92] Mehmed IV sent a victory letter[93] to 'Shah Suleiman His sublime Majesty, of Bahram's onslaught, shah of the throne of magnificence, sovereign of the realm of Ajam',[94] by doing which he 'upheld the pacts of amity'. After 'stressing Ottoman–Safavid friendship', Mehmed IV 'the shahenshah, the cosmic master'[95] summarised the Cretan War, for whose outbreak he blamed the Venetians. Descriptions of Ottoman investments, strength of Venetian fortifications, steadfastness of the defenders, unending contributions from Venetian allies, and the grimness of clashes all highlighted the accomplishment of the Ottoman conquests that followed. The padishah above all emphasised the Empire's ability to concentrate legions called up from faraway lands on one front, the firepower of Ottoman guns, potency of the sappers and miners, and the expertise of the military staff. The Sublime Porte thereby hinted at the overwhelming array of resources with which the Empire could sustain and win long-drawn-out, full-blown wars. The padishah asked the shah to 'undertake festivities and spread the glad tidings' when this letter reached him.

Like his lord 'the sultan of the Two Mainlands and khaqan of the Two Seas, second Alexander the Great, padishah of the Earth',[96] Köprülü Fazil Ahmed Pasha, who as commander-in-chief had brought a victorious end to the war, also sent a letter[97] to Iranian chief vizier Sheikh-Ali Xan Zangana 'his vizierial, regental, deputial, princely Highness'.[98] The grand vizier likewise recounted to his Iranian counterpart how the war had unfolded, remarking above all the conquests of the 'unattainable and prestigious' fortresses of Chania, Rethymno, and the 'impregnable' Candia. The Ottomans had waited so long to deal the deathblow to the Venetians in Crete because of the war with Germany in 1663–4, Köprülü argued, and he spoke of ammunition shipments, troop (re-)deployments and manoeuvers so as to underscore Ottoman military capabilities as well as the administrative set-up and resource base which these rested upon. Narrations of onslaughts, trench operations, artillery bombardments and mine blastings, meanwhile, depicted for Iranians how effectively the Ottomans fielded this potential. The letter's last part, however, differs from that of Mehmed IV:

> As required by unity, honesty, concord, and candor, a cordial letter of glad-tidings has also been written by [me] the Pure-of-Heart to Your deputial, princely Highness. It is appropriate to the requirements of forthrightness and peace that Your side also avoid situations inconsistent with the conditions of the treaty. It has been heard that formerly, Husein Pasha and Yahya Pasha, who were the banner bearers of rebellion and banditry in Basra, as a resort, so-to-say took refuge there [in Iran] from the sway of the padishah's vanquishing wrath and, in the vicinity of [Safavid] patronage, found admission to comfort and security. This unbecoming affair is contrary to the steady friendship between us. Previously, when the hell-blazing flames of the [padishah's] sovereign wrath had willed to melt down the evil and exhausted existence of Husein Pasha, who had embarked upon banditry, and the amassing of the [Ottoman] Triumphal Troops at that frontier had become necessary, and when correspondence had taken place for the expediency that no development inconsistent with peace be considered [by the Safavids] from this move [of the Ottomans], it had been correctly replied [by the Iranian chief vizier], in accordance with the ceremonies of unfaltering cordiality, in the musk-masked writing, that in no way would any favour or help, which would be in violation of the peace, be perpetrated towards the mentioned bandit.
>
> As matters stand, it is apparent that admitting those bandits, who took refuge there [in Iran], into the zone of patronage is this very help to those bad-charactered ones; it is evident that consenting to those who oppose [the Ottomans] here is itself contrary to the conditions of cohesion – may this undesirable affair not upset the source of affinity! It is appropriate of the situation that You affirm the pillars of affection by delivering – seized and bound – the bandits, who are the pacers of the valley of banditry, to the revered vizier, Our esteemed and high-standing brother, governor of Baghdad, the preeminent [Firari Kara] Mustafa Pasha.[99]

Sharing the news that the Ottoman Empire conclusively overcame the Republic of Venice and its allies was a fitting occasion to 'speak softly and carry a big stick' towards the Safavids. Köprülü Ahmed, rather than saying it out loud, drew instead a likeness of what he wanted the Iranians to keep in mind: the Empire could wage, keep up, and win full-blown wars against two great powers at the same time even when its separate armies were fielded in warzones on different continents and even when an uprising shook the imperial sway at a borderland faraway from both theatres of war, not to speak of what the Empire could score in an eastern campaign when not busy anywhere else. Forwarding this message in a non-embittering way, by rubbing it into the account of victory against the Venetian alliance, was a welcome opportunity to show teeth to the Safavids. And the Sublime Porte did not let this opportunity go by the board. The letter's content aside, the *inscriptio* which it put together for Sheikh-Ali Zangana also lays this bare, for it entitled the Iranian chief vizier as a high prince, whereas it was then the norm for the Ottoman grand vizier to be acknowledged at a kind of kingly degree, setting the Ottoman premier above his Iranian colleague. As with the padishah and the shah, the Ottoman grand vizier and the Safavid chief vizier too were counterparts by office and not peers by rank.

As to be understood from a cross-reading of the chronologies of the last Basran showdown and the siege of Candia, by the time these letters reached the Safavid court it had already driven Basra's overthrown lords out of Iran and afterwards these two took shelter in India, becoming incorporated into the Mughal service nobility. Therefore, the Safavids could safely argue that they had neither helped nor sheltered the outlaw pashas. And in all likelihood it happened so, because the Sublime Porte seems to have stopped protesting the Shahdom for harbouring these runaway pashas.

The conclusion of the Cretan War resounded in the contacts between the Ottomans' eastern and western neighbours, or rivals. In late 1669 or early 1670, Shah Suleiman sent a letter to the head of the losing side, Domenico II Contarini the doge of Venice, wherein he spoke of the 'protraction of [Venice's] war with Ottoman legion[s] on island Crete', and said that he had now learned of the peace after the Republic had given up the whole island.[100] In February/March 1670, Shah Suleiman granted an audience to Bogdan (Gurdziecki) the ambassador of Poland, and Mateos Avanik (a.k.a. Mgr. Iovhanesean/Matthieu Hovannes) the archbishop of Nakhchivan, both the ambassador and the archbishop having set out for Iran back in 1668. Ambassador Bogdan came to discuss trade, but was also entrusted with talking the Shah into teaming up with Poland–Lithuania and Russia in an alliance against the Ottomans. Archbishop Avanik brought letters from King Louis XIV of France, Pope Clemens IX, the Duke of Tuscany and the Doge of Venice calling on the shah to enter the Cretan War against the Ottomans.[101]

The coalition, however, had already broken up by the time of the audience, let alone that the Safavids would in all likelihood reject the calls even if these had reached the shah before the end of the war, as shown by all former and later attempts of this kind. Shah Suleiman turned down both invitations, and all available information hints that he would not to go into war against the Ottomans, regardless of when and how. The ending of the Cretan War must have only strengthened the shah's hand by affording him a sound justification. That from 1668 to 1670 too, as before, Iran outright rejected Polish and Russian offers of alliance against the Empire, harbingered the fate of like attempts in the 1670s, 80s and 90s.

On 5 April 1671, following the fulfillment of the land survey in southern Iraq, the imperial court shifted Firari Kara Mustafa Pasha from Baghdad to Basra.[102] (Silahdar) Kız Husein Pasha took the former marshal's stead in Baghdad on 9 May.[103] Now Basra too had a vizier-pasha (of three standards) rather than a pasha (of two standards),[104] which meant more Ottoman sanction power at the southernmost flank of the Iranian border. The Empire's annexation of the principality of Basra had reshaped the balance of power in the Persian Gulf between the Ottomans and the Safavids, and Basran governorship's raise to governor-generalship was one of the outcomes thereof. All was said and done. In November of the same year, Shah Suleiman's 'superintendent' and his 'head of the household servants' crossed the border from Erivan into the Empire for a long, non-official trip to Hejaz via Erzurum.[105] Ottoman–Safavid relations at the beginning of the 1670s were friendly enough for the shah's two high-ranking household officials to roam in the Empire for almost a year.

Away from the Iranian border, war had broken out in March 1672 between the Ottoman Empire and the Polish–Lithuanian Commonwealth over the Right-Bank Ukraine and its Cossacks. The Imperial Army, led by Mehmed IV himself, joined later by Petro Doroshenko's Cossack and Khan Selim I Giray's Crimean troops, took the fortress of Kamieniec-Podolski on 27 August. The Turks' further advance into Poland ended up in King Michael Wisniowiecki's bid for peace. The Peace of Buczacz, drawn up on 17 October, transferred the province of Podolia as a whole from the Commonwealth to the Turks, confirmed the Right-Bank Ukraine as Turkish-tributary under the hetmanship of Petro Doroshenko, and set down a yearly cash 'present' to be paid by the king to the padishah.[106]

Meanwhile, the good neighbourhood between the Sublime Porte and the Shahdom went on. The Safavids seem not to have reacted to the defection of an Iranian *xan* who, in 1672, after falling out of the shah's graces, sought shelter in the Ottoman state and became lodged in Scutari, the news of which spread to Constantinople on 1 June.[107] The Iranian–Ottoman border remained at rest. In January 1673, Çelebi Hasan Pasha, after reconfirmation as governor of Basra by a commissary coming from the Sublime Porte,[108] sent his sergeant of ceremonies[109] on a mission to the shah's court. This emissary reached Isfahan on 16 August 1673, and after making known that Çelebi Hasan wished to uphold the friendly relations, he discussed the regulations on the passage of Iranian pilgrims from Basra.[110]

Poland–Lithuania may have signed a peace with the Sublime Porte, but this did not mean that it gave up the hope of weakening the Ottoman Empire by having the Iranians attack it. In June 1673, John Sobieski, the great hetman of Poland, sent a letter to the shah with a Spanish cleric, Pedro Cubero Sebastian, and proposed building a military coalition against the Ottomans. A couple of months later, in September, the Russian ambassador Konstantin Khristoforov showed up in Isfahan. Housed at a royal dwelling and invited by Chief Minister Sheikh-Ali Zangana to talk secretly, Khristoforov said that Tsar Alexei wished to wage war against the padishah together with Poland–Lithuania and asked Iran to join. But Shah Suleiman declined, saying that Iran might set on Iraq but only if and after Russia and Poland had started and furthered the war. The chief vizier too spoke against breaking the Peace of Zuhab, reminding that European partners had erstwhile forsaken Iran by signing early peace treaties with the Sublime Porte. In the autumn of the next year, the Polish great hetman's emissary too would hear the same answer at his audience with the shah.[111] The Shahdom thus warded off another wave of Polish and Russian attempts to draw Iran into war against the Empire.

Amidst the Russian diplomacy in Isfahan, in 1673, the shah's commanders somehow concluded that the Ottomans would soon strike Iran, and therefore reviewed the troops, stocks and ordnance in the provinces along the western border. The building of a bulwark at the eastern side of the Erivan fortress, having begun a year ago, also continued, and would be finished the next year. The Safavids even recruited villagers to fill up Erivan's garrison. When Shah Suleiman headed out towards Kazvin in autumn 1673, it looked as if the Safavids were getting ready for a war, though afterwards nothing further happened in that direction.[112] Nothing on the Ottoman side of the border that could have triggered this restlessness in Iran stands out either. The Safavids' 1673 call-up must therefore have stemmed from wrong intelligence. And the measures died off evidently as soon as the misunderstanding became clear. The following year, however, again resulting from incorrect information, and at the same time as the handover of the Polish great hetman's abovesaid letter to the shah, a similar but more critical situation came about. Now the roles in the misunderstanding were switched.

This time, misleading hearsay about the Safavids startled the imperial court in eastern Europe. On 29 June 1674, at the way-stop of Isaccea in eastern Romania, as the Imperial Army marched towards Poland with

Mehmed IV and Köprülü Ahmed at its head, presentations came in from borderland governors warning that some things in breach of the peace were unfolding on the Iranian side.[113] Follow-up correspondence between the governorates in Iraq and the imperial court backed up this news. Mehmed Molla Çelebi, the judge of Baghdad, in an undated letter to the grand vizier, confirmed an earlier report of his: in Iran some governors and a few thousand troops had gathered, they were waiting in Huvayza, Ottoman officials in Iraq did not know why, but there was yet no unrest on the west side of the border.[114]

Next came Çelebi Hasan Pasha of Basra's letter to an agha, most likely the grand-vizieral steward, who might be called the Empire's pre-modern minister of the interior: the pasha had readied Basra's yearly tax and would take it to Baghdad himself together with a company of the Baghdad Local Service and the Bedouins of Abrushoğlu amir-Dindin as well as Mahzaoğlu amir-Nasir. But the pasha's spies, coming back from Huvayza-Iran on the eve of departure, had told that someone named Namubarak had risen up. After gathering the (Iranian-subject) tribes in the region and writing to those that dwelled farther, Namubarek had promised them the whole of Basra's yearly tax if they all set on the governor's caravan. That was why Çelebi Hasan had halted the journey until troops from Baghdad reached them. Namubarak had also teamed up with chieftains from the (Ottoman-subject) Mesopotamian Marshes by buying them over, and was keeping their sons as surety to the deal. This growing upheaval, if not nipped in the bud, could cost the Empire not only that year's tax from Basra but also the province of Basra as a whole, emphasised Çelebi Hasan. He pledged himself to fight to the death, but also warned worriedly that if not thwarted with enough force, this Bedouin coalition involving Safavid-subject tribes would shake the Ottomans' sway at the Iranian border, and cost the grand vizier dearly. He wanted the agha to forward this cry for help himself to the grand vizier.[115]

An upcoming crisis with Iran the grand vizier did not take lightly. In an undated letter, Köprülü Ahmed instructed Çelebi Hasan to wait, in line with Mehmed IV's decree, for the right time to step in. The governor of Basra meanwhile was to ready everything in utmost secrecy, not share this with anyone or lay bare his goal until the time of action, and to this end even make up separate pretexts if need be. Those in the service of the padishah, said the grand vizier, 'should think ahead, favour the Sublime State's reputation', and not repeat the well-known mistakes of forerunners.[116] The imperial court did not want the governor of Basra to intervene at this stage, lest this trigger a clash at the Iranian border before reinforcements could arrive.

1660–1682: The Persian Gulf

This news from around the Persian Gulf bothered the imperial court at a time when the Empire's main strength was concentrated near Poland, with Mehmed IV himself leading the imperial campaigns in 1673 and 1674 and the Crimean Khan as well as his army partaking in each one.[117] An entanglement with Iran at this time was the last thing the Ottomans needed. The imperial court was wary of taking a hasty step upon unconfirmed news and triggering an Iranian war when already fighting at the Ukrainian borderland.

The Ottomans took substantial measures to thwart a cross-border scramble, which they named a state matter of top priority. Arnavut Abdurrahman Abdi Pasha the commander of the Janissary Corps, an outstanding veteran of the siege of Candia against Venice, was forthwith made governor of Baghdad and ordered to ride thither at messenger speed from the Imperial Army then in eastern Romania marching north towards Poland. Kız Husein Pasha was accordingly shifted from Baghdad to Basra. The subsidiary government in Constantinople was made to ship great amounts of gear and ammunition from the capital to Van through Trebizond and to Baghdad through Alexandretta over Birejik. The governors of Raqqa, Mosul and Shahrizor were called up to guard middle Iraq. More papers speaking of Iranian military movements near Baghdad came in to the Imperial Army on 8 July 1674 at the way-stop of Zernish village in Moldavia, by the river Pruth. This further worried the imperial court: Aleppo's governor Kaplan Mustafa Pasha, who in this Polish war had served first as marshal of the Lviv campaign and later as general of the Imperial Army division gathered at Moldavia's capital Jassy, and who had experience of the Iranian borderland from his earlier governorships of Baghdad and Van, was now made governor of Diyarbekr and likewise hurriedly dispatched thither with messenger speed together with his own battalion and provincial troopers.[118] Diyarbekr, after all, situated one step behind the frontline provinces of Van and Baghdad, was a winter quarters for the Imperial Army in an Iranian war, while its provincial and governorate troops were natural participants in Iranian campaigns. One hundred further Household cannoneers were also sent to Baghdad on 29 August to join the Household and Local cannoneers already manning the fortress.[119]

Unrest on the southern flank of the Iranian border and the intervention coming all the way from Wallachia-Moldavia must have been the occasion for the imperial chancellery to write out a fresh copy of Shah Safi's 1639 writ of pledge ratifying the Peace of Zuhab, drawn up sometime between the summer of 1674 and March 1675.[120] The involvement of tribes from Iran in the uprising of a Bedouin coalition in southern Iraq might lead to a clash between Ottoman and Safavids troops. And if it came to that, citing the exact terms of the peace would be critical in making or rejecting an accusation of breach of peace.[121]

Only after Arnavut Abdi Pasha reached his post on 26 August 1674 did the Ottomans find out that the news was groundless: the hearsay had spread even within the fortress of Baghdad, but there was no Iranian military movement near the border. Nevertheless, the new governor had the fortifications repaired to soothe the public and increase the feeling of security. The incoming military shipments to Baghdad he also kept hold of, thereby topping up the fortress's stocks of food and ammunition.[122] These measures notwithstanding, the situation remained jumpy. After a disagreement about whether the Ottoman or the Safavid officials had the right to collect the customs toll at a border crossing to the north of the Persian Gulf ended up in a fight involving deaths, Arnavut Abdi declared a state of emergency and embarked upon a crackdown on those accused of providing intelligence to Iranians and plotting to abduct his family and belongings.[123] Military staff who had ties with Iran were also removed from service.[124]

Mistaken news of Iranian military activity at the border had most likely spread as Ottoman officials belatedly learned of the Iranians' mobilisation that, as we have seen, was itself triggered by earlier wrong information. The Ottomans first wrote that the Iranian mobilisation's goal was unknown and that no border breach was in sight. Ottoman reports drawn up after beholding the restlessness at the Iranian side of the border, which itself had been triggered by untrue hearsay, became in turn another mistaken intelligence, this time for the Empire, in that misgivings arose as to what the Safavids had in mind. Reciprocal call-ups in reaction, first, to incorrect news and, then, to a bloody brawl at the customs, pulled the pin out of the grenade, but it could be plugged back in before the blast.

Vassals by the border never ceased to provide the states with pretexts for hostilities if so wished. On 4 June 1675, the Mahmudi margrave of Khoshab, to the south of Van, sent a mission bearing a letter to the Safavid court: the padishah was meaning to undo the Mahmudis' fiefdom rights to Khoshab, and the margrave offered to become the shah's vassal in return for keeping his status. Shah Suleiman, after talking this over with his ministers, answered that he would not breach the peace, and advised the margrave to get on well with the Ottoman court.[125] Nor did third parties stop calling on Iran to wage war against the Empire. On 20 July, another Russian mission led again by A. Priklonskii and Konstantin Khristoforov reached the Safavid court: Tsar Alexei was asking the shah to set on the Ottomans with an army of 20,000. After the last few years' talks, the tsar now awaited a definitive answer, and a lag in answering he would take as rejection. The shah consulted with his officials at a meeting on 5 August, and then he turned down the bid, emphasising that it was in Iran's best interest to uphold the peace with the Empire even if this entailed breaking a deal with Russia.[126]

As this stillborn crisis at Kurdistan between the Sublime Porte and the Shahdom played itself out in 1675, the Polish–Turkish war in western Ukraine continued with the Imperial Army led this time by Marshal Şişman Ibrahim Pasha and the Crimean Khan. The following year, the Turks won the war, and in October 1676 the Peace of Zurawno confirmed the Polish losses.[127] Business at the Iranian border meanwhile went back to normal, as the mobilisations and counter-mobilisations triggered by mistaken news cooled off. In 1677, however, a new war broke out over the Ukraine, this time between the Russians and the Turks, when Petro Doroshenko cast off Turkish overlordship and handed over Chyhyryn, the hetmanate's capital until 1669, to Russia. Marshal Sheitan Ibrahim Pasha and Selim I Giray Khan of Crimea fell short of expectations in the 1677 campaign, wherefore Mehmed IV discharged the former and dethroned the latter. He made Grand Vizier Merzifonlu Kara Mustafa Pasha commander-in-chief in 1678, and fielded the newly enthroned Khan of Crimea, Murad Giray, to back him up. The Turks took Chyhyryn on 12 August and then tore it down. Yuri Khmelnytsky was installed as the new Turkish-tributary hetman of the Right-Bank Ukraine. The Peace of Bakhchysarai with Russia in 1681 would confirm the Turks' sway over the hetmanate and their right to keep the newly fortified positions along the Dnieper.[128]

Meanwhile low-key, non-political contacts between the Empire and Iran continued to take place,[129] but this stillness did not last long. In 1680 another hearsay spread in Iran's western borderlands, that this time the Ottomans were marching upon Erivan with 50,000 troops. Shah Suleiman forthwith appointed a marshal to raise an army of some 50–60,000 men. It soon showed, though, that putting together and keeping up such a force was beyond the capacity of Iran's strained resources.[130] The Shahdom was lucky that the aforesaid hearsay turned out to be false, thanks to which the Safavids could step down from high alert and dodge the embarrassing exposure of its own weakness.

A near-complete lull reigned between Constantinople and Isfahan in the few years that followed this last round of mistaken hearsay and counter-mobilisation. In the autumn of 1682, a mission from Dagestan's Shamkhal showed up at the Ottoman court. Only documented by a treasury memorandum for the emissary's subsidies given by the state from

11 to 20 October, this contact otherwise went down quietly, seemingly without leaving behind an extant diplomatic letter, imperial decree or chronicle entry.[131] On the one hand, by this mission, Buday Shamkhal may have asked for Ottoman help against a likely Russian onslaught.[132]

On the other hand, taken together with the earlier mission from Dagestan to the Sublime Porte fourteen years before, this contact may have refreshed Dagestan's homage to the Ottomans so that the Shamkhalate could seek help from them in a later emergency. There was no reason for the Sublime Porte not to welcome having an Ottoman-friendly ruler beyond the Empire's borders to the northwest of Iran. In the long run, the post-1639 Dagestan–Ottoman ties, which had begun with the Adrianople–Derbend diplomacy of 1668 and which this low-profile mission of 1682 fostered, would be deadly for the Safavids in the events leading up to their downfall. Thus began the 1680s, without the slightest foretoken that Iranian–Ottoman relations, and pre-modern diplomacy in Islamdom more generally, would be revolutionised just a few years later. The cards were about to be reshuffled in the Middle East.

Notes

1. Matthee, 'Basra', 67.
2. Farooqi, 'Mughal-Ottoman Relations', 98, 103.
3. Rota, 'Safavid Persia and its Diplomatic Relations with Venice', 151.
4. See Floor, *The Persian Gulf*, 484.
5. Abdi Paşa, *Vekâyi-nâme*, 236; al-Kaʾbi, *Zâd ul-Musâfir*, 20–1; *Tarih-i Raşid*, 80; Nazmizade, *Gülşen-i Hulefâ*, 277.
6. BOA, *Mühimme d.* 94. ent. 159.
7. Thomas Winkelbauer, *Österreichische Geschichte 1522–1699: Ständefreiheit und Fürstenmacht. Länder und Untertanen des Hauses Habsburges im konfessionellen Zeitalter Teil 1* (Wien: Ueberreuter, 2003), 151–7; Hammer von Purgstall, *Geschichte* vol. 6, 106–25, 128–46; İnalcık, *Devlet-i Aliyye III*, 75–102; Uzunçarşılı, *Osmanlı Târihi* vol. 3/1, 402–13.
8. Fındıklılı Mehmed, *Zeyl-i Fezleke*, 403; *Tarih-i Raşid*, 66.
9. Farooqi, 'Mughal-Ottoman Relations', 101–4.
10. Davide Trentacoste, 'The Marzocco and the Shir o Khorshid: The Origin and Decline of Medici Persian Diplomacy (1599–1721)', *Cyber Review of Moden Historiography* 24 (2021): 34–5.
11. Abdi Paşa, *Vekâyi-nâme*, 236; al-Kaʾbi, *Zâd ul-Musâfir*, 20–1; *Tarih-i Raşid*, 80; Nazmizade, *Gülşen-i Hulefâ*, 277. This Uzun Ibrahim Pasha of Banyaluka, a Bosnian (*Anonim Osmanlı Vekayinamesi*, 125; Fındıklılı Mehmed, *Zeyl-i Fezleke*, 165, 251, 376, 403; Murat Yıldız, 'Osmanlı Devlet Teşkilatında Bostancı Ocağı' (PhD diss., Marmara University,

2008) 279–80, 288), should not be mistaken for the other contemporary Uzun Ibrahim Pasha, an Albanian (Fındıklılı Mehmed, *Zeyl-i Fezleke*, 354, 369, 372, 397) who was then commander of the Janissary Corps.

12. Fındıklılı Mehmed, *Zeyl-i Fezleke*, 422–3; Ğurabzade, *ᶜUyûn Akhbâr*, 271a. In his exposition to the imperial government dated 21 March 1667, Gurji Kenan Pasha wrote that Ismail, the margrave of the tribe Zangana, had not participated in the Basran campaign in violation of the decree ordering him to do so, not sent troops to the siege of Qurna in violation of the law setting down one of the terms of his margraveship as patrolling during mobilisations, not kept his tribe under discipline, but helped bandits and oppressed the poor. His steward and the elders of the tribe had also filed a complaint about him. Gurji Kenan Pasha voted in support of appointing Ismail's son Omar as the new margrave, for the tribesmen supported him. See BOA, *İbnülemin – Askeriye*, 1656. Also see *İbnülemin – Askeriye*, 608.
13. *Tarih-i Raşid*, 80; Nazmizade, *Gülşen-i Hulefâ*, 277–9. For the sizes of armies and contingents, see Matthee, 'Basra', 68.
14. Nazmizade, *Gülşen-i Hulefâ*, 279–80; al-Kaᵓbi, *Zâd ul-Musâfir*, 32–3; Matthee, 'Basra', 68.
15. Matthee, *Persia in Crisis*, 126.
16. Fındıklılı Mehmed, *Zeyl-i Fezleke*, 423; Mühürdar Hasan Ağa, *Cevahirüᵓt-Tevarih*, 294; Müneccimbaşı, *Sahâifuᵓl-Ahbâr*, vol. 3, 743. According to the second source, the name of the herald is Abdulgani Agha.
17. Five hundred purses. One purse of *akçe* (asper): 500 *guruş* (thaler). Mehmet Zeki Pakalın, *Osmanlı Târih Deyimleri ve Terimleri Sözlüğü* vol. 2 (Istanbul: Millî Eğitim Basımevi, 1983), 248.
18. *irsâliyye*.
19. Abdi Paşa, *Vekâyi-nâme*, 236; Nazmizade, *Gülşen-i Hulefâ*, 281–2; *Tarih-i Raşid*, 80; Floor, *Persian Gulf*, 566, 570; Mühürdar Hasan Ağa, *Cevahirüᵓt-Tevarih*, 305; Fındıklılı Mehmed, *Zeyl-i Fezleke*, 423; al-Kaᵓbi, *Zâd ul-Musâfir*, 29–30, 33. In 1666 and 1667, Husein Pasha and Afrasiyab Beğ had to tax the Basrans heavily so as to pay the promised tribute and to keep up their reportedly 18,000-strong military. Matthee, 'Basra', 69.
20. Abdi Paşa, *Vekâyi-nâme*, 227; Fındıklılı Mehmed, *Zeyl-i Fezleke*, 423–4; Mühürdar Hasan Ağa, *Cevahirüᵓt-Tevarih*, 295.
21. Walî-kulu Shamlu, *Qisasuᵓl-Khâqânî* vol. 2 (HS 1373), 16–22.
22. Engelbert Kaempfer, *Am Hofe der persischen Großkönigs (1684–1685), das erste Buch der Amoenitates Exoticae*, ed. and trans. Walther Hinz (Leipzig: K. F. Koehler Verlag, 1940), 35–7.
23. *mîrzâ*.
24. İnalcık, *Devlet-i Aliyye III*, 103–4; Uzunçarşılı, *Osmanlı Târihi* vol. 3/1, 414–15, 419.
25. Abdi Paşa, *Vekâyi-nâme*, 257; *Tarih-i Raşid*, 92; Nazmizade, *Gülşen-i Hulefâ*, 283–4; Fındıklılı Mehmed, *Zeyl-i Fezleke*, 456, 495–6; Matthee, 'Basra', 69; Floor, *Persian Gulf*, 566.

26. *balyemez.*
27. *shâhî darb-zan (büyük döğücü).*
28. Fındıklılı Mehmed, *Zeyl-i Fezleke*, 496; Mühürdar Hasan Ağa, *Cevahirü'*t-*Tevarih*, 390, 397.
29. For a detailed list of war materials used as debit from the Imperial Armory and the Baghdad armory on this campaign, see the register compiled by Abdi the castellan of Baghdad: BOA, *Başmuhasebe Cebehane-i Amire Kalemi d.* 18367.
30. (*sadâret/rikâb-i humâyûn/âsitâna*) *qâimmaqâm(ı).*
31. BOA, *Sadaret Mektubi Kalemi b.* 1/61. Carrying no date, the letter was classified by the archivist as belonging to the year H 1073 (1662–3). However, it is most likely that the actual date is late summer of 1667. The letter is signed 'from the affectionate and candid Mustafa (*min al-muhibb-i mukhlis Mustafa*)', and the address is to the 'felicitate, esteemed, and eminent Highness, my brother the Pasha of imposing glory (*saadetlu ve izzatlu ve raf'atlu karındaşım paşa-yi jalilu'ş-şân hazratleri*)'. This signature and address were reserved for letters written from a superior to an inferior in Ottoman internal hierarchy: M. Kütükoğlu, *Osmanlı Belgelerinin Dili*, 223, 227. There were only two officials superior in rank to an army marshal: certainly the grand vizier, and arguably the vice grand vizier – in case one was appointed when the grand vizier himself was on campaign as commander-in-chief: see [Şâir] *Abrurrahman Abdi Paşa Kanunnâmesi*, 24, 45–6 for the vice grand vizier's powers, indicating this office's (at least) equality in rank with the vizier-marshal, over all other viziers. So, this Mustafa should be none other than vice grand vizier of the time Merzifonlu Kara Mustafa Pasha. His first term in this post was in 1663–4 and the second in 1666–9. While Pamuk Mustafa Pasha and Firari Kara Mustafa Pasha (second term), respectively, governed Baghdad for short terms in 1664, they led no campaigns to Basra that would have fitted in with this letter. Merzifonlu's second term as Köprülü Fazil Ahmed Pasha's vice grand vizier, however, perfectly overlaps with the time of the 1667 campaign that Firari Mustafa Pasha undertook in his third term at Baghdad. Another bit of evidence backing this up comes from the letter (*Sadaret Mektubi Kalemi b.* 1/62) classified next to the one above, carrying likewise no date but marked with the year H 1073 by the archivist. In this letter, Mustafa the governor-general of Baghdad asks an inferiour carrying the title *efendi* (again, apparent from the words used in the signature and the address) to intercede on his behalf so as to disassociate him from the arranged marriage with the imperial princess Fatime, Ahmed I's daughter, on the grounds that he did not have the financial means with which to make the implied payments and expenditure. This Mustafa should be none other than our Firari Mustafa Pasha who had been serving his third term at Baghdad since 9 April 1667. Because Fatime Sultan was actually married off to Kozbekçi Yusuf Pasha the governor-general of Ochakov-Silistra on 3 September 1667 and that the imperial

court must not have lost time in finding this next suitable candidate, this letter and the preceding one may have been written shortly before this marriage took place.
32. BOA, *Sadaret Mektubi Kalemi b.* 1/61. In yet another letter which must have been sent around the same time (the archival dating H 1087 is inaccurate), Merzifonlu Kara Mustafa asked Firari Kara Mustafa to postpone the debt claims of the merchants from whom Yahya had borrowed until Yahya was installed in Basra: *Sadaret Mektubi Kalemi b.* 2/11.
33. Topkapı, *Evrak*, 854/11: on this day, an on-site courthouse sitting was held in Yahya's lodging in the neighbourhood of Eski Nişancıpaşa. Balı b. Ali, the judge of Constantinople, sent Mawlana Mehmed Efendi b. Abdulbaqi to preside as his representative, Yahya himself was there, and Kurt Ali Agha deputised for vice grand vizier Merzifonlu, who was in Adrianople and who for this hearing was in turn named the deputy of none other than Mehmed IV. Such a high-profile gathering called for high-ranking witnesses, among whom were Hasan Agha the overseer of the state shipyards, three further aghas, and three clergymen posted to Basra; Yahya Pasha thereby acknowledged that he owed Mehmed IV 35,000 Dutch thaler and pledged to hand in this amount in Baghdad to Shahin Agha sent ahead of Governor-general Firari Mustafa Pasha to collect the said debt; Mehmed Efendi b. Abdulbaqi wrote down the proceeding, and judge Balı b. Ali signed off on the deed. In less than a month, the imperial chancellery took over the deed. The logging of Yahya's personal debt to Mehmed IV in a judge's attestation is unlikely to have been for that share of Basra's yearly lump-sum tax that was to be paid to the Privy Treasury rather than the Central Treasury; the state did not need an attestation if it had to prosecute a governor who defaulted on a tax payment or a political pledge. And to justify Yahya's tax collection in Basra, his imperial diploma of appointment would be enough. This attestation, then, must have been drawn up to put in writing a loan that the padishah had given from his Privy Purse to help towards the ongoing investment to uproot the Afrasiyaboğlu establishment from Basra.
34. BOA, *Divan Beylikçi Kalemi b.* 50/68.
35. Nazmizade, *Gülşen-i Hulefâ*, 284–5; al-Kaʾbi, *Zâd ul-Musâfir*, 13–14, 28, 38; Matthee, 'Basra', 69.
36. Kaempfer, *Hofe der persischen Großkönigs*, 45, 57.
37. *sarıca*.
38. BOA, *Ali Emiri – Mehmed IV*, 11910.
39. Mühürdar Hasan Ağa, *Cevahirüʾt-Tevarih*, 391; Nazmizade, *Gülşen-i Hulefâ*, 285.
40. Fındıklılı Mehmed, *Zeyl-i Fezleke*, 496.
41. Fındıklılı Mehmed, *Zeyl-i Fezleke*, 496–7; Mühürdar Hasan Ağa, *Cevahirüʾt-Tevarih*, 392; Müneccimbaşı, *Sahâifuʾl-Ahbâr*, vol. 3, 746; Nazmizade, *Gülşen-i Hulefâ*, 286–7; al-Kaʾbi, *Zâd ul-Musâfir*, 37–8.

42. *sağ[-kol] Gönüllüler.*
43. *sekban.*
44. *sarıca.*
45. Fındıklılı Mehmed, *Zeyl-i Fezleke*, 496–9; Mühürdar Hasan Ağa, *Cevahirü'␠t-Tevarih*, 392–5; Nazmizade, *Gülşen-i Hulefâ*, 286–8; Ğurabzade, *ᶜUyûn Akhbâr*, 271a; al-Kaʾbi, *Zâd ul-Musâfir*, 39–41; Müneccimbaşı, *Sahâifuʾl-Ahbâr*, vol. 3, 746.
46. *hujjat* by Hasan Efendi.
47. BOA, *Ali Emiri – Mehmed IV*, 3981.
48. Matthee, 'Basra', 70.
49. Here 'Bâb-i Âhanîn', the Arabo-Persianised version of the city's Turkish name 'Demirkapı'.
50. *aᶜlâ.*
51. BOA, *Ali Emiri – Mehmed IV*, 83/9897.
52. BOA, *Ali Emiri – Mehmed IV*, 96/11333; BOA, *Ali Emiri – Mehmed IV*, 25/2797. It seems from the logs that the emissary's consumption cost the state 300 aspers daily, for each ten-day span amounted to 3000 aspers.
53. *khâss.*
54. 'hâkimân-i Shamkhâl'. BOA, *Ali Emiri – Mehmed IV*, 83/9860: the state's purchase of 'bolsters and packs for the dispatch (*şilte ve bohça-hâyi irsâliya*)' to the Shamkhal.
55. Bülbül, 'Kumuk Türkleri ve Tarku Şamhallığı', 74–6.
56. Fındıklılı Mehmed, *Zeyl-i Fezleke*, 499–501; Mühürdar Hasan Ağa, *Cevahirü'␠t-Tevarih*, 396; al-Kaʾbi, *Zâd ul-Musâfir*, 42; Floor, *Persian Gulf*, 569.
57. al-Kaʾbi, *Zâd ul-Musâfir*, 42; Matthee, *Persia in Crisis*, 132. Afrasiyaboğlu Husein first made promises to seek support from the Portuguese for winning back Basra, but to no avail. He next showed up in India in 1669. Becoming titled Islam Xan Rûmî at the Mughal court, where he also had his son Afrasiyab admitted, he stayed there until his death in 1676. Fındıklılı Mehmed, *Zeyl-i Fezleke*, 499–501; [Muhammad Mufîd Mustawfî Bâfqî,] *Mukhtasar-i Mufîd (Joğrâfyâ-yi Îrân-zamîn dar ᶜAsr-i Safavî)*, ed. Iraj Afşar (Tehran: Bunyâd-i Mawqûfât-i Doktor Mahmûd Afshar, HS 1390), 42–3; Farooqi, 'Mugal-Ottoman Relations', 106–8, 400.
58. Abdi Paşa, *Vekâyi-nâme*, 328; *Tarih-i Raşid*, 102.
59. The Basran Local Service consisted of the following companies: a castellan, local Janissaries, right-flank Enlistees, left-flank Enlistees, Bachelors, local armourers, local cannoneers, the Guards. See the signers of the collective petition in BOA, *İbnülemin – Şükr-ü-Şikayet*, 47.
60. *Rikâb-i Humâyûn.*
61. *feth-nâme.*
62. Nazmizade, *Gülşen-i Hulefâ*, 288–9; Matthee, 'Basra', 71.
63. BOA, *Divan Beylikçi Kalemi b.* 53/3. Firari Mustafa Pasha's dispatches to the centre must have arrived in June or July 1668; the decree written onto

1660–1682: The Persian Gulf

this exposition and prescribing a travel licence for the return of the three commissaries to Baghdad was issued on 3 June 1668. Mehmed IV sent his congratulatory script along with a *sarâsar*-kind sable fur, one jewelled sword, and three palanquins from the Privy Treasury to the marshal with Musâhib Khalil Agha: Fındıklılı Mehmed, *Zeyl-i Fezleke*, 500.

64. BOA, *Divan Beylikçi Kalemi b*. 53/21: decree issued to Baghdad's governor-general, Basra's governor and Basra's judge. The income items logged in the survey were to be allotted among the Central Treasury, the Privy Purse, fiefs and the province's treasury. The governorate councils of Basra and Baghdad and the Imperial Registry would each get a copy of the final log.
65. BOA, *Divan Beylikçi Kalemi b*. 53/21. Three copies of the Local Service registers were to be kept respectively in Constantinople, Baghdad and Basra. Salaries were to be paid from the provincial treasury of Basra. A later copy of a decree issued on 18 August 1668 gives the total strength of the Locals as 2,100 instead of the original 2,750. Appointments to fill later vacancies were to be made only with the approval of Baghdad's governors-general (ibid). The new Local Service register was also requested to be sent to the Grand Vizier's headquarters, the encampment of the Imperial Army in Crete: BOA, *Beylikçi Kalemi b*. 53/24.
66. BOA, *Sadaret Mektubı Kalemi b*. 2/13.
67. BOA, *Sadaret Mektubı Kalemi b*. 1/68.
68. Nazmizade, *Gülşen-i Hulefâ*, 289; Ğurabzade, *ʿUyûn Akhbâr*, 271b.
69. *İstanbul Kadı Sicilleri 55, Rumeli Sadâreti Mahkemesi 127 Nolu Sicil (H. 1090–1091/M. 1679–1680)*, eds Akman, Soydemir and Sarıcaoğlu (Istanbul: Kültür A.Ş., 2019), 133, ent. 94. This entry is the registration by the highest courthouse of Ottoman Europe (Rumeli qazi-ʿaskarliği/sadârati), in Istanbul, of a business transaction and a property donation on 31 January 1680 between Mustafa Çelebi b. Ahmed Efendi and Abdulhalim Efendi b. Abdullah, the former judge of Basra. In all likelihood, Abdulhalim Efendi b. Abdullah referred to in 1680 as the former judge of Basra is the same Abdulhalim Efendi, the judge of Basra in 1669.
70. BOA, *İbnülemin – Şükr-ü-Şikayet*, 47; BOA, *İbnülemin – Askeriye*, 733; BOA, *Divan Beylikçi Kalemi b*. 57/15 (this later attestation by Abdulhalim Efendi logs the date of Yahya's escape as 9 March).
71. BOA, *Divan Beylikçi Kalemi b*. 57/15; Matthee, 'Basra', 71.
72. BOA, *İbnülemin – Şükr-ü-Şikayet*, 47.
73. *fatwâ*.
74. BOA, *İbnülemin – Dahiliye*, 630.
75. BOA, *Sadaret Mektubı Kalemi b*. 1/72.
76. BOA, *Sadaret Mektubı Kalemi b*. 1/73.
77. BOA, *Sadaret Mektubı Kalemi b*. 2/58.
78. The bookkeeper, the Locals' chief and another Local officer were accused of inappropriate conduct, and imprisoned in the fortress of Baghdad at the

grand vizier's behest: Nazmizade, *Gülşen-i Hulefâ*, 289; Matthee, 'Basra', 71.
79. BOA, *Ali Emiri – Mehmed IV*, 11600: a short register in Turkish on the sponsors of Afrasiyaboğlu Husein and Yahya pashas within Basra; a collective petition and cover letter in Arabic by Basran elders to the imperial court dated mid-December 1670, and a register in Persian of Basra's neighbourhoods logging the houses, their conditions and owners – all drawn up after the end of the Yahya Pasha affair.
80. *bölükbaşı*.
81. BOA, *İbnülemin – Askeriye*, 733; BOA, *Divan Beylikçi Kalemi b.* 57/16.
82. Abdi Paşa, *Vekâyi-nâme*, 328; Nazmizade, *Gülşen-i Hulefâ*, 288–90; *Tarih-i Raşid*, 102; Matthee, 'Basra', 71; Fındıklılı Mehmed, *Zeyl-i Fezleke*, 574; Floor, *Persian Gulf*, 573.
83. In 1671, Yahya Pasha too ended up in India like his former master Afrasiyaboğlu Husein. Received cordially, he was admitted into Mughal service nobility and proved to be a successful military commander: Farooqi, 'Mughal-Ottoman Relations', 109, 400; Ğurabzade, *ʿUyûn Akhbâr*, 271b.
84. BOA, *Divan Beylikçi Kalemi b.* 57/15, 57/16.
85. Karaçelebi-zade, *Ravzatüʾl-Ebrar Zeyli*, 325–7; *Tarih-i Raşid*, 101.
86. Ajam Mehmed Pasha, who was transferred from the subgovernorship of Chernomen in Thrace to that of Şebinkarahisar in northeastern Anatolia on 3 March 1683, one day after the departure of the Imperial Army with Mehmed IV at its head, from the field of Adrianople (see Fındıklılı Mehmed, *Zeyl-i Fezleke*, 795), is probably the same Mehmed Pasha.
87. BOA, *Divan Beylikçi Kalemi b.* 57/16; BOA, *Divan Beylikçi Kalemi b.* 74/48.
88. BOA, *Divan Beylikçi Kalemi b.* 57/16. Hasan Efendi, the judge of the Imperial Army, also drew up another attestation with the same content and sides on 14 October: BOA, *Sadaret Mektubı Kalemi b.* 1/80; BOA, *Divan Beylikçi Kalemi b.* 74/48. Also see BOA, *Divan Beylikçi Kalemi b.* 57/72.
89. 'yeni açılmış'.
90. BOA, *İbnülemin – HattıHümayun*, 342.
91. Setton, *Venice, Austria, and the Turks*, 193–235; Uzunçarşılı, *Osmanlı Târihi* vol. 3/1, 415–21; İnalcık, *Devlet-i Aliyye III*, 104.
92. The emissary's name is omitted in the surviving copy of the imperial letter.
93. *Asnâd u Mukâtabât, 1038–1105*, 250–7.
94. 'ʿâlî-hazrat, ... Bahram-sawlat, ... shâh-i sarîr-i hashmat, ... farmân-farmâ-yi mulk-i ʿAjam ... Suleiman Shah'.
95. 'shahenshah ... sâhib-qirân'.
96. 'sultânuʾl-Barrayn, khâqânuʾl-Bahrayn, sânî-yi Iskandar-i Zul-Qarnayn, ... pâdishâh-i Rûy-i Zamîn'.
97. Rami Mehmed, *Munshaʾât*, ff. 19a–21a; *Asnâd u Mukâtabât, 1038–1105*, 258–64.

1660–1682: The Persian Gulf

98. 'janâb-i vazârat-maʾâb, niyâbat-iyâb, wakâlat-intisâb . . . iyâlat-iyâb'.
99. Ibid.
100. See the shah's letter in Fekete, *Einführung in die persische Paläographie*, 535–8, tables 225–6.
101. Rota, 'Safavid Persia and its Diplomatic Relations with Venice', 151; Rudi Matthee, 'Iran's Ottoman Diplomacy During the Reign of Shah Sulayman I (1077–1105/1666–94)', in *Iran and Iranian Studies: Essays in Honor of Iraj Afshar*, ed. Kambiz Eslami (Princeton: Zagros, 1998), 154–5; Colette Ouahes and Willem Floor (trans. and ann.), *A Man of Two Worlds: Pedros Bedik in Iran 1670–1675* (Washington, DC: Mage Publishers, 2014), xxii–xxiii; Kołodziejczyk, *Polish-Lithuanian Commonwealth with Safavid Iran*, 89–92.
102. Abdi Paşa, *Vekâyi-nâme*, 347.
103. Nazmizade, *Gülşen-i Hulefâ*, 292–3. A copy of the survey register was sent to the central government and another copy was kept in Basra. After the survey and before his next appointment, Firari Mustafa Pasha returned to Baghdad in late April 1671.
104. I understand this from the correspondence between Firari Mustafa Pasha (as governor-general of Basra) and his successor in Baghdad, Silahdar Kız Husein Pasha. The latter too was a vizier, as indicated by his title and by the definition of his office: Nazmizade, *Gülşen-i Hulefâ*, 293, 297; *Tarih-i Raşid*, 149. Normally, owing to his vizierial grade and given Baghdad's watch over Basra as prescribed by the state, the governor-general of Baghdad would be expected to have precedence over that of Basra. However, the titulature Firari Mustafa Pasha used in his correspondence with Kız Husein Pasha is that which was used in Ottoman diplomatics when a superior addressed an inferior. This could not have been the case if Firari Mustafa Pasha had not kept his vizierial grade and without his former mandate as marshal: BOA, *Sadaret Mektubı Kalemi b.* 1/75.
105. *Journal of Zakʾaria of Agulis*, 110.
106. Dariusz Kołodziejczyk, *Ottoman–Polish Diplomatic Relations (15th–18th Centuries): An Annotated Edition of ʿAhdnames and Other Documents* (Leiden: Brill, 2000), 144–8.
107. Antonie Galland, *İstanbulʾa Ait Günlük Hâtırat (1672–1673)* vol. 1, ed. and trans. Nahid Sırrı Ödik (Ankara: Türk Târih Kurumu, 2000), 150.
108. The commissary who brought the diploma (*manshûr*; or *barʾat* (charter) for appointments below that of three[or two?]-standard pashas) also took over the estate of the late Firari Mustafa Pasha: Matthee, 'Basra', 72; *Chronicle of Events Between the Years 1623 and 1733 Relating to the Settlement of the Order of Carmelites in Mesopotamia (Bassora)*, ed. Hermann Gollanz (London: Oxford University Press, 1927), 333.
109. *salâm/alkış çavuşu*.
110. Chardin, *Seyahatnâme*, 413.
111. Konstantin Khristoforov had followed up on an earlier Russian mission in

1672 by A. Priklonskii: Chardin, *Seyahatnâme*, 447; *Journal of Zakʾaria of Agulis*, 117–18, 124; Matthee, 'Iran's Ottoman Diplomacy', 156–7.
112. *Journal of Zakʾaria of Agulis*, 117–18, 124; Matthee, 'Iran's Ottoman Diplomacy', 152, 156–7.
113. Abdi Paşa, *Vekâyi-nâme*, 426; *Tarih-i Raşid*, 181.
114. Topkapı, *Evrak*, 243.
115. BOA, *Divan Beylikçi Kalemi* b. 72/98 (H 1085).
116. *Majmûʿa-i Mukâtabat*, 21b–22a. Aside from the content, the only information we have is provided in the title given by the compiler of the correspondence volume: 'is gone from Köprülü-zade Fazıl Ahmed Pasha to the governor of Basra'. Nothing recorded by the sources other than this title helps date this letter.
117. Kołodziejczyk, *Ottoman–Polish Diplomatic Relations*, 148–9.
118. Abdi Paşa, *Vekâyi-nâme*, 426–7; *Tarih-i Raşid*, 181; Sarı Mehmed, *Zübde-i Vekâiyât*, 48; Fındıklılı Mehmed, *Zeyl-i Fezleke*, 659, also see 630–58.
119. BOA, *Cevdet – Askeriye*, 43935.
120. BOA, *İbnülemin – Hariciye*, 4/407.
121. In the given timespan, only the developments of June and July 1674 could reasonably have brought on the reproduction of the Safavid ratification of the Peace of Zuhab. For if a breach came from the Iranian side of the border, the Sublime Porte must have wanted to base its reaction upon the Safavid version of the treaty. The reproduction was in all likelihood not made for archive keeping, but for practical use in a live crisis. Moreover, in this reproduction, the chancellery used red ink for Quranic verses and Prophetic sayings within a text otherwise written in black: this practice was more conventional in prestigious documents, such as imperial letters or diplomas, which could be shown to a third party to exercise the power they warranted, rather than in copies made to refresh archival logs. Furthermore, the handwriting of this reproduction is outstandingly clear. The scribe wrote in so-to-speak block letters, and the script is free from any artistic stylisations that would boost the document's artistic worth but make its reading less flowing. Such readability hints that the reproduction must have been meant to be physically shown to Safavid addressees likely in talks or disagreements. So careful a finishing would not have been done on a reproduction made for the archives.
122. Nazmizade, *Gülşen-i Hulefâ*, 298–9; *Tarih-i Raşid*, 133, 148.
123. Chardin, *Voyages* vol. 9, 232–3.
124. BOA, *İbnülemin – Askeriye*, 1297: Arnavut Abdi's exposition asking the imperial court to give somebody named Ali the fief formerly held by the feudal trooper Husein who had fled to Iran six or seven years earlier. The request was granted on 8 February 1676.
125. Chardin, *Voyages* vol. 9, 243.
126. Chardin, *Voyages* vol. 9, 337–8; Matthee, *Persia in Crisis*, 131. Matthee deems it probable that 'the decision to defuse the mounting tension may

have been informed by the reaction of the Ottomans who, meanwhile, had moved artillery and other military equipment from Alexandretta to Baghdad. Ottoman intimidation similarly may have determined the outcome ...': Matthee, 'Iran's Ottoman Diplomacy', 157. While this cannot be ruled out, Safavid shahs' successive rejections of each offer to make Iran part of an anti-Ottoman alliance hint at a longer-term state policy rather than at isolated occasions for rejection in each case (ibid).

127. Kołodziejczyk, *Ottoman–Polish Diplomatic Relations*, 148–9.
128. Uzunçarşılı, *Osmanlı Târihi* vol. 3/1, 429–33.
129. For example, a mastership licence (*khilâfat-nâma*) survives from the year 1678, drawn up by the Safavid deputy-grandmaster's (*khalîfetuʾl-khulafâ*) office, promulgated by Shah Suleiman himself in his capacity as grandmaster of the Kızılbaş order, and issued to Seyyid Muhammad Tahir, the Sufi-master (*khalîfe*) of the Kavi community in the Akçadağ banner in Ottoman eastern Anatolia. The addressee had visited the Safavids' court, in all likelihood the order's headquarters in Ardabil. See Karakaya-Stump, *Kizilbash in Ottoman Anatolia*, 231–4.
130. Matthee, *Persia in Crisis*, 135–6.
131. BOA, *İbnülemim – Hariciye*, 2/231.
132. Bülbül, 'Kumuk Türkleri ve Tarku Şamhallığı', 77–8.

Afterword

The history of Ottoman–Safavid relations progressed in three stages. The first period runs from the Safavids' state formation in 1500 up to the settlement of Amasya in 1555. The second, which begins in 1555, comes to an end with the Peace of Zuhab in 1639. Over these 140 years marked by conflict, the Ottomans first thwarted onslaughts towards Anatolia, then wrested Kurdistan and Iraq, and finally consolidated their hold on these conquests. Our familiarity with the studies on these 140 years of strife have instilled in us a habit of thinking about Ottoman–Safavid relations mainly in terms of warfare, and conditioned us to deem eventless the later decades from 1639 to the downfall of the Savafid monarchy in 1722. Implied in this outlook is that as soon as the fighting ended, the two sides became unwilling to deal with each other, and settled to abide by a peace that rested only on non-aggression and a roughly sketched border.

As I hope to have shown in this book, however, this was not the case. Rather, from 1639 onwards, the Ottoman Empire and Safavid Iran thoroughly engaged one another by courtly diplomacy and near-constant interactions at the border. They swapped missions, sent letters, bargained, regulated an interstate hierarchy, struck deals, confronted each other, and went through crises that threatened to imperil the very foundations of the peace. This diplomacy was not only ceremonial; it held substantial stakes. Both states also strived to gain the upper hand in borderlands time and again by stirring up insubordination, staging shows of strength, crushing uprisings, furthering their sway, disputing the line of demarcation, demanding compensation for breaches and running spies. And they did all this while upholding their formal friendship.

Following the Peace of Zuhab, it took the parties almost four years of intensive diplomacy to overcome the complications, which had arisen after the signing and hindered the treaty's enforcement. Relations remained tense in the 1640s, when unsettled border disputes and Venetian attempts to draw Iran into the Cretan War prompted the Ottomans to field an Imperial Army near the Iranian border at Armenia, testing the soundness

Afterword

of the treaty. Nevertheless, peace persisted through not only these brittle moments but also the longer-running tensions and mobilisations around the Persian Gulf. Such chronic entanglements and the diplomatic contacts tackling them set the agenda of Ottoman–Safavid dealings throughout the 1650s, 60s and 70s. Underpinning relations throughout this period, as indeed had been the case since the late 1510s, was the Safavid acknowledgement of Ottoman superiority in hierarchy and in the scale of power on every platform where the two sides dealt with each other.

This book stops at the year 1682. But the story it tells does not. The terms of the Peace of Zuhab would continue to premise Ottoman–Safavid relations in the decades thereafter, as the two states set about building an actual alliance, which was something unheard-of in their mutual history over the earlier two centuries. This rapprochement would come to pass thanks to both outside factors and underlying bilateral dynamics. The Sublime Porte and the Shahdom would even go as far as to entrust the safety of their shared border to each other and acknowledge themselves as brothers and allies in an everlasting peace – all while the Ottoman–Safavid inequality remained in place and the Ottomans performed further shows of might for the Safavids to behold. Even uprisings of international scale upsetting whole Imperial and Iranian provinces in Kurdistan and in the Persian Gulf could not break this trend: the traffic of delegations and correspondence between Adrianople–Baghdad and Isfahan throughout the Ottomans' war against the Holy League (1684–99) would take the cooperation with the Safavids even a step further. From 1701 onwards, however, with the favourable international setting gone and an anti-Ottoman Iranian government in power, diplomatic strifes and border clashes would haunt relations. Nevertheless, both states would keep on paying occasional lip service to their brotherhood, alliance and everlasting peace, and no war between them would break out until the Afghan overthrow of the Safavid monarchy in 1722. My next book will handle this post-1682 episode of the history narrated in the present work.

Unlike the assumption that has become part of our received knowledge, notwithstanding the lack of research to back it up, diplomacy and contacts between the two parties after the 1639 Peace of Zuhab were anything but eventless. Thanks to better documentation, and without war as an agenda-setter to weigh down all other matters to at best secondary importance, it becomes evident that relations in this period were at least as manifold as in earlier stages. As it comes to light, when not waging war against one another, the Ottomans and the Safavids shuttled diplomatic missions and found substantial agenda to bargain on. The full significance thereof can be grasped only by considering each individual affair throughout this peacetime together with the trends they highlight.

The workings of this detente carry implications not only for the timespan before it, but also for the wider field of premodern eastern diplomacy. The studied case suggests that we need to be more careful to not over-represent military campaigns and war-related diplomacy in our attempts to understand early modern interstate dealings in the Middle East. This present study offers a salutary reminder that premodern Middle Eastern diplomacy was not premised on war alone; peacetime interactions prove to have been no less consequential in begetting substantial content. The axioms of received historiographical wisdom may thus require emendation as we set about evaluating anew the principles of diplomacy in the premodern Middle East, which turns out to have been much more complex, hierarchically structured, regulated, multi-faceted and elaborate than we previously thought.

Bibliography

Primary Sources

Abdülkâdir Efendi. *Topçular Katibi Abdülkâdir (Kadrî) Efendi Târihi*. Edited by Ziya Yılmazer. Ankara: Türk Tarih Kurumu, 2003.

[Abdurrahman Abdi Paşa, Şâir.] *Abdurrahman Abdi Paşa Kanunnâmesi*. Edited by H. Ahmet Arslantürk. Istanbul: Okur Kitaplığı, 2012.

Abdurrahman Abdi Paşa, [Şair]. *Vekâyi-nâme*. Edited by Fahri Ç. Derin. Istanbul: Çamlıca, 2008.

Afshar, Iraj (ed.). 'Du Farmân-i Safavî Marbût ba Ravâbit-i Îrân u Lahistân.' *Râhnamây-i Kitâb* 5 (1962): 581–5.

[of Agulis, Zakaria.] *The Journal of Zakᵓaria of Agulis*. Edited and translated by George A. Bournoutian. Costa Mesa, CA: Mazda Publishers, 2003.

Andersen, Jürgen, and Volquard Iversen. *Orientalische Reise-Beschreibungen*. Schleswig: Fürstliche Druckerei durch Johan Holwein, 1669.

Anonim Osmanlı Vekayinamesi (H. 1058–1106/M. 1648–1694). Edited by Ramazan Aktemur as an MA thesis, Istanbul University, 2019.

Astarâbâdî, Seyyid Husein. *Târîkh-i Sultânî az Shaykh Safî tâ Shâh Safî*. Edited by Ihsân Ishrâqî. Tehran: Intishârât-i ᶜIlmî, HS 1366.

[Bâfqî, Muhammad Mufîd Mustawfî.] *Mukhtasar-i Mufîd (Joğrâfyâ-yi Îrânzamîn dar ᶜAsr-i Safavî)*. Edited by Iraj Afşar. Tehran: Bunyâd-i Mawqûfât-i Doktor Mahmûd Afshar, HS 1390.

Bayâz-i Daftarkhâna-i Humâyûnî-yi Davlat-i Îrân-i ᶜAsr-i Safavî. Edited by Mansur Sefatgol. Tokyo: Research and Information Center for Asian Studies, Institute for Advanced Studies on Asia, University of Tokyo, 2023.

Bîzhan. [*Sahîfa-i Girâmî*]. Published in Giorgio Rota, *La vita e i tempi di Rostam Khan (Edizione e Traduzione Italiana del Ms. British Library Add 7,655)*. Vienna: Verlag der Österreichische Akademie der Wissenschaften, 2009.

BOA. (Başkanlık Osmanlı Arşivi, Ottoman State Archives of Turkey). Collections used:
  Ali Emiri – Ahmed III
  Ali Emiri – Ibrahim
  Ali Emiri – Mehmed IV
  Ali Emiri – Murad IV
  Ali Emiri – Mustafa II

Bâb-ı Âsafî Defterhâne-i Âmire Defterleri
Başmuhasebe Cebehane-i Amire Kalemi Defterleri
Cevdet – Askeriye
Cevdet – Hariciye
Divan Beylikçi Kalemi Belgeleri
Hatt-ı Humayun
İbnülemin – Askeriye
İbnülemin – Dahiliye
İbnülemin – Hariciye
İbnülemin – HattıHümayun
İbnülemin – Şükr-ü-Şikayet
İbnülemin – Tevcihat
Mühimme Defterleri
Name-i Humayun Defterleri
Sadaret Mektubi Kalemi Belgeleri

Chardin, Jean. *Chardin Seyahatnâmesi: İstanbul, Osmanlı Toprakları, Gürcistan, Ermenistan, İran 1671–1673*. Translated by Ayşe Meral, edited by Stefanos Yerasimos. Istanbul: Kitap Yayınevi, 2013.

Chardin, Jean. *Voyages du Chevalier Chardin en Perse, et autres lieux de l'Orient*. Paris: le Normant, Imprimeur-Libraire, 1811.

Chronicle of Events Between the Years 1623 and 1733 Relating to the Settlement of the Order of Carmelites in Mesopotamia (Bassora). Edited by Hermann Gollanz. London: Oxford University Press, 1927.

Evoğlu, Haydar Beyg. *Majmaʿuʾl-Inshâ*. Manuscript from British Library, Ms. Add. 7668.

Fekete, Lajos (ed.). *Einführung in die persische Paläographie: 101 Dokumente*. Published by György Hazai. Budapest: Akademiai Kiado, 1977.

Feridun, Ahmed Bey. *Münşeatü's-Selâtîn* vol. 1. [Istanbul]: Takvimhâne, H 1275.

Fındıklılı, Silahdar Mehmed Ağa. *Zeyl-i Fezleke*. Published in Nazire Karaçay Türkal, 'Silahdar Fındıklılı Mehmed Ağa. Zeyl-i Fezleke (1065 – 22. Ca. 1106 / 1654 – 7 Şubat 1695).' PhD diss., Marmara Üniversitesi, 2012.

Galland, Antonie. *İstanbulʾa Ait Günlük Hâtırat (1672–1673)*. Edited and translated by Nahid Sırrı Ödik. Ankara: Türk Târih Kurumu, 2000.

Ğurabzade, Ahmed b. Abdullah Baghdadi. *ʿUyûn Akhbâr al-Aʾyân*. Manuscript from the British Library, MS 23309.

Hibrî, Abdurrahman Efendi. *Defter-i Ahbâr*. Published in Muhittin Aykun's MA thesis 'Abdurrahman Hibrî Efendi, Defter-i Ahbâr (Transkripsiyon ve Değerlendirme).' Marmara Üniversitesi,, 2004.

İstanbul Kadı Sicilleri 55, Rumeli Sadâreti Mahkemesi 127 Nolu Sicil (H. 1090–1091/M. 1679–1680). Edited by Akman, Soydemir and Sarıcaoğlu. Istanbul: Kültür A.Ş., 2019.

al-Kaʾbi, Fathullah b. ʿAlwaan. *Zâd ul-Musâfir wa Luhnat ul-Muqîm wal-Hâdir*. Baghdad: Matbaʾat ul-Maʾârif, 1958.

Bibliography

Kaempfer, Engelbert. *Am Hofe der persischen Großkönigs (1684–1685), das erste Buch der Amoenitates Exoticae*. Edited and translated by Walther Hinz. Leipzig: K. F. Koehler Verlag, 1940.

Karaçelebizade, Abdülaziz Efendi. *Ravzatü'l-Ebrar Zeyli*. Edited by Nevzat Kaya. Ankara: Türk Tarih Kurumu, 2003.

Karaçelebizade, Abdülaziz Efendi. *Ravzatü'l-Ebrar*. Published in İbrahim Özgül, 'Ravzatü'l-Ebrâr [Kara Çelebi-Zade Abdülaziz Efendi'nin Ravzaü'l-Ebrâr Adlı Eseri (1299–1648) Tahlil ve Metin].' PhD diss., Atatürk Üniversitesi, 2010.

Karaçelebizade, Abdülaziz Efendi. *Zafername*. Published in Nermin Yıldırım's MA thesis 'Kara Çelebizâde Abdülaziz Efendi'nin Zafername Adlı Eseri (Tarihçe-i Feth-i Revan ve Bağdad): Tahlil ve Metin.' Mimar Sinan Üniversitesi, 2005.

Katib Çelebi, Hacı Halife Mustafa. *Fezleke*. Published in Zeynep Aycibin, 'Kâtib Çelebi. Fezleke. Tahlil ve Metin. I-II-III.' PhD diss., Mimar Sinan Üniversitesi, 2007.

Kazvini, Muhammad Tahir Wahid. *ʿAbbâsnâma, yâ Sharh-i Zindagânî-yi 22-Sâla-i Shâh ʿAbbâs-i Sânî (1052–1073)*. Edited by Ibrahim Dihgân. Erâk: Kitâb-furûshi-yi Dâvûdî-yi Erâk, 1329.

Kazvini-Isfahani, Muhammad Yusuf Walih. *Khuld-i Barîn [Îrân dar Zamân-i Shâh Safî vu Shâh ʿAbbâs-i Duvvum]*. Edited by Muhammad Rizâ Nasiri. Tehran: Anjuman-i Âsâr u Mafâkhir-i Farhangî, 2003.

Khâjagî-Isfahânî, Muhammad Masûm b. *Khulâsatu's-Siyar*. Edited by Iraj Afshar. Tehran: Intishârât-ı ʿIlmî, 1358.

Majmûʿa-i Mukâtabat. Manuscript from Österreichische Nationalbibliothek, *Orientalische Handschriften*, Cod.Mixt. 371.

Majmûʿa-i Makâtib. Manuscript from Staatsbibliothek zu Berlin, *Orientabteilung*, Ms. or. quart. 1577.

Muahedat Mecmuası II. Ankara: Türk Târih Kurumu, 2008.

Mühürdar, Hasan Ağa. *Cevahirü't-Tevarih*. Published in Ebubekir Sıddık Yücel, 'Mühürdar Hasan Ağa'nın Cevâhirü't-Tevârihi.' PhD diss., Erciyes Üniversitesi, 1996.

Müneccimbaşı, Derviş Ahmed Dede Efendi. *Sahâifu'l-Akhbâr* III. Translated by Ahmed Nedim. Istanbul: [Matbaa-i Amire], 1285.

Naima, Mustafa Efendi. *Târih-i Naʾîmâ*. Edited by Mehmet İpşirli. Ankara: Türk Tarih Kurumu, 2007.

Nasiri, Mirza Naqi. *Titles and Emoluments in Safavid Iran: A Third Manual of Safavid Administration*. Edited by Willem Floor. Washington, DC: Mage Publishers, 2008.

Navâî, AbdulHusein (ed.). *Asnâd u Mukâtabât-i Siyâsî-yi Îrân az Sâl-i 1038 ta 1105*. Tehran: Bunyâd-i Farhang-i Îrân, HS 1360.

Nazmizade, [Hüseyin] Murteza [Efendi]. *Gülşen-i Hulefâ: Bağdat Tarihi 762–1717*. Edited by Mehmet Karataş. Ankara: Türk Tarih Kurumu, 2014.

Nihâdî, Hacı Halife Mustafa. *Târih-i Nihâdî*. Published in Hasine Biga, 'Târih-i

Nihâdî (1b-80a) (Transkripsyon ve Değerlendirme).' MA thesis, Marmara Üniversitesi, 2004.

Özkasap, Hande Nalan, 'Târih-i Nihâdî (152b–233a) (Transkripsiyon ve Değerlendirme).' MA thesis, Marmara Üniversitesi, 2004.

Ralamb, Claes. *İstanbul'a Bir Yolculuk 1657–1658*. Translated by Ayda Arel. Istanbul: Kitap Yayınevi, 2008.

Rami, Mehmed, *Munshaʾât*. Manuscript from Österreichische Nationalbibliothek, HO 179.

Raşid, Mehmed Efendi, and Çelebizade, İsmail Asım Efendi. *Tarih-i Raşid ve Zeyli*. Edited by Abdülkadir Özcan, Yunus Uğur, Baki Çakır and Ahmet Zeki İzgöer. Istanbul: Klasik, 2013.

[von Reningen, Simon Reniger.] 'Die Hauptrelation des Kaiserlichen Residenten in Constantinopel Simon Reniger von Reningen 1649–1666.' Edited by Alois Veltze, *Mittheilungen des K. und K. Kriegs-Archivs* N.F. vol. 12, 98.

Sarı, Mehmed Paşa. *Zübde-i Vekâiyât: Tahlil ve Metin (1066–1116/1656–1704)*. Edited by Abdülkadir Özcan. Ankara: Türk Târih Kurumu, 1995.

Sarı Abdullah Efendi and İbrahim Çelebi Cevri. *Dastûruʾl-Inshâ*. Manuscript from Süleymaniye Kütüphanesi, *Nur-ı Osmaniye* no. 4304.

Schmid [von Schwarzenhorn], Johann Rudolf. *Finalrelation 1–4 vom 12. November 1643*. Published in Peter Meienberger, *Johann Rudolf Schmid zum Schwarzenhorn als kaiserlicher Resident in Konstantinopel in den Jahren 1629–1643*. Bern: H. Lang: 1973.

Shamlu, Walî-kulu bin Davud-kulu. *Qisasuʾl-Khâqânî*. Edited by Sayyid Hasan Sâdât Nâsirî. Tehran: Sâzmân-i Châp u Intishârât-i Vazârat-i Farhang u Irshâd-i Islâmî, 1371.

Solakzâde, Mehmed Efendi. *Târih*. Istanbul: Mahmud Bey Matbaası, H 1298.

of Tabriz, Arakʾel. *Book of History*. Translated by George A. Bournoutian. Costa Mesa: Mazda Publishers, 2010.

Tafrishî, Abûlmafâkhir. *Târîkh-i Shâh Safî*. Edited by Muhsin Bahrâm-Nijhâd. Tehran: Mîrâs-i Maktûb, HS 1388.

Târîkh-i Safaviyân: Khulâsatuʾl-Tavârîkh & Târîkh-i Mullâ Kamâl. Edited by Ibrahim Dihgân. Arâk: Châp-i Farvardîn, HS 1334.

Tavernier, Jean-Baptiste. *Tavernier Seyahatnâmesi*. Translated by Teoman Tunçdoğan. Istanbul: Kitap Yayınevi, 2010.

Topkapı Sarayı Müzesi Arşivi (Topkapı Palace Archives). Collections used:
Defter
Evrak

Türkman, Iskandar Beyg Munshî. *Zayl-i Târîkh-i ʿÂlam-ârâ-yi ʿAbbâsî*. Edited by Ahmed Suhayli Khvânsârî. Tehran: Châpkhâna-i Islâmiya, 1317.

Uysal, Satiye Büşra, 'Tarih-i Nihâdî (80b–152a) (Transkrispyon ve Değerlendirme).' MA thesis, Marmara Üniversitesi, 2004.

Vecihi, Hasan Efendi. *Tarih-i Vecihi*. Published in Buğra Atsız, *Das Osmanische Reich um die Mitte des 17. Jahrhunderts. Nach den Chroniken des Vecihi*

Bibliography

(1637–1660) und des Mehmed Halifa (1633–1660). Munich: Dr. Dr. Rudolf Trofenik, 1977.

Zıllı, Evliya Çelebi b. Derviş Mehemmed. *Evliyâ Çelebi Seyahatnamesi*. Istanbul: Yapı Kredi Yayınları, 2011.

Secondary Sources

Afyoncu, Erhan (ed.) *Venedikli Elçilerin Raporlarına Göre Kanuni ve Şehzade Mustafa*. Istanbul: Yeditepe Yayınevi, 2015.

Ágoston, Gábor. *Guns for the Sultan: Military Power and Weapons Industry in the Ottoman Empire*. Cambridge: Cambridge University Press, 2009.

Akkutay, Ülker. *Enderun Mektebi*. Ankara: Gazi Üniversitesi Basın-Yayın Yüksekokulu Basımevi, 1984.

Allouche, Adel. *The Origins and Development of the Ottoman–Safavid Conflict 906–962/1500–1555*. Berlin: Schwarz, 1983.

Ateş, Sabri. 'Treaty of Zuhab, 1639: Foundational Myth or Foundational Document?' *Iranian Studies* 52, no. 3–4 (2019): 411–20.

Aydın, Dündar. *Erzurum Beylerbeyiliği ve Teşkilatı: Kuruluş ve Genişleme Devri, 1535–1566*. Ankara: Türk Tarih Kurumu, 1998.

Babayan, Kathryn. 'The Waning of the Qizilbash: The Spiritual and the Temporal in the Seventeenth-Century Iran.' PhD diss., Princeton University, 1993.

Bacque-Grammont, Jean-Louis. 'The Eastern Policy of Süleyman the Magnificent.' In *Süleyman the Second and His Time*, edited by Halil İnalcık and Cemal Kafadar, 219–28. Istanbul: The Isis Press, 1993.

Baltacıoğlu-Brammer, Ayşe. 'The Formation of Kızılbaş Communities in Anatolia and Ottoman Responses, 1450s–1630s.' *International Journal of Turkish Studies* 20 (2014): 21–48.

Baltacıoğlu-Brammer, Ayşe. *Politics of Sectarianism in the Middle East: Ottoman Sunnism, Safavid Shiism, and the Kızılbaş*. Forthcoming.

Bilge, Reha. *1514 Yavuz Selim ve Şah Ismail: Türkler, Türkmenler ve Farslar*. Istanbul: Giza Yayınları, 2010.

Bilge, Sadık Müfit. *Osmanlı Çağı'nda Kafkasya 1454–1829*. Istanbul: Kitabevi, 2015.

Bülbül, İsmail. 'Başlangıcından Rus Hakimiyetine kadar Kumuk Türkleri ve Tarku Şamhallığı.' PhD diss., Sakarya Üniversitesi, 2011.

Burton, J. Audrey. 'Relations between the Khanate of Bukhara and Ottoman Turkey, 1558–1702.' *International Journal of Turkish Studies* 5, no. 1–2 (1990–1): 83–104.

Cantemir, Demetrius. *The History of the Growth and Decay of the Othman Empire*. Translated by N. Tindal. London: Crown in Ludgate Street, 1734.

Cevrioğlu, Mahmut Halef. 'Ottoman Foreign Policy during the Thirty Years War.' *Turcica* 49 (2018): 195–235.

Diyanet, A. Ekber. *İlk Osmanlı-İran Anlaşması (1555 Amasya Musâlahası)*. Istanbul: İstanbul Üniversitesi Edebiyat Fakültesi, 1971.

Eberhard, Elke. *Osmanische Polemik gegen die Safawiden im 16. Jahrhundert nach arabischen Handschriften.* Freiburg im Breisgau: Klaus Schwarz Verlag, 1970.

Eberhard, Elke Niewöhner. 'Machtpolitische Aspekte des osmanisch-safawidischen Kampfes um Bagdad im 16./17. Jahrhundert.' *Turcica* 6 (1975): 103–27.

Emecen, Feridun. *Zamanın İskenderi, Şarkın Fatihi. Yavuz Sultan Selim.* Istanbul: Yitik Hazine Yayınları, 2010.

Farooqi, Naimur Rahman. 'Mughal-Ottoman Relations: A Study of Political and Diplomatic Relations between Mughal India and the Ottoman Empire, 1556–1748.' PhD diss., University of Wisconsin-Madison, 1986.

Faroqhi, Suraiya. 'Trade between the Ottomans and Safavids: The Acem Tüccarı and Others.' In *Iran and the World in the Safavid Age*, edited by Willem Floor and Edmund Herzig, 237–52. London: I. B. Tauris, 2012.

Floor, Willem. 'The *Khalifeh al-kholafa* of the Safavid Sufi Order.' *Zeitschrift der Deutschen Morgenländischen Gesellschaft* 153, no. 1 (2003): 51–86.

Floor, Willem. *The Persian Gulf: A Political and Economic History of Five Port Cities 1500–1730.* Washington, DC: Mage Publishers, 2006.

Floor, Willem. *Safavid Government Institutions.* Costa Mesa: Mazda Publishers, 2001.

Floor, Willem, and Mohammad H. Faghfoory. *The First Dutch–Persian Commercial Conflict: The Attack of Qeshm Island, 1645.* Costa Mesa: Mazda Publishers, 2004.

Fragner, Bert G. *Die 'Persophonie': Regionalität, Identität und Sprachkontakt in der Geschichte Asiens.* Berlin: Das Arabische Buch, 1999.

Gandjei, Tourkhan. 'Turkish in the Safavid court of Isfahan.' *Turcica* 21–3 (1991): 311–18.

Gökbilgin, M. Tayyib. 'Arz ve Raporlarına Göre İbrâhim Paşaʾnın Irakeyn Seferiʾnde İlk Tedbirleri ve Fütuhatı.' *Belleten* 21, no. 83 (1957): 449–82.

Gündoğdu, Abdullah. 'Türkistanʾda Osmanlı İran Rekabeti (1583–1598).' In *Uluslararası Osmanlı Târihi Sempozyumu (8–10 Nisan 1999) Bildirileri,* edited by Gökçe Turan, 141–52. Izmir: Türk Ocakları İzmir Şubesi, 2000.

Güngörürler, Selim. 'Diplomacy and Political Relations between the Ottoman Empire and Safavid Iran, 1639–1722.' PhD diss., Georgetown University, 2016.

Güngörürler, Selim. 'Islamic Discourse in Ottoman-Safavid Peacetime Diplomacy after 1049/1639.' In *Historicizing Sunni Islam in the Ottoman Empire,* edited by Tijana Krstic and Derin Terzioğlu, 470–500. Leiden: Brill, 2020.

Güngörürler, Selim. 'The Qizilbash in Anatolia after 1630: Sidelined and Estranged.' In *Iranian/Persianate Subalterns in the Safavid Period: Their Role and Depiction: Recovering 'Lost Voices',* edited by Andrew J. Newman, 83–98. Berlin: Gerlach Press, 2022.

von Hammer-Purgstall, Joseph. *Geschichte des Osmanischen Reiches.* Vol. 5. Graz: Akademische Druck- u. Verlagsanstalt, 1963.

Bibliography

Hammer von Purgstall, Joseph. *Geschichte des Osmanischen Reiches*. Vol. 6. Pest: C. A. Hartleben's Verlag, 1830.

Imber, Colin. 'The Persecution of the Ottoman Shiites According to the Mühimme Defterleri 1565–1585', *Der Islam* 56 (1979): 245–73.

İnalcık, Halil. *Devlet-i Aliyye II – Tagayyür ve Fesad (1603–1656)*. Istanbul: Türkiye İş Bankası Kültür Yayınları, 2014.

İnalcık, Halil. *Devlet-i Aliyye. Osmanlı İmparatorluğu Üzerine Araştırmalar III: Köprülüler Devri*. Istanbul: Türkiye İş Bankası Kültür Yayınları, 2015.

Jahânbakhsh, Sawâqib. 'Sâzmân-i Sipâh u Sâhib-mansibân-i Nizâmî-yi ᶜAsr-i Shâh Safî.' *Faslnâma-i ᶜIlmî-Pizhûhishî-yi Târîkh-i Islâm u Îrân-i Dânishgâh-i az-Zahrâ*, 23rd year, new period, issue 14 (*payâpay 101*) (Summer 1391): 1–52.

Jahânbakhsh, Sawâqib, and Tâhira Zakii. 'Tahlîl-i Zamînahâ-yi Muâᶜhada-i Zuhâb u Payâmadhâ-yi ân bar Davlat-i Safaviya.' *Faslnâma-i Pizhûhishhâ-yi Târîkhî (Muâvanat-i Pizhûhish u Fannâvârî-yi Dânişgâh-i Isfahân)* 3 (Fall 1395): 1–24.

Kafadar, Cemal. 'A Rome of one's own: reflections on cultural geography and identity in the Lands of Rum.' *Muqarnas* 24 [History and Ideology: Architectural Heritage of the 'Lands of Rum'] (2007): 7–25.

Karakaya-Stump, Ayfer. *The Kizilbash/Alevis in Ottoman Anatolia: Sufism, Politics and Community*. Edinburgh: Edinburgh University Press, 2020.

Katko, Gaspar. 'The Redemption of the Transylvanian Army Captured by the Crimean Tatars in 1657.' In *The Crimean Khanate between East and West (15th–18th Century)*, edited by Denis Klein, 91–106. Wiesbaden: Harrassowitz Verlag, 2012.

Kılıç, Orhan. *XVI. ve XVII. Yüzyıllarda Van (1548–1648)*. Van: Van Belediye Başkanlığı Kültür ve Sosyal İşler Müdürlüğü, 1997.

Kılıç, Remzi. *Kanuni Devri Osmanlı-İran Münasebetleri 1520–1566*. Istanbul: IQ Kültür ve Sanat Yayıncılık, 2006.

Kocaaslan, Murat. *Kösem Sultan. Hayatı, Vakıfları, Hayır İşleri ve Üsküdar'daki Külliyesi*. Istanbul: Okur Kitaplığı, 2014.

Kołodziejczyk, Dariusz. *Ottoman–Polish Diplomatic Relations (15th–18th Centuries): An Annotated Edition of ᶜAhdnames and Other Documents*. Leiden: Brill, 2000.

Kołodziejczyk, Dariusz. (ed.), *The Relations of the Polish–Lithuanian Commonwealth with Safavid Iran and the Catholicosate of Etcgmiadzin*. Warsaw: Archiwum Glowne Akt Dawnych, 2017.

Kubbealtı Lügatı. Edited by İlhan Ayverdi. Istanbul: Kubbealtı Neşriyatı, 2011.

Kunt, İ. Metin. *Sancaktan Eyalete. 1550–1650 arasında Osmanlı Ümerâsı ve İl İdâresi*. Istanbul: Boğaziçi Üniversitesi Yayınları, 1978.

Küpeli, Özer. 'Osmanlı-Safevi Münasebetleri (1612–1639).' PhD diss., Ege Üniversitesi, 2009.

Küpeli, Özer. *Osmanlı-Safevi Münasebetleri (1612–1639)*. Istanbul: Yeditepe Yayınları, 2014.

Kütükoğlu, Bekir. *Osmanlı-İran Siyasi Münasebetleri (1578–1612)*. Istanbul: Fetih Cemiyeti Yayınları, 1993.

Kütükoğlu, Mübahat. *Osmanlı Belgelerinin Dili (Diplomatik)*. Istanbul: Kubbealtı Akademisi Kültür ve San'at Vakfı, 1994.

Maeda, Hirotake. 'On the Ethno-Social Background of Four Gholâm Families from Georgia in Safavid Iran.' *Studia Iranica* 32, no. 2 (2003): 243–78.

Mahdavi, Abdurriza Hushang. *Târîkh-i Ravâbit-ı Khârijî-yi Îrân*. Tehran: Muassasa-i Intisharat-i Amir-i Kabir, HS 1349.

Matthee, Rudi. 'Between Arabs, Turks and Iranians: The Town of Basra, 1600–1700.' *Bulletin of the School of Priental and African Studies, University of London* 69, no. 1 (2006): 53–78.

Matthee, Rudi. 'Iran's Ottoman Diplomacy During the Reign of Shah Sulayman I (1077–1105/1666–94).' In *Iran and Iranian Studies: Essays in Honor of Iraj Afshar*, edited by Kambiz Eslami, 97–126. Princeton: Zagros, 1998.

Matthee, Rudi. 'The Ottoman–Safavid War of 986–998/1578–90: Motives and Causes.' *International Journal of Turkish Studies* 20, no. 1–2 (2014): 1–20.

Matthee, Rudi. *Persia in Crisis: Safavid Decline and the Fall of Isfahan*. London: I. B. Tauris, 2012.

Matthee, Rudi. 'Safavid Iran and the "Turkish Question" or How to Avoid a War on Multiple Fronts.' *Iranian Studies* 52, no. 3–4 (2019): 513–42.

Matuz, Josef. 'Vom Übertritt osmanischer Soldaten zu den Safawiden.' In *Die islamische Welt zwischen Mittelalter und Neuzeit: Festschrift für Hans Robert Roemer zum 65. Geburtstag*, edited by Ulrich Haarmann, 402–15. Beirut: Orient-Institut der Deutschen Morgenländischen Gesellschaft, 1979.

Mazzaoui, Michel M. *The Origins of the Safavids: Şhiism, Sufism, and the Ghulat*. Wiesbaden: Franz Steiner Verlag, 1972.

Murphey, Rhoads. 'The Functioning of the Ottoman Army under Murad IV (1623–1639/1032–1049): Key to the Understanding of the Relationship between Center and Periphery in Seventeenth-Century Turkey.' PhD diss., University of Chicago, 1979.

Murphey, Rhoads. 'Süleyman's Eastern Policy.' In *Süleyman the Second and His Time*, edited by Halil İnalcık and Cemal Kafadar, 229–48. Istanbul: The Isis Press, 1993.

Newman, Andrew J. *Safavid Iran: Rebirth of a Persian Empire*. London: I. B. Tauris, 2006.

Nyitrai, Istvan. 'The Third Period of the Ottoman–Safavid Conflict: Struggle of Political Ideologies (1555–1578).' In *Irano-Turcic Cultural Contacts in the 11th–17th Centuries*, ed. E. M. Jeremias, 161–76. Piliscsaba: The Avicenna Institute of Middle Eastern Studies, 2003.

Ouahes, Colette, and Willem Floor. (trans. and annot.). *A Man of Two Worlds: Pedros Bedik in Iran 1670–1675*. Washington, DC: Mage Publishers, 2014.

Pakalın, Mehmet Zeki. *Osmanlı Târîh Deyimleri ve Terimleri Sözlüğü*. Vol. 2. Istanbul: Millî Eğitim Basımevi, 1983.

Bibliography

Panaite, Viorel. *The Ottoman Law of War and Peace: The Ottoman Empire and Tribute Payers*. Boulder: East European Monographs, 2000.

Parmaksızoğlu, İsmet. 'Kuzey Irak'ta Osmanlı Hakimiyetinin Kuruluşu ve Memun Bey'in Hatıraları.' *Belleten* 37, no. 146 (1973): 191–230.

Parsadust, Menuchihr. *Shah Tahmasb-i Avval*. Tehran: Shirkat-i Sahami-yi Intishar, HS 1381.

Pedani, Maria Pia. 'The Sultan and the Venetian *Bailo*: Ceremonial Diplomatic Protocol in Istanbul.' In *Diplomatisches Zeremoniell in Europa und im Mittleren Osten in der Frühen Neuzeit*, edited by Ralph Kauz, Giorgio Rota and Jan Paul Niederkorn, 287–99. Wien: Verlag der Österreichischen Akademie der Wissenschaften, 2009.

Perry, John. 'Cultural currents in the Turco-Persian world of Safavid and post-Safavid times.' In *New Perspectives on Safavid Iran*, edited by Colin P. Mitchell, 85–96. London: Routledge, 2011.

Perry, John. 'The historical role of Turkish in relation to Persian of Iran.' In *Iran and the Caucasus V. Research Papers from the Caucasian Centre for Iranian Studies, Yerivan*, edited by Garnik Asatrian, 193–200. Tehran: International Publications of Iranian Studies, 2001.

Posch, Walter. *Osmanisch-safavidische Beziehungen (1545–1550): Der Fall Alkas Mirza*. Vienna: Verlag der Österreichischen Akademie der Wissenschaften, 2013.

Râznihân, Muhammad Hasan, and Anvar Khâlandî. 'Jihat-gîrî-yi Siyâsat-i Khârijî-yi Safaviyân dar Mas'ala-i Munâzaᶜât-i miyân-i Dawlat-i Osmânî vu Uvrupâ (az Muᶜâhada-i Zuhâb tâ Suqût-i Safaviyân).' *Mutâlaᶜât-i Târîkh-i Islâm* 24 (seventh year, spring 1394): 83–116.

Reychman, Jan, and Ananiasz Zajaczkowski. *Handbook of Ottoman-Turkish Diplomatics*. Revised and translated by Andrew S. Ehrenkreutz. The Hague: Mouton, 1968.

Riyâhî, Muhammad Amîn. *Zabân u Adab-i Fârsî dar Qalam-rav-i Osmânî*. Tehran: Intishârât-i Pâzhang, 1369.

Roemer, Hans Robert. 'The Safavid Period.' In *The Cambridge History of Iran* 6, edited by Peter Jackson and Laurence Lockhart, 189–350. Cambridge: Cambridge University Press, 1986.

Römer, Claudia. "Die osmanische Belagerung Bagdads 1034–35/1624–25. Ein Augenzeugenbericht.' *Der Islam* 66 (1989): 119–36.

Roosen, William James. *The Age of Louis XIV: the Rise of Modern Diplomacy*. London: Routledge, 1976.

Roosen, William. 'Early Modern Diplomatic Ceremonial: a Systems Approach.' *The Journal of Modern History* 52, no. 3 (1980): 452–76.

Rota, Giorgio. 'Caucasians in Safavid Service in the 17th Century.' In *Caucasia between the Ottoman Empire and Iran, 1555–1914*, edited by Raoul Motika and Michael Ursinus, 107–20. Wiesbaden: Reichert Verlag, 2000.

Rota, Giorgio. 'The Death of Tahmâspqolî Xân Qâjâr According to a Contemporary Ragusan Source.' In *Iran und iranisch geprägte Kulturen. Studien zum 65.*

Geburtstag von Bert. G. Fragner, edited by Markus Ritter, Ralph Kauz and Birgitt Hoffmann, 54–63. Wiesbaden: Dr. Ludwig Reichert Verlag, 2008.

Rota, Giorgio. 'Safavid Persia and its Diplomatic Relations with Venice.' In *Iran and the World in the Safavid Age*, edited by Willem Floor and Edmung Herzig, 149–60. London: I. B. Tauris, 2012.

Savory, Roger M. 'The Emergence of the Modern Persian State under the Safavids.' Reproduced in his *Studies on the History of Safavid Iran*. London: Variorum Reprints, 1987.

Savory, Roger M. 'The Office of *Sipahsâlâr* (Commander-in-Chief) in the Safavid State.' In *Proceedings of the Second European Conference of Iranian Studies held in Bamberg, 30th September to 4th October 1991*, edited by Bert G. Fragner, Christa Fragner, Gherardo Gnoli, Roxane Haag-Higuchi, Mauro Maggi and Paola Orsatti, 597–615. Roma: Istituto Italiano Per Il Medio Ed Estremo Oriente, 1995.

Savory, Roger M. 'Tajlu Khanum: Was She Captured by the Ottomans at the Battle of Chaldiran, or not?' In *Irano-Turcic Cultural Contacts in the 11th–17th Centuries*, edited by E. M. Jeremias, 217–31. Piliscsaba: The Avicenna Institute of Middle Eastern Studies, 2003.

Schwarz, Florian. 'Writing in the Margins of Empires – the Huseinabadi Family of Scholiasts in the Ottoman–Safawid Borderlands.' In *Buchkultur im Nahen Osten des 17. und 18. Jahrhunderts*, edited by Tobias Heinzelmann and Henning Sievert, 151–98. Bern: Peter Lang, 2010.

Setton, Kenneth M. *Venice, Austria, and the Turks in the Seventeenth Century*. Philadelphia: The American Philosophical Society, 1991.

Shukurov, Rustam. 'The Campaign of Shaykh Djunayd Safawî against Trebizond (1456 AD/860 H).' *Byzantine and Modern Greek Studies* 17, no. 1 (1993): 127–140.

Sohrweide, Hanna. 'Der Sieg der Safawiden in Persien und seine Rückwirkungen auf die Schiiten Anatoliens im 16. Jahrhundert.' *Der Islam* 41 (1965): 95–223.

Söylemez, Faruk. 'Anadolu'da Sahte Şah Ismail İsyanı.' *Erciyes Üniversitesi Sosyal Bilimler Enstitüsü Dergisi*, no. 17 (2004): 71–90.

Sümer, Faruk. *Safevi Devletinin Kuruluşu ve Gelişmesinde Anadolu Türklerinin Rolü*. Ankara: Güven Matbaası, 1976.

Süreyyâ, Mehmed. *Sicill-i Osmânî*. Istanbul: Târih Vakfı Yurt Yayınları, 1996.

Tekindağ, Şahabettin. 'Yeni Kaynak ve Vesikaların Işığı Altında Yavuz Sultan Selim'in İran Seferi.' *İstanbul Üniversitesi Edebiyat Fakültesi Tarih Dergisi* 17, no. 22 (1968): 49–78.

Trentacoste, Davide. 'The Marzocco and the Shir o Khorshid: The Origin and Decline of Medici Persian Diplomacy (1599–1721).' *Cyber Review of Moden Historiography* 24 (2021): 21–41.

Tucker, Ernest. 'From Rhetoric of War to Realities of Peace: The Evolution of Ottoman–Iranian Diplomacy through the Safavid Era.' In *Iran and the World in the Safavid Age*, edited by Willem Floor and Edmund Herzig, 81–90. London: I. B. Tauris, 2012.

Bibliography

Turan, Şerafettin. *Kanuni'nin Oğlu Şehzade Bayazid Vak'ası*. Ankara: Türk Tarih Kurumu, 1961.

Türk Diyanet Vakfı İslam Ansiklopedisi. 46 volumes. Istanbul: Türk Diyanet Vakfı, 1988–2016.

Uluçay, M. Çağatay. 'Sultan İbrahim Deli mi, Hasta mıydı?' *Tarih Dünyası* (series 1) 2, no. 11 (1950): 479–80.

Uluskan, Murat. 'Dîvân-ı Hümâyun Çavuşbaşılığı (XVI. ve XVI. Yüzyıllar).' MA thesis, Marmara Üniversitesi, 1998.

Unat, Faik Reşit. *Osmanlı Sefirleri ve Sefaretnameleri*. Edited by Bekir Sıtkı Baykal. Ankara: Türk Tarih Kurumu, 1968.

Uzunçarşılı, İsmâil Hakkı. *Osmanlı Devleti Teşkilatlarından Kapıkulu Ocakları I: Acemi Ocağı ve Yeniçeri Ocağı*. Ankara: Türk Tarih Kurumu Basımevi, 1988.

Uzunçarşılı, İsmâil Hakkı. *Osmanlı Devletinin Merkez ve Bahriye Teşkilatı*. Ankara: Türk Târih Kurumu, 1948, repr. 1998.

Uzunçarşılı, İsmâil Hakkı. *Osmanlı Târihi*. Vol. 3/1. Ankara: Türk Târih Kurumu, 3rd edn 1983.

Uzunçarşılı, İsmâil Hakkı, Ibrahim Kemal Baybura, Ülkü Altındağ (eds). *Topkapı Sarayı Müzesi Osmanlı Saray Arşivi Kataloğu: Fermanlar. I. Fasikül*. Ankara: Türk Târih Kurumu, 1985.

Weineck, Benjamin. *Zwischen Verfolgung und Eingliederung: Kızılbaş-Aleviten im osmanischen Staat (16.–18. Jahrhundert)*. Ergon Verlag: Baden-Baden, 2020.

Winkelbauer, Thomas. *Österreichische Geschichte 1522–1699: Ständefreiheit und Fürstenmacht. Länder und Untertanen des Hauses Habsburges im konfessionellen Zeitalter Teil 1*. Vienna: Ueberreuter, 2003.

Yıldız, Murat. 'Osmanlı Devlet Teşkilatında Bostancı Ocağı.' PhD diss., Marmara University, 2008.

Yıldız, Sara Nur. 'Ottoman Historical Writing in Persian, 1400–1600.' In *A History of Persian Literature*, vol. X, edited by Charles Melville, 436–502. London: I. B. Tauris, 2012.

Yinanç, Refet. *Dulkadir Beyliği*. Ankara: Türk Tarih Kurumu, 1989.

Index

Abaza Hasan Pasha, 121–2
Abaza Mehmed Agha, 138
Abaza Mehmed Pasha, 5, 92–3, 95
Abbas I, 5, 56, 62, 86
Abbas II, 66–70, 86, 91, 93, 97–9, 102, 105–8, 112, 114–16, 118–20, 122, 125, 130, 137, 143, 145–6
Abbas-kulu Beyg, 65
Abdi (dizdar), 168
Abdulaziz Khan, 99
Abdulgani Agha, 167
Abdulhakim, 109, 134
Abdulhalim Efendi b. Abdullah, 152–3, 155, 171
Abdulkadir Agha, 152
Abdullah Agha, 128
Abdullah Pasha, 128, 132
Abdullah b. Ahmed, 153
Abdunnebi Çavuş, 145–6
Abdurrahim Bey, 105, 107
Abrushoğlu amir-Dindin, 162
Abubakr, 128
Adilcevaz, 132
Adniya b. Shahhasan, 134
Adrianople, 64, 130, 138, 142, 145, 147, 149, 166, 169, 172, 177
Aegian, 117
Afghan, 177
Afrasiyab, 68
Afrasiyaboğlu, 43, 102, 106–8, 115, 141, 142, 146–7, 151, 154, 156
  Afrasiyab Bey, 145–6, 167

Ahmed Bey, 105–7, 115–16
  Ali Pasha, 53, 73, 82, 93, 105
  Fathi Bey, 105–7, 115
  Husein Pasha, 105–10, 115–16, 118, 141–51, 153–4, 156, 158, 167, 170, 172
  Mir-Mahmud, 148
Afşar, 6, 110
Afşar, Kalb-Ali Xan, 45, 52, 137
Afşar, Genç-Ali Xan, 111–14, 136
Afşar, Silsüpür Kalb-Ali Soltan/Xan, 118–20, 138
Ahlat, 132
Ahmed (kedkhuda), 127
Ahmed Agha, 73
Ahmed Efendi, 152
Ahmed I, 168
Ahmed III, 74
Akçadağ, 175
al-Ahsa, 73, 105–6, 142, 144–6
Ajam, 16, 42, 49–50, 63, 90, 92, 99, 113, 155, 157, 172
Akhaltsikhe, 112
Akkoyunlu, 2
Alacaatlı Hasan Agha, 94
Albania, 167
Aleppo, 62, 74, 91, 108, 110, 116, 122, 143, 163
Alexander the Great, 44, 67, 119, 157
Alexandretta, 163, 175
Alexei, 161, 164
Ali Agha, 66
Ali b. Abdan, 152

Index

Ali b. Abdullah, 134
Ali beyg, b. Ahmed, 134
Ali Pasha, 127
Alqas, 4
Altıncı Ahmed Agha, 96
Amasya, 4, 6, 30, 176
Amık, 132
Anatolia, 1–4, 16, 30, 44, 74, 79, 91–2, 118, 122, 136, 139, 172, 175–6
Andersen, Jürgen, 100–1, 133
Anna Khanum, 67
Aqara, 106
Arab, 30, 43, 76, 148
    Arabia, 49, 105, 141, 145
    Arabic (language), 22–3, 34, 172
Arabgir, 30
Arakel, 141
Aras, 127
Ardabil, 2, 5, 136, 175
Ardalan, 5, 43, 120–1
Arja, 106, 148
Arjesh, 69–70, 132
Armenia, 3–4, 10, 25, 43, 90, 92–3, 95–6, 99–101, 113, 116, 176
Arnavut Abdurrahman Abdi Pasha, 163–4, 174
Arnavut Bektaş Agha, 37, 40, 42, 76
(Arnavut) Uzun Ibrahim Pasha, 167
Asia, 98, 110, 130
Astrakhan, 98
Atabegli-Jaqeli, 43, 123
    Arslan Mehmed Pasha, 123, 140
    Rustam Pasha, 123
    Sefer Pasha, 90
Aurangzib, 141, 143
Austria, 34
Avanik, Mateos (Matthieu Iovhanesean/Hovannes), 159
Avlonya, 9, 37
Avraman, 77
Azerbaijan, 2–6, 10, 19, 25, 38–9, 43, 52, 71, 90, 93–5, 100, 103–5, 111–15, 117, 143

Baban Suleiman Bey (the elder), 60–1
Baden, 34
Badrah, 77
Baghdad, 4–7, 9–10, 19, 25, 36–43, 45–7, 52–4, 56–8, 60–1, 66–7, 70, 73–6, 78, 81–2, 90–2, 95–103, 105–9, 113, 115–16, 118–21, 129, 133–5, 139, 141, 143–4, 147–9, 152, 154–6, 158, 160, 162–4, 168–9, 171, 173, 175, 177
Bagration, 43, 113, 123
    Archil, 123–4
    Vakhtang V, 123
Bâğ-i Jinân, 77
Bahchekapı, 45
Bahram, 157
Bajilan, 154
Bakhchysarai, 165
Baku, 4
Balı b. Ali, 169
Balkan, 30
Balkh, 98
Bani Khalid, 73
Bani Lam, 66, 69, 86, 103
Banu Ka'b, 154
Banyalukalı (Kabasakal Kadirullah) Uzun Ibrahim Pasha, 143–5
Bashir (the agent), 51
Basra, 10–11, 43, 53, 73, 82, 93, 102, 105–11, 115–16, 118, 120, 135, 141–63, 167–74
Bastam, 97
Bavaria, 34
Bayazid II, 3
Bayazid (prince), 4
Bayazid (town), 65
Bayazid Square, 58, 87
Bayburtlu Katırcı Kara Ibrahim (pasha), 122
Bedouin, 73, 107, 141, 144, 146–8, 153–4, 162–3
Behdinan Ebusaid Bey, 104
Belgrade, 78, 142

Benli Omer Agha, 111, 136
Berda, 56
Beyat, 154
Bıyıklı Dervish Mehmed Pasha, 41–2, 45, 52–4, 66, 76, 86
Bihbehan, 107, 150
Biredos, 110
Birejik, 163
Bitlis, 111–12, 114, 132, 135
Boğazkesen (Rumelihisarı), 48
Bohemia, 34
Bolu, 47
Bosnalı Suleiman Efendi, 101
Bosnia, 132
Bosphorus, 48
Boynueğri Durak Agha, 58
Bozok, 30
Böğürdelen, 109, 135
Brandenburg, 34
Brandy, Willy, 7
Buczacz, 160
Budak Mukri Soltan, 60
Budakoğlu Mehmed, 144
Budapest, 78, 129, 132
Buday, 149, 166
Bukhara, 10, 98–9, 131
Bursa, 122
Burun Qasim Yadigar Ali Soltan, 130
Burun Qasimoğlu Mehemmed-kulu, 98–9, 131, 138
Byzantium, 2, 16, 30

Caesar, 50
Cairo, 39
Candia (Heraklion), 74, 92, 100, 117, 146, 154, 157, 159, 163
Canik, 30
Canikli Boynuyaralı Mehmed Pasha, 117
Caspian, 149–50
Catholic, 100
Caucasus, 2, 5, 124, 136, 150, 152
Central Accounting (*Başmuhâsebe*), 87

Central Treasury (*Khazîne-i Âmire*), 83, 106, 115–16, 145, 150, 169, 171
Chagatay, Kütük Mehemmed-kulu Beyg, 40–1, 44–7, 49, 52, 81
Chaldiran, 3
Chaluchiya, 106
Chania, 74, 76, 90, 92, 124, 157
Chehel-Sotun, 119
Chernomen, 172
Chevlan, 110
Childir, 43, 90, 123, 140
Chinggis, 98
Christian, 30, 125
Chyhyryn, 165
Civankapıcıbaşı Sultanzade Mehmed Pasha, 125
Clemens IX, 159
Cold War, 7
Constantinople, 8, 16, 38, 42, 45–8, 51–3, 56–9, 61–4, 67–70, 79, 87, 90, 92, 97–102, 106, 108–9, 116, 117–18, 120–1, 123, 130, 141–2, 146–7, 156, 160, 163, 169, 171
Contarini, Alvise, 63
Contarini, Domenico II, 159
Cossack, 160
Crasso, Francesco, 63
Crete, 9, 11, 90–2, 95–6, 100, 117, 121, 124, 146, 154, 157, 159–60, 171, 176
Crimea, 5, 103, 121, 160, 163, 165
Croat, 34
Cyrus, 50
Czech, 34

Çağangediği, 77
Çelebi Hasan Pasha, 160–2
Çepni Ismail Beyg, 45–6
Çiftelerli Osman Pasha, 40
Çorum, 30, 118
Çubukköprü, 40
Çukursa'd, 4, 19, 25, 43, 45, 52, 62, 93–4, 128

Index

Dadiani, 43
Dagestan, 103, 117, 122–4, 149–50, 152, 165–6
Damascus, 40, 48
Dar Beni-Esed, 148
Dardanelles, 90, 117, 121
Dargazîn, 77
Darna, 41–3, 54, 77
Dartang, 41–3, 54, 77
Davudpaşa, 45
Daylam, 49
Delfino, Giuseppe, 117
Deli Abdi Agha, 132
Deli Dilaver Pasha, 146
Deli Husein Pasha, 91–2, 100, 117
Demircioğlu, 132
Derbend, 149, 166
Dervish Husein, 93
Dervish Mehmed Agha, 88
Dev Kara Murad Agha/Pasha, 70, 111, 115, 117, 119
Dilaver Agha, 87
Divriği, 30
Diyala, 40, 96
Diyarbekr, 38, 42, 44–7, 53, 79, 90, 112, 121, 129, 138, 143, 145–6, 149, 155, 163
Dnieper, 165
Dominican, 91, 143
Doroshenko, Petro, 160, 165
Dulkadir, 74
Dumdumi, 110
Dunbuli, 110, 113, 136
Durak, 107, 150–1, 153, 155
Dzierzek, Prandota, 91

Egri, 132
Egypt, 6, 42, 78, 130
Emir Reshid (Ali Shedid), 144
English, 102
Ergani, 46
Erivan, 4–6, 19, 25, 37–8, 42–3, 46, 52, 56–7, 61–2, 65, 86, 91–2, 94–5, 113, 126, 128, 160–1, 165

Erzincan, 2
Erzurum, 4–6, 10, 19, 25, 43, 55, 76, 78, 86, 92–4, 100, 112, 116, 123, 126, 128, 140, 160
Esed Aka, 114
Eski Nişancıpaşa, 169
Ethiopia, 152
Euphrates, 107, 121, 139
Europe, 7, 9–10, 16–17, 19, 22–4, 26, 29, 31, 34, 61, 101, 125, 130, 139, 143, 171
Evliya Çelebi, 94, 112–14, 127, 136
Eyub, 97, 119

Falluja, 107
Fathi Beşe, 153
Fatime (sultan), 168
Feres, 143
Ferhadpaşa Palace, 87
Fiandra, Antonio de, 91
(Firari) Kara Mustafa Pasha, 101, 103, 146, 148–9, 151–2, 154–6, 158, 160, 168–70, 173
Florence, 100
France, 125, 159

Ganja, 5
Gazi Mehmed Agha, 127
German, 34, 57, 61, 63, 91, 100–1, 142–3, 145
   German (language), 132
   Germany, 26, 34, 100, 109, 157
Georgia, 4–5, 25, 43, 69–71, 90, 93, 105, 111, 117, 122–4, 128, 140, 152
Ghinayizade Ali Efendi, 110–11
Gilan, 136
Giray, Mehmed Khan IV, 121
Giray, Murad Khan, 165
Giray, Selim Khan I, 160, 165
Giraylu Aliyar Xan, 45
God, 44, 59–60, 68–70
Gökdolak, 114
Gökmeydanı, 114

Göynük, 47
Greek, 30
    Greece, 155, 157
Gurdziecki, Bogdan, 159
Guria, 43, 123
    Gurieli, 43
Gurji Çalık Deli Dilaver Pasha, 128–9
Gurji Ibrahim Pasha, 143
Gurji Kenan Pasha, 143, 146, 167
Gurji Temres Bey, 111, 113
Gümüşlükümbet, 94–5
Gürdelen, 153

Habsburg, 24, 26, 34, 57, 61, 123, 142
Hagia Sophia, 59, 84
Haji Agha, 144
Haji Bey, 134
Haji Ebubekr Bey, 152–3
Hakkari, 132
Hamadan, 6, 77
Hamza Agha, 76
Hamza (mirza), 5
Hamzapashaoğlu Mehmed Agha, 38, 41, 45, 47, 49–52, 56, 58–9, 81
Hanafi Mehmed Efendi, 98, 118, 130
Hanover, 34
Hâridât, 73
Haruniya, 41
Hasan Agha, 169
Hasan Bey, 60
Hasan beyg b. Mehmed, 134
Hasan Efendi, 172
Hasan Pasha, 128
Haseki Mehmed Pasha, 121, 139
Haydar (mirza), 5
Haydar (shaykh), 2
Hejaz, 160
Hidayat, 154
Hizir Agha, 108–9
Holy League, 177
Hospitaller, 124
Husein (the messenger), 55
Husein Efendi, 153
Huseinpasha, 58

Household (*Kapıkulu*), 25, 29, 42–3, 55, 58, 70–1, 74–6, 84, 93–6, 101, 110, 122, 126, 132–3, 149, 154, 156, 163
Hungary, 35, 64, 121–3, 142–3, 152
    Hungarian, 34–5
Husrevpaşayeğeni Suleiman Bey, 132
Huvayza, 43, 101–3, 107, 133, 149–51, 153–4, 156, 162

Ibrahim (Ottoman monarch), 9, 48–51, 53–6, 59, 61–5, 67–9, 74, 81, 83, 92–3, 97–9, 118, 130
Ibrahim Agha, 76, 144
Ibrahim Pasha, 95–6, 129
Ibshir Mustafa Pasha, 109–12, 115, 121, 136
Ilicz, Jerzy, 91
Ilyas Agha (haseki), 101
Imadiya, 104, 133
Imamiazam, 75
Imereti, 43, 83, 105, 113, 123, 128, 140
Imperial
    Army (*Ordu-yi Humâyûn*), 29, 39–42, 44, 46–7, 73–4, 90, 92, 101, 122, 143, 145–9, 157, 160–1, 163, 165, 171–2, 176
    Council (*Dîvân-i Humâyûn*), 22, 42, 45, 48, 58–59, 62–4, 67, 78, 81, 83–4, 86–8, 90, 99, 111, 118, 145
    Court (*Rikâb-ı Humâyûn*), 21, 38, 46, 51, 59, 70, 83, 86–7, 119, 128, 142, 153, 172
    Gate (*Bâb-i Humâyûn*), 59
    Inner Court (*Enderûn–i Humâyûn*), 22
    Marquee (*Otağ-i Humâyûn*), 36, 62, 73
    Navy (*Donanma-i Humâyûn*), 92
    Outer Court (*Bîrûn-i Humâyûn*), 21
    Registry (*Defterhâne-i Hâkânî*), 74, 171

Index

India, 45, 47, 52–3, 56, 64, 67, 95,
   97–8, 103–4, 106, 116–18, 120,
   131, 141, 143, 151, 155, 159, 170
Iraq, 3, 6, 9–10, 36, 41–3, 45, 47,
   52–3, 66, 71, 95–6, 101–4, 109,
   141, 144–5, 147, 151, 155–7,
   160–3, 176
Isaccea, 161
Isfahan, 8, 16, 25, 28, 51–2, 56, 64–5,
   82, 90–1, 99–100, 102–3, 105,
   107, 109, 112–15, 119–20, 142,
   145, 156, 161, 177
Islam, 6, 29, 140, 166
Ismail (imposter shah), 4
Ismail (kedkhuda), 128
Ismail I, 2–3
Ismail II, 4
Italian, 34, 143

Jâf (77)
Jafar Pasha, 60
Jalali, 92
Jamshid, 68
Janissary, 36–7, 40, 43, 58, 60, 67,
   70, 74–6, 83–4, 90, 92, 96, 98,
   100–1, 108, 132–3, 142, 146,
   148, 151–4, 163, 167
Jassân, 77
Jassy, 163
Jesuit, 125
Jewazer, 106
Jidda, 152
Junayd, 2
Jundi Mehmed Agha, 96

Kağıthane, 62
Kajar, 6, 62, 76
Kajar, Akçakoyunlu Tasmasp-kulu
   Xan / Amirguneoğlu Yusuf
   Pasha, 48, 56, 62–4
Kajar, Koca Kayıtmaz Murtaza-kulu
   Xan, 111–12, 114, 136
Kajar, Yirmidört Ibrahim Xan, 53, 56,
   58–64, 84

Kakheti, 43
Kamianets-Podilskyi, 74, 160
Kandahar, 45, 47, 56, 66, 80, 97–8,
   101–5, 118, 129, 144
Kapıcıbaşı Mustafa Agha / Pasha, 155
Kaplan Mustafa Pasha, 163
Kara Murtaza Pasha, 105–8, 110–11,
   113, 115–16, 122, 134
Kara Ulus, 108–9, 134
Karabakh, 5, 43, 56, 94
Karadağlu Maqsud Soltan, 37–9, 65,
   67–9, 87–8
Karakaş Ali Agha, 143
Karaki, Mirza Habibullah, 52
Karaki, Mirza Muhammad Mahdi,
   145–6
Karam Vays b. Shahwali, 134
Karaman, 2, 74
Kars, 4, 41, 43, 65, 90, 94, 123–4,
   127–9, 132
Kartalkayası, 155
Kartli, 43, 113, 123
Kavi, 175
Kay-Khusrav, 49
Kazvin, 44–6, 68–71, 161
Keçiqale, 127
Kemankesh Kara Mustafa Pasha, 9,
   36–8, 40–4, 46–51, 54–5, 59–61,
   63–5, 67, 69–70, 72, 76, 79,
   84–5, 87, 128
Kerden, 6
Kerha, 101–3, 133
Kesikdeveboynu, 132
Khalaf Beyg/Xan, 45
Khalid, 66
Khalife-Soltan, Alaaddin Husein, 98
Khalil Agha (musahib), 171
Khalil Çavuş, 128
Khalt, 152
Khanki, 41
Khazali, 66
Khmelnytsky, Yuri, 165
Khojazade Mesud Efendi, 116
Khorasan, 67

Khoshab, 45, 164
Khoy, 45–6
Khristoforov, Konstantin, 161, 164, 173
Khudadad, 114, 136
Khusrav, 99, 118
Kız Husein Pasha, 160, 163, 173
Kızılbaş, 2–3, 21–3, 36–7, 45, 54, 65, 92, 100, 102–5, 155, 175
Kızılca, 77
Kızılribat, 41, 108, 134
Kirmanshah, 25, 41, 43, 46, 108–9, 120
Kirkuk, 43, 54–5
Koca Sinan Agha, 64
Kose Ismail Agha, 119–20, 138–9
Kotur, 46, 65, 77, 113
Konya (Iconium), 2, 122
Kozbekçi Yusuf Pasha, 168
Köprülü Mehmed Pasha, 117–19, 121–2, 138
Köprülü Fazil Ahmed Pasha, 142, 145–6, 153, 157–8, 162, 168, 174
Kuşlar, 108, 148
Kuhigiyula, 107
Kur Husein-xanoğlu, 101
Kurd, 60, 73, 75–6, 103–4, 110, 120, 124, 146
Kurdistan, 3–4, 6, 42–3, 105, 115, 123, 165, 176–7
Kurt Ali Agha, 169
Kuruçeşme, 87
Kut, 144, 148
Kuwait, 105
Küçükçekmece, 87
Küçük Hasan Agha / Pasha, 37, 41–2, 46, 48, 51, 53, 55, 75–6, 90

Lahan, 103
Lahrasp Soltan, 103
Larissa, 155, 157
Latin, 22
Lemnos, 121

Levant, 1
Lithuania, 90, 92, 159–61
Local Corps/Service (*Yerlü Kulu*), 5, 40, 74–5, 94, 96, 106–8, 110–11, 128, 132, 135, 146, 148–9, 151–6, 162–3, 170–1
Louis XIV, 159
Lur Husein Xan, 37
Luristan, 103
Lviv, 163

Magazberd, 65, 70, 77, 94, 127–8
Mahmud I, 88
Mahmudi, 132, 164
Mahpeyker Kösem Sultan, 98, 130
Mahzaoğlu amir-Nasir, 162
Maku, 65, 70, 77, 94–5, 113, 127
Malta, 100, 117, 124
Mandaljin, 77
Mansuriya, 106, 144, 148
Marash, 74, 136
Marcello, Lorenzo, 117
Mardin, 38, 73
Mashhad, 103, 120, 130
Mawlana Mehmed Efendi b. Abdulbaqi, 169
Mawlana Sheref, 103
Mazandaran, 49, 52, 94, 105, 130, 145–6
Mecca, 117, 119, 124, 142, 145
Medina, 117, 119, 130
Mediterranean, 1, 10, 90, 95, 100, 117, 122–3, 142
Mehmed IV, 74, 98–9, 110, 116, 118–20, 136, 140, 145–6, 148, 155–8, 160, 162–3, 165, 169, 171–2
Mehmed Agha, 87, 128
Mehmed Agha (haseki), 101
Mehmed Bey, 69–70
Mehmed Efendi, 102
Mehmed Molla Çelebi, 162
Mehmed Pasha, 104, 142, 144
Melet, 67

Index

Merzifonlu Kara Mustafa Pasha, 147, 149, 152, 165, 168–9
Mesopotamia, 91, 106, 144, 148, 153, 162
Middle East, 1, 4, 6, 11, 17, 166, 178
Mihribân (Marîvân), 77
Mingrelia, 43, 105, 140
Mintiqa, 139
Mir-Seyyid, 103
Mirahur Husein Pasha, 79
Mirfattah-oğlu Aka Sadiq Kumshei, 45, 56–8, 83
Mirfattah-oğlu Aka-Tahir Kumshei, 57–8, 83
Mirimanidze, Bektaş Xan, 36–7, 57
Moldavia, 121, 139, 163
Mosul, 37–8, 44, 47, 73–4, 104, 121, 133, 143, 146, 148, 155, 163
Mughal, 10, 45, 47, 56, 64, 80, 97–8, 102–5, 116–18, 120, 141, 143–4, 170, 172
Muhammad (prophet), 72
Muhammad Beyg, 155
Muhammad-Ali Beyg, 67
Muhammad Rashid, 107
Muhammadi-xan Beyg, 120
Muntafiq, 144, 148
Murad II, 2
Murad III, 5
Murad IV, 6, 9, 36–9, 41–50, 52–3, 55–7, 62–4, 66, 73–4, 76, 80–3, 86, 109, 113, 117, 126–7
Muradbakhsh, 120
Murtaza Pasha, 46
Musa Pasha, 103–4, 146
Musabey b. Abdullah, 153
Mushasha, 43, 151, 156
Mustafa (kedkhuda), 127
Mustafa Agha, 127, 153
Mustafa Bey, 94
Mustafa Çelebi b. Ahmed Efendi, 171
Mutafarriqa Qabil Agha, 61, 65, 67

Nadr Muhammad Khan, 98–9
Nagykanizsa / Großkischen, 142, 152
Nakhchivan, 4–5, 38, 65, 94–5, 98, 159
Namubarak, 162
Naqdi (khaja), 113, 136
Naqdi Xan, 45
Naqsh-i Jahan, 119
Nasuhpasha, 5, 78
Nasuhpaşaoğlu Husein Pasha, 78, 86
Navruz Xan, 150
Nevesinli Murtaza Pasha, 129
Nevesinli Salih Pasha, 92, 95–6, 125, 129
Nicomedia, 45
Niksarlı Kilerci Veli Agha, 94
Nixon, 7
Nogaypaşaoğlu Arslan Pasha, 132
Northern War, 121

Ochakov, 168
Oman, 73
Osman, 152

Padishah Bridge, 100
Pamuk Mustafa Pasha, 123, 168
Persia, 16–17, 30
  Persian (language), 1, 16, 22–3, 33–4, 78, 172
  Persian Gulf, 10, 43, 66, 93, 95, 105–7, 109–10, 115–16, 141–2, 145–7, 150–2, 155–7, 160, 163–4, 177
Pinyanishi, 110, 112–14, 136
Pinyaşi, 132
Pir-Ali Beyg, 137
Podolia, 160
Poland, 11, 24, 26, 90–2, 95, 103, 109, 121, 159–61, 163, 165
Portugal, 170
Prevezeli Defterdaroğlu Mehmed Pasha, 92–5, 128–9
Priklonskii, A., 164
Privy Purse (Cîb-i Humâyûn), 145, 169, 171

Pruska, 103
Pope, 91, 100, 109, 125, 143, 159
Pruth, 163

Qabban, 106, 134
Qaim Beyg, 116–17
Qasim (the functionary), 45
Qasim Agha, 141
Qasim Çavuş, 128
Qasr-i Shirin, 6, 42, 46
Qatar, 105
Quran, 174
Qurban-kulu, Haji, 136
Qurna, 73, 106–7, 109, 116, 144–5, 147–9, 151, 153–5, 167

Ragusa, 63
Rajab Agha, 44
Rakoczi, George II, 121
Ramazan Agha, 107
Raqqa, 143, 146, 148, 163
Rethymo, 74, 91, 157
Rojeki, Koca Abdal-khan Beğ, 111, 114
Roman, 1, 16–17, 30, 34
Romania, 161, 163
Rûm (the empire), 16–17, 22, 30
Rûm (the province), 74, 118
Rumelia, 42, 74, 171
Rûmî Islam Xan, 170
Russia, 11, 26, 97, 103, 109, 122, 124, 140, 150, 159–61, 164–6, 173

Saadat-abad, 68
Saakadze, Ali-kulu Xan, 103–4
Saakadze, Rustam Xan, 38, 40–1, 44–6, 50–1, 55, 59–61, 65, 67
es-Sadun, Othman Bey, 148
Sâfî (kedkhuda), 134
Safi (shaykh), 2, 62, 136
Safi (shah), 6, 37–9, 41–2, 44–7, 49–50, 52–3, 56, 59, 61, 64–7, 69, 76, 78, 83, 86, 97, 163
Saint Gotthard, 142

Salih (the messenger), 69–70
Salmas, 110
Samawat, 66
Sangiar, 129
Santis, Domenico de, 91
Sarı Abdullah Efendi, 68
Sarı Ali Agha, 112–14
Sarı Husein Pasha, 143
Sarı Kenan Pasha, 117
Sarı Mehmed Pasha, 143
Sarıca Ibrahim Bey, 46
Saru Taqi, Mirza Muhammad, 51–2, 65, 67, 69, 50, 87
Saru Xan Talish, 42–4, 76
Saturn, 49
Savcı Muhammad Sharif, 119
Saxony, 34
Scutari (Üsküdar), 45, 47–8, 92, 109, 160
Schmid, Johann Rudolf, 57, 63
Sebastian, Pedro Cubero, 161
Sehab, 147
Selim I, 3, 6
Selim II, 4
Seljuks, 139
Semiz Kara Musa Pasha, 96, 129
Serb, 34
Seven Towers (*Yedikule*), 57, 62
Seydi Murad b. Mirza, 108, 134
Seyyid Muhammad Tahir, 175
Seyyid Yusuf Pasha, 123, 143
Shafî Xan, 73
Shah-Jahan, 116, 118, 120
Shahgediği, 110
Shahin Agha, 169
Shahinqala, 65, 70
Shahnavaz Xan, 123
Shahnazar Xan, 140
Shahriban, 40
Shahrizor, 43, 54, 60, 91, 121, 143, 146, 148, 155, 163
Shamkhal, 103, 122–3, 149–50, 165–6
Shamlu, Begdilli Janibek Xan, 38, 42, 52, 67, 69, 82

Index

Shamlu, Begdilli Karakhan Beyg, 38, 52
Shamlu, Biçerlu Murtaza-kulu Xan, 69
Shamsaddîn Amîr, 73
Sharish, 107
Shatir Husein (pasha), 101
Shatt-al-Arab, 109, 144, 147–8, 152
Sheitan Ibrahim Pasha, 140, 143, 145–6, 165
Sherban, Constantine Beg II, 121
Shiite, 37
Shiraz, 102, 151
Shirvan, 4–5
Shirvanshahs, 2
Shushik, 94–5
Siirt, 105
Silistra, 168
Sin, 77
Sivas, 30, 74
Slovakia, 142
Sobiesl, John, 161
Solak Husein, Haji Musallam, 144
Spain, 100
Stefan, George Beg II, 121
Sufiyan, 5
Sulayman I, 3–4, 38
Suleiman (shah, Sam / Safi II), 146, 157, 159–61, 164–5, 175
Suleiman Çavuş, 128
Suleiman Xan, 120–1
Surat, 141
Surkhay II, 103, 122, 149
Surnazen Mustafa Pasha, 116
Suveyb, 148, 153
Sweden, 121
Syria, 2, 6, 42, 62, 74
Szigetvar, 142

Şebinkarahisar, 172
Şişman Ibrahim Pasha, 165

Tabriz, 3–6, 19, 25, 43–4, 51, 55, 81, 94, 104, 111–14, 132, 136

Tahmaps I, 3–4
Tahtıvan, 132
Tani, Antonio, 143
Taqi Xan, 114
Tarhuncu Sarı Ahmed Pasha, 104
Tarku, 122
Tavşantaşlı Tezkireci/Hezarpare Ahmed Pasha, 96, 129
Tayyar Mehmed Pasha, 36, 86
Temesvar, 64
Tenedos, 117
Tezkireci Musa Efendi, 71
Thessaly, 155
Thirty Years War, 61
Thrace, 143, 149, 172
Tırnakçı Malak/Melek Ahmed Pasha, 47, 53, 75, 110–15, 132, 136
Tiepolo, Giovanni, 90
Tigris, 107, 121, 129, 139
Timur, 117
Timurtaş, 145
Tokat, 138
Tokmak Ali, 128–9
Topal Mehmed Agha, 40
Topal Mehmed Pasha, 121
Topkapı Palace, 45, 47, 58–9, 97
Toprakqale, 114
Transylvania, 117, 121–2, 139, 142
Trebizond, 2, 155, 163
Tripoli, 62, 74
Turk, 1–2, 16, 22–3, 26, 30, 34, 49, 61, 90, 92, 100, 117, 121, 129, 139, 142–4, 157, 160, 165
  Turkish (language), 16, 22–3, 30, 33–4, 78, 101, 132, 135, 172
  Turkey, 16
Tuscany, 91, 143, 159
Tuzluka, 122
Türkman Nadr-Ali Beyg, 42

Ujvar (Neuhäusel / Nove Zamky), 74, 142
Ukraine, 160, 163, 165
Urmia, 110–14, 136–7

199

Ustajlu, Taqi Beyg, 38
Uzbek, 10, 52–3, 95, 98–9

Van, 3–4, 6, 10, 25, 41, 43, 45–6, 49, 51, 53–5, 67, 69, 81, 90, 100, 103–4, 110–14, 124, 131, 136–7, 143, 163–4
Varad, 74
Varvar Ahmed Pasha, 129
Vasvar, 142–3
Velikent, 122
Venice, 9, 11, 26, 63, 90–2, 95, 100, 109, 117, 121, 123–4, 141–3, 146, 157–9, 163, 176
Vestan, 132
Voyvoda-kızı, 97

Wallachia, 121, 139, 163
Weissenburg, 139
Wisniowiecki, Michael, 160
Wladyslaw IV Vasa, 91, 125
World War One, 7

Yahya Agha/Pasha, 145–56, 158, 169, 172
Yaqub, b. Vaysbeyg, 134
Yaqub Pasha, 73

Yar-Ali Xan, 109, 118
Yekceğiz Bezirganzade Silahdar Mustafa Pasha, 48, 63–4, 78–9
Yusuf Agha, 68–70
Yusufpasha, 119

Zakiya, 148–9, 154–5
Zalim, 43, 77
Zangana, 167
Zangana, Ismail Bey, 167
Zangana, Omar, 167
Zangana, Sheikh-Ali Xan, 108–9, 120, 157, 159, 161
Zayd (the sharif), 142
Zaydan, 66
Zaynalâbidîn Efendi, 71
Zeyne'l-abidin Bey, 105
Zenjir, 46, 65, 77
Zernish, 163
Zuhab, 6–7, 9, 15, 18, 20, 24, 40, 42, 44–8, 52, 58, 60, 63, 65–7, 76, 94, 97, 99, 103, 115, 117–18, 120–1, 132, 136, 150, 163, 174, 176–7
Zulfiqar Agha, 46, 129, 138
Zulfiqar Hill, 90
Zurawno, 165